Modern Historiography
in the Making

Modern Historiography in the Making

The German Sense of the Past, 1700–1900

Kasper Risbjerg Eskildsen

BLOOMSBURY ACADEMIC
LONDON • NEW YORK • OXFORD • NEW DELHI • SYDNEY

BLOOMSBURY ACADEMIC
Bloomsbury Publishing Plc
50 Bedford Square, London, WC1B 3DP, UK
1385 Broadway, New York, NY 10018, USA
29 Earlsfort Terrace, Dublin 2, Ireland

BLOOMSBURY, BLOOMSBURY ACADEMIC and the Diana logo are trademarks of
Bloomsbury Publishing Plc

First published in Great Britain 2022
Paperback edition first published 2023

Copyright © Kasper Risbjerg Eskildsen, 2022

Kasper Risbjerg Eskildsen has asserted their right under the Copyright, Designs and
Patents Act, 1988, to be identified as Author of this work.

Cover image: Father Time is from the front page of Johann Peter von Ludewig, Scriptores
rerum Germanicarum, vol. 2 (Franfurt am Main, 1718). Courtesy Det Kongelige Bibliotek
Copenhagen.

All rights reserved. No part of this publication may be reproduced or transmitted in any
form or by any means, electronic or mechanical, including photocopying, recording, or
any information storage or retrieval system, without prior permission in writing from the
publishers.

Bloomsbury Publishing Plc does not have any control over, or responsibility for, any
third-party websites referred to or in this book. All internet addresses given in this
book were correct at the time of going to press. The author and publisher regret any
inconvenience caused if addresses have changed or sites have ceased to exist, but
can accept no responsibility for any such changes.

A catalogue record for this book is available from the British Library.

A catalog record for this book is available from the Library of Congress.

ISBN: HB: 978-1-3502-7147-0
PB: 978-1-3502-7148-7
ePDF: 978-1-3502-7149-4
eBook: 978-1-3502-7150-0

Typeset by Deanta Global Publishing Services, Chennai, India

To find out more about our authors and books visit www.bloomsbury.com and
sign up for our newsletters.

Contents

List of figures	vi
Acknowledgements	vii
Introduction: Between past and present	1
1 The lecture hall	17
2 The field	35
3 The princely archive	47
4 The art cabinet	57
5 The study	75
6 The state archive	87
7 The seminar	107
Epilogue: The purpose of historiography	119
Notes	125
References	155
Index	179

Figures

1	Engraving of the large lecture hall in the Weigh House in Halle from the beginning of the eighteenth century	31
2	Imprint of Leda, the swan and Amor (1762)	65
3	Imprint of Silenus, Amor and satyrs (1755)	66
4	Reproduction of gravestone (1799)	76
5	A table illustrating that a document, attested by Emperor Otto I in 970, can only be from the tenth century (1799)	80

Acknowledgements

This book started a decade and a half ago, when Christian Jacob asked me to contribute to his encyclopedic project on places of knowledge with a chapter on Leopold von Ranke. One venue of historical knowledge soon grew into multiple. I have presented many versions of the chapters at seminars, workshops and conferences around the world, and I am grateful to everyone who listened and commented. Your names are too many to be mentioned here. I am also thankful to the institutions that have hosted me for longer periods. My investigations into Ranke became a larger project at the Franke Institute for the Humanities and the Morris Fishbein Center for the History of Science and Medicine at the University of Chicago, where I joined an academic environment interested in the entangled histories of the sciences and the humanities. After Chicago, I went to the Science Studies Program at the University of California at San Diego. Many ideas emerged out of discussions with colleagues and students there. Later Lorraine Daston of the Max Planck Institut für Wissenschaftsgeschichte invited me to join her project on the sciences of the archive. The various chapters started to become a book when Christian Jacob invited me back to Paris to deliver a series of lectures at the École des hautes études en sciences sociales. A sabbatical semester at the Department of the History of Science at Harvard University offered an opportunity to finish a rough draft. I am especially indebted to Naomi Oreskes and Steven Shapin, who read the entire draft, as I was writing it, and offered numerous suggestions for improvement. John Brewer intervened as well with helpful advice to the introduction. I would also like to thank my colleagues and students at Roskilde University for constant inspiration and especially Patrick Blackburn, who read through a draft of the manuscript. And I am obliged to friends and colleagues in the growing history of humanities community with whom I have had many conversations about the project over the years. Finally, I should thank my wife, Evelyn, and my daughter, Helena, who patiently have followed me on the journey and offered encouragement along the way.

Several chapters include material from my previous publications. Parts of Chapter 1 appeared in 'Christian Thomasius, Invisible Philosophers, and Education for Enlightenment', *Intellectual History Review* 18, no. 3 (2008): 319–36.[1] Chapter 2 is a revision of 'Exploring the Republic of Letters: German Travelers in the Dutch Underground, 1680-1720', in *Scientists and Scholars in the Field: Studies in the History of Fieldwork and Expeditions*, ed. Kristian H. Nielsen, Michael Harbsmeier, and Christopher J. Ries (Aarhus: Aarhus. University Press, 2012), 425–53. Some of the material in Chapter 3 appeared in 'Inventing the Archive: Testimony and Virtue in Modern Historiography', *History of the Human Sciences* 26, no. 3 (2013): 8–26.[2] Chapter 5 is a revision of 'Relics of the Past: Antiquarianism and Archival Authority in Enlightenment Germany', *Storia della Storiografia* 68, no. 2 (2015): 69–81. Chapter 6 is a revision of 'Leopold Ranke's Archival Turn: Location and Evidence in Modern Historiography', *Modern Intellectual History* 5, no. 3 (2008): 425–53. Chapter 7 is a revision of 'Virtues of History: Exercises, Seminars, and the Emergence of the German Historical Discipline', in *History of Universities*, ed. Mordechai Feingold, vol. 34, no. 1: *A Global History of Research Education: Disciplines, Institutions, and Nations, 1840-1950*, ed. Ku-ming Chang and Alan J. Rocke (Oxford: Oxford University Press, 2021): 27–40. I thank the publishers and editors for allowing me to republish.

Introduction

Between past and present

The age of history

At the end of the nineteenth century, German historical scholarship had grown into a mighty enterprise. All German universities housed seminars for historical research and education, some with extensive libraries, reference works and source editions, working spaces for students and offices for professors and their assistants. German academies funded large editorial projects, which demanded the collaboration of dozens of scholars, who collected millions of notecards. Some scholars had started talking about historical scholarship as *Großwissenschaft* (big scholarship) with an industrialized approach to knowledge production based upon the division of academic labour.[1] German academics easily justified the immense institutional, economic and human resources employed investigating the past. Historical scholarship was not just a branch of scholarship like any other. It was the very foundation of both the humanities and the social sciences. Historical scholarship, they even argued, defined the modern worldview. German academics, of course, also recognized the import of science and technology, the bureaucratic state, secularization, industrialization and urbanization, but, to many, these modernizing forces paled in comparison to the transformative impact of the discovery of the past. Their epoch was, as the historian Hans Prösler declared in 1920, 'the historical age'.[2]

Since the early twentieth century, historians have offered variations of the same grand narrative to explain the prominence of German historical scholarship. According to this narrative, German scholars were inspired by, in Hayden White's formulation, 'a new paradigm of historical comprehension', which first found expression in German philosophy of history, especially in the thought and writings of Johann Gottfried Herder, during the late eighteenth century.[3] The new paradigm, often associated with German historicism, reflected larger changes in the European worldview, which happened in the decades around the French Revolution. These changes, Reinhart Koselleck and later writers have claimed, broke the continuity of tradition and disconnected the past from the present.[4] Modern historical scholarship, White, Koselleck and others have argued, no longer confirmed the universality of human experience, but instead delivered material to different ideologies with conflicting ideas of historical development.

This narrative needs revision. Historical scholarship began its ascent to prominence at German universities during the late seventeenth century, long before Herder and the French Revolution. The funders and founders of the institutions of scholarship were government bureaucrats, state-employed professors and university administrators. Most of them were pragmatists, who detested ideological dreamers and radical reformers. They appreciated history not as a servant of philosophy or ideology, but as an antidote. Historical scholarship uncovered a world of *differences*. These differences proved that contemporary systems of belief were not universal but products of contingencies and choices, and that other ways of interpreting and living in the world were possible and meaningful. Historical scholarship, they believed, thereby prompted contemporaries to reconsider their norms and values and opened the possibility of mutual understanding and gradual reform. History, not philosophy or ideology, made people modern.

History versus theory

At the end of the seventeenth century, only a few scholars defended this view of historical scholarship and the modern world. For the vision to succeed, it first had to be accepted within German universities. This demanded a redefinition of academic knowledge itself. In the scholastic tradition, historical knowledge was considered as an incomplete form of knowledge and as auxiliary to theoretical knowledge.[5] True knowledge was certain and deducible. It explained matters according to their causes and with reference to laws and principles. Universities therefore did not consider historical scholarship as an independent branch of academic knowledge-making or education.[6] Early modern humanists and antiquarians revered the philosophy, literature and art of Antiquity, but historical knowledge only played a secondary role within academic institutions. History did not belong among the seven canonical arts of the philosophical faculty and professorial chairs in history were normally combined positions, usually with philosophy, rhetoric or theology. While professors, especially at Protestant universities, discussed historical material in their courses, this was primarily in the service of other theoretical disciplines. Academics justified their interest in the past by pointing to *similarities*, rather than differences, between past and present. History illustrated universal laws and principles and served as a pedagogical aid. Its place in the curriculum was justified as, with an often-quoted phrase from Cicero, *historia magistra vitae* (history as a teacher of life).[7]

During the eighteenth century, however, historians who had acquired the proper skills and training distinguished themselves from others, who merely wrote about the past. They insisted that historical scholarship produced a particular kind of knowledge, which the theoretical disciplines could not. The authorities, moreover, supported this new academic role for historical scholarship. At the new reform universities of Halle and Göttingen, founded in 1694 and 1737, governments introduced historical studies as a central part of an enlightened university curriculum. Other German universities adopted these curricular reforms and established chairs in history.[8] By the end of the eighteenth century, historical scholarship had become fully integrated into the university.

German bureaucrats and academics embraced historical scholarship exactly because it delivered an alternative. Historical knowledge was fundamentally different from theoretical knowledge and therefore demonstrated the limits of theoretical reasoning. Their initial concern was not the new philosophies and ideologies of the Enlightenment, but rather older theological worldviews. The conflicts between the three major European confessions, Catholicism, Calvinism and Lutheranism, had resulted in two centuries of devastating religious wars and persecution, culminating with the forced exile of French Protestant Huguenots, after Louis XIV's revocation of the Edict of Nantes in 1685. Many late-seventeenth-century scholars blamed metaphysical commitments for these conflicts and for the impossibility of interconfessional dialogue. Factual and empirical knowledge served as an alternative common ground for discussion. In Great Britain, historians of science have argued, the new experimental sciences offered a model for a fact-based dialogue.[9] In the German-speaking parts of Europe, scholars instead turned to historical scholarship. Their empiricism, as the leading thinker of the early German Enlightenment Christian Thomasius formulated the programme in 1688, was a historical 'eclecticism' directed against the 'sectarianism' of scholastic academic philosophy and the confessional order.[10] Instead of committing themselves to one dogmatic system of belief, scholars should explore the many differences of the past.

These empirical investigations also contributed to, what Constantin Fasolt has called, the 'historical revolt'.[11] They questioned older universal histories, which enclosed human history within biblical chronology, starting with the creation of the world approximately 6,000 years earlier, and interpreted the rest of history according to biblical revelation and divine providence. Until the eighteenth century, one dominant narrative focused on the unique historical role of the Holy Roman Empire – a multi-ethnic and multi-lingual conglomerate of states and cities that held together most of central Europe.[12] The Empire was founded with the coronation of Charlemagne as emperor in 800 or, as German historians normally preferred, with the Saxon kings and emperors, starting either when Henry the Fowler became Duke of Saxony in 912, when he was elected as King of East Francia in 919 or when Otto the Great claimed the title as emperor in 962. In European historiography, however, the Empire was given an even longer prehistory as the last of the four world monarchies, prophesized in the Old Testament book of Daniel. It was at once the direct continuation of the ancient Roman Empire and the embodiment of universal Christendom. This interpretation had survived the Reformation, with the three confessions each claiming the position as the true defender of tradition. Across the Empire emerged, to borrow Markus Völkel's phrase, different 'confessional historical cultures'.[13] Protestants emphasized the biblical foundation, while Catholics linked the continuation of the Empire to the Roman Church. Scholarly investigations into the complicated legal and political history of the Empire questioned these continuities and thereby unsettled the confessional order.

The theory of the four world monarchies remained a viable interpretation of German history until the Napoleonic wars and the dissolution of the Holy Roman Empire in 1806. However, increasingly German scholars had to deal with other theoretical and philosophical interpretations of the past as well. Already the natural law thinkers of the seventeenth century, in the German context most importantly Samuel Pufendorf, had employed history to investigate the development of state and society at the expense of older theological universal histories.[14] From the 1740s and onwards, major Enlightenment thinkers, from Montesquieu, Voltaire and Rousseau to Condillac and Condorcet, produced a series of important works that explored society, culture, knowledge and language from the viewpoint of a secularized universal history. Scottish philosophers invented their own version with the so-called 'conjectural history'.[15] These works, as Peter Hanns Reill and others have shown, immediately influenced German debates, and German writers themselves produced noteworthy contributions to the genre.[16] The theoretical and philosophical interpretations also gained political significance, especially after the French Revolution. By the early nineteenth century, the historian Heinrich von Sybel argued in 1856, Germans suffered two versions of 'speculative politics', where 'the left appealed to philosophy, the right to theology'. Historical scholarship still served as an alternative, Sybel claimed, by showing the 'practical lessons of history'. The double task of historians became 'to forcefully enliven the connection between past and present, and to use the old not to exterminate, but to develop further the new'.[17] They should not only show their fellow Germans that reform and progress were possible but also reassure them about the continuities between past and present. There was no eternal theological order, to which the fragmented Germanies could or should return, but there was also no revolutionary necessity, which disconnected the contemporary world from its past.

In 1856, Sybel argued, this battle had largely been won. Germans and German universities had rejected theory and embraced a historical worldview. Others concurred. In 1866, at his inauguration as rector of the University of Munich, the theologian Ignaz von Döllinger summarized the long history of European universities and ended this summary with the triumph of German universities and historical scholarship. The particular gift of the Germans, Döllinger claimed, was 'the historical sense', which allowed them to break 'through the fog of prejudices' and embrace the ideas and worldviews of everyone on earth.[18] During the following decades, German thinkers, most prominently the Berlin philosopher Wilhelm Dilthey, elevated historical scholarship to the model for all knowledge within the humanities and social sciences.[19] The old distinction between true theoretical knowledge and incomplete and auxiliary historical knowledge was gradually replaced by a new distinction between the sciences, the humanities and the social sciences, all considered equals. So, even according to theologians and philosophers, historical knowledge no longer depended upon theoretical knowledge to count as scholarship. At the end of the nineteenth century, historical knowledge was itself the foundation of a large domain of scholarship and, to many, the core of the modern worldview.

History versus historicism

At this moment of triumph, however, German intellectuals started to question the benefits of historical scholarship. They no longer doubted if historical knowledge was knowledge, but instead questioned if it served a moral purpose. The debates about historicism during the Weimar period were especially important for this revision of the German view of the past.[20] In some ways, these debates only confirmed the belief that the modern age was an age of history. In 1922, in an influential book that framed the discussion, the theologian Ernst Troeltsch associated 'historicism' with 'the fundamental historicizing of our knowledge and thinking'.[21] In 1924, the sociologist Karl Mannheim similarly claimed that 'historicism' was not just an option among others but 'an intellectual force with which we must deal, whether we like it or not'. It, he continued, 'is not an idea, it is also not a fashion, it is not even a movement, but the foundation from which we observe social-cultural reality'. History shaped the modern mind, rather as religion had defined Middle Ages and reason had encapsulated the Enlightenment.[22]

The triumph of history, however, was no longer just a cause for celebration. Troeltsch called the first chapter of his book on historicism 'the crisis of history'. Since the end of the seventeenth century, German academics had praised historical scholarship for its ability to challenge the universalism of theology and philosophy. For Troeltsch, this challenge had become a problem. The crisis of history, he explained, was a crisis of 'historical values'.[23] The historicization of European thinking had undermined beliefs in universal norms and values and whatever had been left of these beliefs had perished in the trenches of the First World War. 'Therefore', he argued in an essay the same year, 'we understand the current crisis of historicism as a deeper inner crisis of the age'.[24] Historical scholarship, he further explained, had not caused the crisis. Scholarly publications had become more specialized, impersonal and unoriginal, but this was a necessary consequence of the progress of scholarship and no different than in the natural sciences. The problem was more fundamental, grounded in the worldview of the historical age.

If historical scholarship had not caused the crisis, a different genealogy was needed. The age of history did not emerge in the late seventeenth century, with its institutionalization at German universities, but rather with the rise of modern philosophical relativism in the eighteenth century. The first true historical thinker, according to Troeltsch, was not a history professor but 'Rousseau, the first romantic, who through the denial of all historical values fundamentally raised the problem of the meaning of history'.[25] Troeltsch's book set the standard for all future works about German historicism and helped establish the grand narrative of twentieth-century history of historiography. In 1936, the historian Friedrich Meinecke described historicism as 'one of the greatest spiritual revolutions' in European thought and the second great feat of 'the German spirit' after the Reformation. It was a central 'constituent of modern thinking' and had resulted in 'the relativizing of values' that once had been secured through religion and reason. For Meinecke, like for Troeltsch, German universities or academic scholarship had not caused this 'spiritual revolution'. His magisterial two volumes work on the origins of historicism ended with Leopold von Ranke, but almost all the authors dealt with before him were not university professors. German historicism, according to Meinecke, started with playwright Gotthold Ephraim Lessing and the papal librarian Johann Joachim Winckelmann. The 'three great German thinkers' who shaped modern historicism were the jurist and statesman Justus Möser, the philosopher and clergyman Johann Gottfried Herder and the poet and novelist Johann Wolfgang von Goethe.[26]

In 1968, Georg G. Iggers retold this story to Anglophone readers, with his description of the 'German conception of history', as both a worldview and a philosophical project rooted in German idealism. Iggers started with Herder, who in 1774 first presented 'the historicist position formulated in its radical form: the conception that every age must be viewed in terms of its own immediate values, that there is no progress or decline in history, but only value-filled diversity'. Herder's ideas contained 'the seeds of relativism' because 'all knowledge and all values are related to concrete cultural and historical settings'.[27] In *Metahistory*, Hayden White also associated the 'new paradigm of historical comprehension' with Herder's philosophy of history and ended with the 'crisis of historicism', in which scholars finally realized 'the impossibility of choosing, on adequate theoretical grounds, among the different ways of viewing history'.[28] Similar histories, starting from eighteenth-century philosophical foundations and ending with twentieth-century relativism, can be found in recent works on German historicism.[29]

Many historians also still associate modern historical thinking with a larger transformation of the European worldview during the second half of the eighteenth century. Reinhart Koselleck's account of the history of the modern concept of history has been especially influential. In 1972, Koselleck proposed that Europeans experienced a *Sattelzeit* (threshold period) that fundamentally reshaped the intellectual landscape.[30] This shift announced the end of the ancient order and the coming of modernity. It showed itself in the radically changing meaning of 'basic historical concepts' and, among these, the concept of history. History, Koselleck argued, was no longer considered as a collection of individual facts or examples for moral reflection.[31] There were not many histories, plural, but only one history, singular. The French Revolution in 1789 showed that history resulted in radical breaks and illustrated the distinction between past and present. Historical scholarship did not cause this shift in European historical thought. The 'threshold period' changed how all Europeans viewed the past and therefore also how historians viewed the past. All moderns were disconnected from the past and left, as Peter Fritzsche has claimed, 'stranded in the present'.[32] Recently, François Hartog offered a broader version of this argument, which divides European historical thinking into a series of 'regimes of historicity', but still locates 'Europe's most momentous crisis of time' in the decades around the French Revolution.[33]

These histories of modern relativism and ideology are not without merit. German philosophy of history, and the thought of Herder, probably inspired modern relativism and influenced the ideologies of the nineteenth and twentieth centuries. It may even, as Karl Popper claimed, have prepared the ground for modern totalitarianism.[34] The association of German philosophy of history with relativism and totalitarianism certainly helped discredit the German vision of a historical modernity. However, the debates about historicism during the Weimar period, and their afterlife in later historiography, may say more about the problems and anxieties of the twentieth and twentieth-first centuries than about the German age of history. Earlier generations of scholars were not much concerned about these problems, seldom referred to Herder, and were not familiar with historicism, which only acquired its modern meaning and significance during the debates.

The morals of history

From the late seventeenth century to the early twentieth century, advocates of historical scholarship emphasized its moral and political significance. History had shaped the modern worldview and shaped it for the better. History belonged within German universities not only because knowledge about the past should be considered knowledge, but also because it transformed scholars and students alike into better human beings and delivered a new and better foundation for society. So, before the early twentieth century, most Germans did not associate historical scholarship with relativism or fear that it would destroy all values. Scholars and governments, as evidenced by the many titles and honours bestowed upon historians, remained convinced that knowledge of the past could and should provide moral and political guidance.

The morals of history were not like the morals of theology or philosophy. Historical scholarship did not offer new universal principles for proper behaviour or the organization of society. The confrontation with historical difference, its advocates argued, instead cultivated a new kind of morality and promoted modern virtues, such as open-mindedness and tolerance. History offered perspectives and alternatives and helped people orient themselves in a world of contingencies and change, but also served as a corrective to revolutionary dreams about a sudden and radical remaking of humankind. So, historical knowledge gave moral and political guidance because it was not like theoretical knowledge. It was relevant because it uncovered truths about people that had little resemblance to contemporary Europeans and, at the same time, because it made these truths accessible and intelligible. Historical scholarship both emphasized the distance between past and present and enabled moderns to overcome this distance.

Historiography in the making

Eighteenth- and nineteenth-century Germans especially praised historians for their practical ability to connect past and present. The most important scholars of the age of history, such as Johann Peter von Ludewig, who established the most influential school of historical research of the Enlightenment, and Leopold von Ranke, who often has been celebrated as the founder of the modern historical discipline in the nineteenth century, were known for their technical and methodological skills. Their works did not offer brilliant theoretical insights and were not rhetorical or literary masterpieces. But they did present practical solutions to the problems of historical understanding. Understanding the past was not primarily a question of speculation or imagination but rather of hard scholarly work and countless hours, shifting through notecards, visiting archives and libraries, editioning sources and crafting footnotes.

To appreciate the significance of Ludewig and of Ranke, and the impact of historical scholarship more broadly, it is necessary to investigate these working practices. To borrow an expression from science studies, we must explore historiography *in the making*. We need to follow the processes of knowledge-making and investigate how these processes shaped what was considered knowledge. Such an approach allows us to take historical scholarship seriously as scholarship rather than as an aid to theology and philosophy or as an appendix to modern ideology. In science studies, investigations of 'science in the making' have revealed, Steven Shapin argues, 'how, with what confidence, and on what bases, scientists come to know what they do'.[35] There is no reason why investigations of historiography in the making should not be able to do the same for historians.

This approach differs from the normal approach to the history of historiography. The book does not just investigate the final products of historical research. It does not limit itself, again borrowing an expression from science studies, to *ready-made* historiography. The investigation instead focuses on the everyday life of research and how the challenges and conditions of this life helped make the historical works possible. This emphasis upon the everyday life of research also reveals that the world of historiography was not a very egalitarian world. All the major characters in the book are university professors and all of them are men. Women only entered German universities on somewhat equal terms with men at the beginning of the twentieth century, where the investigation ends.³⁶ The scholars described here did not open the doors. None of them were revolutionaries. They belonged among the privileged, received their salary from the state and worked closely together with administrators and bureaucrats. However, they all had hopes and dreams for a better and more tolerant society. And they believed that historical scholarship could help create this world.

Places of mediation

One way to approach historiography in the making is to visit the venues where scholarship was made.³⁷ Like modern experimental science, modern historical scholarship was fiercely empirical. Historians produced a particular kind of knowledge, different from the knowledge of other disciplines, because they based their conclusions upon the sources. The most important insight in modern critical historical scholarship, the Berlin historian Johann Gustav Droysen declared in 1868, was 'that the foundation of our studies is the examination of the "sources", from which we create' and 'that the pasts no longer lie immediately before us, but only in a mediated way'.³⁸ Only through the meeting with tangible evidence could scholars bring history alive and make it relevant in the present. The sources offered a material bridge between past and present and allowed for mediation across time. Unlike modern experimental scientists, historians could not produce their data themselves. The remains of the past were unique and not immediately available. They first had to be located and studied somewhere. Scholars had to travel to archives, observe antiquities in art cabinets and museums, collect inscriptions in ruins and excavation sites and interview witnesses in the field. Their research practices were, as Robert Kohler has noted about biological field studies, 'not the placeless practices of labs but practices of place'.³⁹

Often the physical venues, such as the princely archive or the art cabinet, preceded the German age of history. However, before the eighteenth century, the principal purpose of these venues was not to mediate between past and present. The princely archive was primarily a repository of documents that supported the legal and territorial claims of the prince. The art cabinet served the education and display of taste. To access the past, scholars had to remake these venues as places of mediation and invent practical solutions to transform sources into evidence. These solutions ensured that the materials were not manipulated or forgeries and circumvented the interests and preferences of collectors. Other practical measures, from footnotes to source editions, guaranteed that the scholars' colleagues and students could trust their findings and understand their research practices. Over time, this scholarly engagement transformed the venues. Princely archives became modern research archives, whose guardians were no longer state servants but trained historians. Private art cabinets became university research collections and museums, where objects were acquired according to scholarly interests and questions.

Other places of mediation served the transformation of evidence into historical knowledge. For German historical scholarship the most important places could be found at, or in the proximity to, universities. The experimental sciences, as they developed during the seventeenth century, first established themselves in venues outside the university.[40] German historical scholarship, on the contrary, was almost from the beginning a university enterprise. With a few notable exceptions, the most influential scholars in the field were university professors. Many of their books were written as textbooks and lectures. Students also encountered historical scholarship at university. The norms, skills and personal qualities of modern historians were acquired through education. Like the princely archive or the art cabinet, however, German universities had to be remade to allow for mediation. This transformation of the university demanded not only a redefinition of academic knowledge but also that professors refurbished the places of teaching and research. Within the university, they created venues, where they and their students could approach the distant past. Some venues, such as research collections or seminar libraries, allowed scholars and students to investigate and compare the remains of the past. Other venues, such as the private lecture hall, enabled them to disregard the conventions of the surrounding society and investigate ideas and opinions considered distasteful and dangerous.

Summary and chapter outline

This book recounts a series of episodes in the history of the German engagement with the past. The history of historical scholarship is not presented as series of disembodied arguments, developing over time and culminating with Goethe, Hitler or modern relativism. It is instead described through different practical solutions to the problems of knowing the past. Each chapter focuses upon a place of mediation. The first three chapters discuss the new moral and political purpose of history during the early Enlightenment and how this purpose was reflected in the everyday working life of German scholars. *The lecture hall* investigates developments at the University of Halle and especially the thought and teaching of Christian Thomasius, the most prominent philosopher of the period. Thomasius rejected the ideal of *historia magistra vitae*, but nonetheless insisted upon the importance of historical studies across the curriculum. He used historical differences to refute confessional dogmatism and as an instrument of moral education. The chapter investigates how Thomasius reimagined the university, including the design and location of the lecture hall, to enable this education.

The field discusses the Göttingen professor Christoph August Heumann, who founded the world's first journal for history of philosophy and wrote the most influential textbook on the history of scholarship in the eighteenth century. The chapter focuses upon his journey to Holland in 1705 before his tenure at Göttingen. On the journey Heumann interviewed religious and intellectual dissenters and tested claims in contemporary history writing. He uncovered how historical works were instruments in larger political and religious battles of the time and therefore were read and discussed among the dissenters themselves. His journey, along with similar journeys made by young German academics during the period, can also be considered as a continuation of Thomasius' educational programme, which employed the investigation of differences in moral education. *The princely archive* discusses the Halle professor Johann Peter von Ludewig, who founded the influential school of *Reichshistorie* (imperial history). Ludewig rejected the ideal of *historia magistra vitae* as well as the theory of the four world monarchies, but he was no less critical of the new moralizing uses of history of his Enlightenment colleagues. He instead emphasized political and juridical benefits, especially the rediscovery of ancient Germanic freedoms threatened by the universalism of theology and Roman law. This new political and juridical function demanded that scholars first transformed princely archives into venues for the production of historical knowledge.

The fourth and fifth chapters describe developments in historical scholarship in the middle of the eighteenth century. *The art cabinet* discusses the Halle professor Christian Adolph Klotz, who was arguably the most controversial figure in the German academic world during the 1760s. Klotz employed ancient art to reintroduce the hedonism and paganism of Antiquity and to challenge not just confessional control but Christianity as such. Among Klotz's most vocal critics was Johann Gottfried Herder. The chapter shows how Herder developed early versions of his philosophy of history as well as the modern concepts of *Kultur* (culture) and *Zeitgeist* (spirit of time) in opposition to Klotz. Herder did not develop these concepts because philosophy had convinced him that the past was incomprehensible or irrelevant to the present, but, on the contrary, to counter the moral and political threat of historical scholarship. *The study* discusses the Göttingen professor Johann Christoph Gatterer, who founded specialized journals for historical research, published numerous textbooks and established the first institute for historical research, the Königliche Institut der historischen Wissenschaften, in 1764. Focusing upon a minor controversy about a medieval gravestone, the chapter investigates how he utilized these different resources as well as his large private collection of documents to establish his scholarly authority. The problem for Gatterer was no longer the influence of theology in society. He instead worked to justify history as an independent branch of academic knowledge-making. He demarcated academic history writing from the writings of antiquarians, who insisted upon the importance of connoisseurship and personal experience, as well as from the works of thinkers, who engaged in conjectures and reconstructions. Gatterer thereby also placed himself in opposition to the new philosophical histories of the Enlightenment.

The last two chapters deal with developments within the historical discipline of the nineteenth century. *The state archive* investigates the Berlin professor Leopold von Ranke and his use of historical scholarship to counter the revolutionary philosophies and philosophical histories of his time. The chapter focuses on his first longer archival journey to Austria and Italy between 1827 and 1831. The archives that Ranke visited were not traditional princely archives, but centralized state archives created in the late eighteenth and early nineteenth centuries. The chapter discusses how the work in these archives shaped Ranke's political viewpoints and how, in turn, Ranke's archival research model, which has dominated in the historical discipline ever since, helped further these viewpoints. *The seminar* shows how modern institutionalized forms of instruction forced scholars to rethink the purpose of historical education. The chapter focuses upon Ranke's most prominent student, the Göttingen professor Georg Waitz, who resisted the shift towards institutionalization. Waitz continued a form of private instruction, invented by Ranke, which aimed at the education of future researchers. These courses were housed not at the university but in Waitz's study at home and emphasized the moral dimension of historical education. The new institutional seminars, on the contrary, had their own rooms in the buildings of the university. They did not primarily aim at moral or political education but at vocational training of future secondary school teachers. To Waitz, institutionalization did not signal the success of historical scholarship but, on the contrary, its demise. At its moment of triumph, German historical scholarship was forgetting its purpose.

1

The lecture hall

The present is not the past

The German vision of a historical modernity arrived at the University of Leipzig in the fall of 1687 with an unusual spectacle, one which outraged the German academic community.[1] In the words of one contemporary, 'in the Republic of Letters arose such crowds and horrid brawls, as had not been observed in ordinary life since the Turks besieged the imperial Residence' a few years earlier.[2] The reason for the commotion was not a military invasion, but something as ordinary and unremarkable for a university town as a new course offered by a young lecturer named Christian Thomasius. But there was nothing ordinary about this course. Thomasius entitled his lecture programme 'How One Should Imitate the French in Everyday Life', and used an introduction to courtly life by the Spanish Jesuit Baltasar Gracián as a textbook. He discussed recent French salon literature and lectured in German instead of the usual academic Latin. His sartorial style was even less traditionally professorial. 'It is a longstanding habit in Leipzig', one critical observer noted, 'that doctors, when they dispute, appear at the lectern in black clothing and robes, and this habit is observed by all reasonable people. . . . How did mister Thomas behave here? Whimsically, he comes in colorful clothing with a rapier, hanging from a nifty golden waist belt'.[3]

If many of Thomasius's colleagues were outraged, the Leipzig students were thrilled. Another contemporary critic complained that 'the guzzling and drinking gatherings in Leipzig' revered 'master Thomas' and that 'some young people at university, who still have school-dust in their eyes, see him as the hero of our century and deem him the light of the world'.[4] But Thomasius's choices of literature, language and clothing were not just pandering to youth.

He wanted to remind his students that the university was a part of the world and that the world was constantly changing. Nothing made the historicity of the world more evident than the recent influence of French fashions in German everyday life. As he explained in the opening of his lecture programme:

> There can be no doubt, and it has already been noticed by many, that if our forefathers, the ancient Germans, now should be revived and come back to Germany, they would not feel at all that they were in their fatherland and with their compatriots. They would much rather imagine that they stayed in a foreign country with strange and entirely different people. Such big changes have happened here in, I will not say a thousand, but just some hundred years. Among these changes, and not most insignificant, is that in those times the French had no special esteem among the Germans, but today everything here has to be French. French clothing, French food, French utensils, French manners, French sins, yes even French sicknesses are everywhere popular.[5]

When professors failed to recognize the changes in the world around them, they could not prepare their students to live and work in this world.[6] The university did not supply the knowledge and skills that were necessary to survive at court and in polite society. French scholarly ideals appealed to Thomasius because they merged the world of learning with that of polite society. Proper gallantry, he argued in his 1687 lecture programme, was 'something mixed, composed of je ne sais quoi, of the proper way to do something, of the art of living as customary at court, of reason, scholarship, a good judgment, politeness, and joyfulness, and opposed to all cohesion, affectation, and indecent ungainliness'. Students should not have to choose between the university and the surrounding world but imitate French 'honnête, scholarship, beauté d'esprit, un bon goût, and galanterie' and, Thomasius claimed, 'when one combines all these parts, finally there emerges un parfait homme sage, or a perfectly wise man, whom one can employ in the world for intelligent and important matters'.[7]

These French ideals were appealing not only because they prepared university candidates for polite society, but also because they offered an alternative to the traditional role of scholars as guardians of the confessional state.[8] After the Reformation of the sixteenth century, the European map had been divided between three major confessions, Catholicism, Calvinism and, as in Thomasius's Saxony, Lutheranism. The European states enforced religious uniformity within their borders and European confessional disagreements had resulted in centuries of religious wars and intolerance. Universities, as Thomasius pointed out, played a central role in these conflicts and injustices.[9] The universities were not just venues for the pursuit and dissemination of knowledge, but also, especially in the Protestant parts of Europe, repressive instruments of religious orthodoxy. Professors persecuted dissenters, enforced moral standards, administered censorship and delivered the arguments that justified the confessional state. They described the state as a representative of a divine order, based upon eternal metaphysical principles, and denied the legitimacy of diverging ideas, beliefs and viewpoints. The untimely customs and clothing of academics reinforced their role as guardians of these eternal principles. When academics behaved differently, they not only set themselves apart from their contemporaries but also indirectly insisted upon their right to define the moral and political order and to persecute those who disagreed with their judgements. Thomasius's fashionable clothing and emphasis upon historical change questioned whether academics should play this role as well as the place of the university within society.

After his 1687 lectures, Thomasius involved himself in a series of controversies, in which he argued against Lutheran orthodoxy and for tolerance among Protestants.[10] He not only addressed an academic audience but also appealed to the broader reading public, especially through his entertaining and illustrated literary journal, *Monatsgespräche* (Monthly Conversations). Thomasius's colleagues at the University of Leipzig did not ignore these provocations. Already in January 1688, shortly after the publication of the first issue of the *Monatsgespräche*, the theology professor and member of the Saxon censorship commission, Valentin Alberti, attempted to have the journal forbidden. In March 1690, the Saxon authorities intervened and prohibited Thomasius to publish or lecture.[11] He was forced into exile in Brandenburg-Prussia, where the confessional divide between the Calvinist princely house of Hohenzollern and the majority Lutheran population made arguments for religious tolerance seem more reasonable. Thomasius remained here for the rest of his life, as a professor at the new University of Halle. This exile to Halle enabled Thomasius to develop a new educational programme, which aimed to teach students to embrace the world and overcome the prejudices and intolerance of the confessional state.

The past is not the present

Thomasius's first larger publication after his arrival in Halle was his *Einleitung zur Vernunfft-Lehre* (Introduction to the Art of Reasoning) of 1691. The book offered the first draft of Thomasius's new educational programme. Already in his dedication, Thomasius praised the mayor of Leipzig, Adrian Stegern, as an example of a new kind of scholar. Although Stegern in his daily life was occupied with public duties and worldly affairs, he also embodied various scholarly characters. As a theologian, Stegern was without prejudice. As a lawyer, he was a man of practice and familiar with natural law. However, above all, Thomasius celebrated the mayor as a model *Weltweiser* (philosopher):

> A righteous philosopher I understand to be a man, who possesses a sharp and penetrating reason and always reasons fairly and concisely; who is well-familiar with the common and most useful instrument of all studies, by which I mean history; who begins his philosophy with self-reflection and, through the subduing of his passions seeks to acquire his highest good, the inner peace of the soul; who next to this knows the wickedness of the world, and . . . in conversations with people penetrates into their inner thoughts and uses this knowledge for the benefit of the common good. . . . Yes, finally one who organizes all his activities so that one in these notices a rightful decorum, without which all philosophy would be vain and pure pedantry.[12]

This definition of the philosopher differed considerably from the usual definitions at the time. Most of his contemporaries considered philosophy as a central part of theoretical knowledge and the philosopher as a representative of theoretical knowledge. In 1694, the dictionary of the Académie française described the philosopher, following standard scholastic definitions of theoretical knowledge, as someone 'who applies himself to the study of the sciences and who seeks to know the effects by their causes and by their principles'.[13] Thomasius instead associated philosophy, to borrow a phrase from Pierre Hadot, with 'a way of life'.[14] To become philosophers, students should know not just how to explain the world, but also how to act in the world and to live among their contemporaries. They had to learn to control their thoughts and feelings, to realize their limitations and human fallibility, and to empathize with the thoughts and feelings of others.

Similar ideals of philosophy as a way of life, Matthew Jones has argued, prevailed among some seventeenth-century natural philosophers, who used mathematics and the study of nature 'to acknowledge, to characterize, and to compensate for human epistemic and affective limits'.[15] For Thomasius, historical studies fulfilled this function. In 1688, in his *Introductio ad philosophiam aulicam* (Introduction to Court Philosophy), Thomasius emphasized the importance of the history of philosophy in the battle against the dogmatism and intolerance of the academic community. The history of philosophy illustrated that the philosophical principles of his colleagues were not universal but merely the beliefs of particular sects of philosophers.[16] As an alternative to this kind of 'sectarian' philosophy, Thomasius advocated an individualized and pragmatic 'eclecticism', where the philosopher selected freely between the many different arguments and ideas that the history of philosophy offered and used these to construct his own philosophy.[17] History was a training ground, where the students could exercise self-control, open-mindedness and empathy with others, as well as a source of alternative ideas and arguments.

After arriving in Halle, Thomasius further developed his educational programme and invented new ways to use historical differences and disagreements in the intellectual and moral education of students. He also re-emphasized the distinction between past and present. In his most comprehensive programme for educational reform, an introduction to academic studies for law students, Thomasius investigated older arguments for the use of history in moral education and especially the tradition of *historia magistra vitae*. Starting from the commentary and notes of Isaac Casaubon's 1609 edition of Polybius, and the works of the most significant early modern writers on the art of history, from Jean Bodin to Gerardus Johannes Vossius, he summarized arguments for why history illustrated moral and political principles. He immediately rejected almost all of these arguments and described it as 'obviously foolish' when 'one reads [history] to improve in grammar or oratory or to employ it in conversations in society, or to brawl about moral and political matters'. Historical examples, he claimed, were seldom applicable to contemporary politics and law, not only because there were few good examples to emulate, but also because 'the ailments and defects in one state are not like in others'. Thomasius was also convinced that the ancient and early modern writers overestimated the effect that historical works had upon their readers. 'Those', Thomasius argued, 'make a big mistake, who maintain that the reading of history brings not only understanding of good and bad, but also the demand for good'.[18] The study of history did not result in prudent actions, seldom delivered any helpful advice for good governance, and did not even bring comfort in times of trouble.

Thomasius nonetheless insisted that the study of history helped the student in 'the improvement of himself'. The particulars of history, and especially those that were 'absent and bygone', delivered an empirical basis of human knowledge. History and philosophy were 'the two eyes of wisdom'[19] and supplemented one another. Historical knowledge was important not because it was auxiliary to theoretical knowledge, and delivered examples to illustrate philosophical principles, but because it was different from theoretical knowledge. The many variations of history taught the students other lessons than philosophy and even served as a remedy to excessive philosophizing. They proved how ideas that seemed to be universal and natural, were in reality arbitrary, contingent and the results of historical processes. They illustrated the folly of men and showed how emotions and passions shaped opinions and beliefs. They reminded readers that prejudices and foolishness were as common among the rich, nobles, scholars and clergymen as among the poor, uneducated and laymen. The study of history, Thomasius explained, could be considered as 'agreeable, necessary, and useful':

> [History] is agreeable because of the endless transformation and the account of such matters appeals immediately to the senses, and because it reveals the most hidden secrets of human desires in all estates. We can prove the necessity of history in many ways. Without [history] human reason is blind, and its thoughts are, as with a deaf and blind [person], completely confused; a human being will never be liberated from prejudices, if he doesn't, with the help of history, understand the origin of prejudices. We can prove the usefulness of history to all of humankind because it is the second eye of wisdom. The philosophers need the history of wisdom and of sects, the physicians natural [history], the jurists and theologians political [history] and church history.[20]

Exercising the self

In some ways, Thomasius's pedagogical routines were traditional, following the conventions of European universities since the Middle Ages. He started with lectures and ended with exercises, testing the students' comprehension and correcting mistakes and misinterpretations. However, to transform the lecture hall into a venue for discussion and moral introspection, Thomasius differentiated this conventional scheme according to degrees of privacy. The more private his classes were, the more he encouraged the students to examine themselves and to investigate different kinds of arguments. Early modern German universities normally distinguished between public and private classes. Public classes were offered by ordinary or full professors, who received their salary from the state. Students could follow these classes free of charge. Private classes were offered not only by ordinary professors, but also by extraordinary professors, who held temporary positions, and *Privatdozenten* (private lecturers), who had no permanent salary and needed the permission of the university to offer classes. To attend these private classes, students would normally have to pay fees.[21]

At the University of Halle, Thomasius was an ordinary professor and offered both public and private classes. He normally started with public lectures and afterwards gathered students for his private classes. On the surface, there was little difference between his public lectures and the first hour of his private classes. Thomasius continued lecturing and some of these lectures, such as those on moral philosophy, were also free of charge.[22] His private class in the following hour was more exclusive and only for a small group of selected students, allowing for independent reflection. Here, Thomasius did not comment upon a book but explained his own philosophy. In this so-called *collegium privatissimum* (most private class), he demanded active participation, taught his students to doubt, and engaged them in 'a continuous examination'.[23] Students who attended all these classes, Thomasius promised, could complete their university education in two or three years.

Thomasius's concerns about privacy reflected his experiences at the University of Leipzig. During the late 1680s, the Pietist August Hermann Francke caused a considerable commotion at the university with his biblical classes, which questioned Lutheran orthodoxy. Francke, Thomasius later reported, partly provoked his opponents by removing his class from his house to a public lecture hall, where he attracted large crowds of students and so challenged the Leipzig theologians. Thomasius considered his own association with Francke as 'one of the major reasons why my . . . adversaries in Leipzig wanted to deprive me of life, honor, and property'.[24] He even suspected that his association with the Pietists had inspired his opponents to have 'spies at my lectures who wrote down what I said'.[25] In 1688, Thomasius had started offering philosophy classes in a 'domestic lecture hall' in Leipzig, without the permission of the university or the philosophical faculty, although he was only a lecturer and not yet a professor.[26]

Most likely, Francke's biblical classes were also an inspiration for Thomasius's intensive exercises. Francke instructed his students to disregard previous opinions and investigate Scripture for themselves. Such close readings served not only erudition but also self-improvement. Already in the foundational programme of the German Pietists, the *Pia desideria* (Pious Desires) of 1675, Philipp Jakob Spener recommended such exercises for university students. 'Theology', Spener claimed, 'is a habitus practicus and does not only consist of scholarship'. The students should therefore participate in 'all kinds of exercises . . . in which the minds are accustomed and trained in those matters that belong to praxis and the edification of oneself'.[27] Another possible Leipzig inspiration for Thomasius's style of teaching was the early modern disputational classes, where students took turns as opponents and respondents. These disputations were normally staged in the professorial home and were only for paying students. The University of Leipzig also housed a number of private societies, where students actively participated in the academic discussions.[28]

Thomasius combined the spiritual exercises of the Pietists with the disputational classes of early modern universities to create a new education for Enlightenment philosophers. Johann George von Raumer, who participated in Thomasius's educational programme from May 1692, described the experience. Raumer arrived in Halle well prepared. He was at the end of his studies and had already read Thomasius's books. However, immediately at their first meeting, Thomasius told him 'that all this is worth nothing and that if I believed him, I would forget everything I already knew'. Thomasius explained that he needed a further two years of private education and that this would cost him 80 silver Thaler. Two years later, Thomasius ordered Raumer to leave Halle again, since he considered his education complete. While in Halle, Raumer dedicated most of his time and energy to his studies with Thomasius. Four hours each week he played ballgames with friends, two hours were occupied with dancing lessons, and one hour he trained his Italian. The rest of his time was spent with Thomasius. The classes alone lasted four to five hours each day. In his free time, Raumer had to prepare for the intense exercises in the *collegium privatissimum*, which often focused upon historical topics. Thomasius here taught him and the other students to empathize with people from the past and to explore their inner selves through comparisons. For rhetoric, each student had to 'choose a subject from ancient or modern history and write apologies, either orations or letters, in German or Latin'.[29] The students wrote these papers independently and received Thomasius's corrections and comments later. The exercises in moral philosophy were even more demanding. The students here learned to analyse themselves as well as others by using historical examples as well as Thomasius's revised version of the Hippocratic theory of temperaments:[30]

> he exercised us for a long time in the praxis or – as we called it – the art of knowing oneself and others well. Yes, he demanded from us in his privatissimum that each [first] should describe his own temperament in writing and hand it over to him, and then [describe the temperament] of other participants . . . yes, even [the temperament] of Thomasius himself. In this way, we made one another blush and laugh. Later, he gave us assignments about such temperaments from holy and secular history; I, for example, had to work out the temperaments of King David and Emperor Charles V and explain my conclusions.[31]

Thomasius's private exercises created a space in which the students could safely investigate their thoughts and feelings. When they first entered his class, they were not calm philosophers, but blushed and laughed when confronted with one another's weaknesses. Self-reflection and openness demanded a personal transformation. Thomasius's innovative educational techniques supported this process. His use of writing, instead of the traditional oral tests, objectified the students' reactions on paper and created observational distance. The comparison with historical figures, such as King David or Charles V, similarly delivered distance and provided the students with a mirror for self-reflection. While Thomasius rejected the ideal of *historia magistra vitae* and doubted the uniformity of human experience over time, he still used historical examples in moral education. To the 'sincere reader', he argued, history still presented 'all kinds of images of virtues and vices' and could be instrumental for students who attempted to overcome their 'folly'.[32]

In his *Kurtzer Entwurf der politischen Klugheit* (Short Sketch of Political Prudence), Thomasius further explained this position and emphasized the benefits of historical examples in different educational contexts. Examples helped students reflect on and understand larger principles. For 'public lectures, where all kinds of listeners show up', he recommended that one should focus upon historical examples that made 'the listeners alert and awake in them the desire also to learn the foundational rules'. For 'selected listeners, who already have reached the proper age and are dedicated to regimentation', he recommended that instead one start with a textbook explaining the principles and use examples in oral instruction. The examples here served the purpose that 'the listeners gradually accustom themselves to reflection. But when a learner has accustomed himself a good part to this, one only needs the examples, so that the mind can relax a bit with these and make itself much more adept to further meditation'.[33] For these pedagogical purposes, it didn't even seem to matter if the historical examples were true or fictitious. He recommended a shocking story from early Roman mythology, Romulus's mass abduction of Sabine women, as starting point for a discussion of justice, decency and public welfare.

Thomasius probably also found inspiration for his exercises in the methodological discussions of the time and especially in the sceptical critique of history writing, known as historical Pyrrhonism.[34] The name Pyrrhonism was derived from ancient sceptic philosopher Pyrrho of Elis. Early modern scholars rediscovered Pyrro's ideas through the writings of Sextus Empiricus. They were widely discussed in the scholarly community during the seventeenth century and had a large impact on prominent thinkers, such as Michel de Montaigne and Pierre Bayle. The central claim of Pyrrhonism was that nothing could be known with certainty and that our assumptions about the world rested upon conflicting evidence. Historical Pyrrhonism applied this claim to historical knowledge in particular and questioned the validity of the surviving sources. The sources reflected the writers' personal beliefs and loyalties and only offered partial and partisan views of the events. To counter these critical arguments, scholars attempted to find reasons for *fides historica* (historical belief) in the written record, proposed rules for determining the trustworthiness of historians and witnesses, and argued that, even if certainty was unattainable, historical knowledge could be more or less 'probable'.

For Thomasius, the problem of knowing the past was closely connected to the problem of knowing oneself. When approaching historical examples, he instructed his students in 1713, they should first understand 'the general condition of human nature and the particular temperament of the person, who is dealt with' as well as the particularities of his time and of the country he lived in. Secondly, they should determine to which degree 'the history writer can be trusted'. The solution to this problem of trust involved a series of questions to the motivations, working and writing practices, and moral character of the historian. Students should ask whether the historian was 'partisan or much too credulous; where he has his [information] from; if he reveals some love or hatred or another affect?' Finally, Thomasius argued, 'if one wants to acquire an accurate idea of the actions and cleverness of those persons, who are described in histories: one must possess a correct understanding of oneself and of human nature'.[35] The procedures for investigating the past and for knowing oneself mirrored one another and were mutually dependent.

Exercising equality

When Thomasius delivered his lectures on 'How One Should Imitate the French in Everyday Life' at the University of Leipzig in 1687, his challenge had been to convince the academic community to accept the historicity of the world. For this purpose, he had advocated French scholarly ideals, which merged the world of learning with polite society. In Halle, he continued this effort and introduced decorum – or the art of governing conduct – as a part of the curriculum in practical philosophy. However, in his classes, Thomasius faced a different problem. To teach his students to examine their thoughts and feelings, and to empathize with the thoughts and feelings of others, he not only had to overcome the prejudices of the academic community, but also the hierarchies of society. His problem was not that his students did not recognize the realities of the world outside of the lecture hall, but rather that these realities interfered with the self-examination and free exchange of ideas, arguments and opinions within the lecture hall. The composition of his students made these concerns especially acute. Raumer remembered that August Hermann Francke, who was called to Halle in December 1691, had women in his audience, 'while Thomasius only taught men'. He also recalled that 'a large number of young men of distinction had followed [Thomasius from Leipzig] or arrived later in Halle'.[36] Thomasius himself claimed that his first Halle lectures attracted more than fifty auditors, many of whom were of high nobility.[37]

In his classes, Thomasius suppressed these social differences. In Spener's model spiritual exercises, students should read the Bible in an atmosphere of 'confidentiality and friendship' and the instructor should teach by example rather than by authority.[38] Thomasius went even further. He declared that his *Einleitung zur Vernunfft-Lehre* was written for 'all reasonable human beings', independent of social standing and gender.[39] He calculated tuition according to income and the poorest students participated free of charge. Raumer recalled that Thomasius immediately prohibited the students from calling him 'your Excellency' and that none of the students received special treatment because of their background. Thomasius, more than any other professor, Raumer explained, 'accustomed youth to a lovable candor and unrestraint'.[40] Thomasius often warned his students about what awaited them if they enrolled in his classes, where he would disregard riches, rank and nobility. Inside the lecture hall, nothing but talent mattered and 'the nature and reason of distinguished and rich people are not different or better than that of inferiors and subordinates'. Thomasius's own arguments and opinions were also open for questioning. '[T]he more they doubt me, yes, the sharper they oppose me', he claimed, 'the more pleased I will be'.[41] Learning to become an eclectic philosopher not only demanded that the students test the opinions of past philosophers, but also that they question the arguments of their teacher and disregard his authority. The philosopher, Thomasius explained to his students in 1713, must 'be careful that he doesn't, under the pretense of eclectic philosophy, introduce a new sect, that is, that he doesn't persecute those who are not of his opinion; he must rather grant his audience exactly the same freedom that he has employed himself'.[42]

Even forewarned, students were sometimes surprised by the candid tone. Zacharias Conrad von Uffenbach, who from 1701 attended Thomasius's two-year programme, remembered that his teacher 'used to flavor his lectures, almost to excess, with jokes and buffoonery, and, often violating decorum, also with scoffing judgments and anecdotes about his colleagues and other learned men'. Laughter and embarrassment not only distanced Thomasius's students from themselves but also taught them to question learned authorities, including the professors at the University of Halle. Uffenbach bemoaned that his fellow students adopted Thomasius's style. During the discussions, they were transformed into 'rather tasteless followers and defenders of contradicting principles'. 'Yes, frankly speaking', Uffenbach continued, 'almost all of Thomasius' auditors suffer from the weakness that they make a great effort to cultivate newer, odder, and more paradoxical opinions, and, therefore, normally appear difficult, suspect, and hostile to other people, especially those from the clerical estate'.[43] One of these clergymen, the minister Martin Günter, who briefly visited Thomasius's class on canon law in 1721, also recalled the disrespectful manner. Thomasius, Günter complained, 'made it his main job to mock the theologians of Wittenberg and Leipzig through and through, and, at the same time, scandalously turning many wonderful commonplaces upside down or even scornfully ridiculing previous interpretations'. Günter later disputed some of Thomasius's comments. The philosopher did not ignore the difficult visitor, but, on the contrary, 'kept me with him in his library for two and a half hours, even though I wanted to leave several times'.[44]

Only a few students at the time could participate in Thomasius's intensive two-year programme, and, in the spring of 1701, he changed his teaching routines to accommodate the increasing number of students arriving in Halle. He abandoned the *collegium privatissimum* and only offered public and private classes. The private classes would be much cheaper and open for all students, but Thomasius ensured that he would continue teaching the same way.[45] He also still encouraged his students to raise their doubts and contradict him in class. These new open private classes immediately tested the limits. Already in October 1701, Thomasius protested that lecture notes made by students were circulating around the city. 'I', Thomasius declared, 'hereby publicly protest against these [notes]. I do not accept them, or acknowledge them as my own, unless they agree with my other published works'. Thomasius was especially distressed that some students who only sporadically visited his classes propagated ideas that 'appear either ridiculous or absurd or even dangerous and Godless'. He therefore decided again to close his private classes to the public, allowing only students who signed up at the beginning of the semester.[46]

One student, Johann Gottfried Zeidlern, who in April 1701 published a collection of lecture notes from Thomasius's classes commented upon his teacher's dislike of such collections. According to Zeidlern, Thomasius had allowed him to publish the notes without edits, but had warned against the dangers of misreadings and misunderstandings. He admonished that his lectures were 'oral', delivered to 'young people' and not intended for a larger audience. Much would be incomprehensible, since different viewpoints were presented in a theatrical fashion upon the lectern and 'he in his discourse presents sometimes the persona of the opponent and sometimes [the persona] of the respondent, in the manner of a [disputational] class or a dialogue, which his audience quite easily noticed through change of tone or voice'. This 'variation of voices' did not come across well in writing. In the lecture hall, one also encountered 'vulgar and free similitudes and expressions, many digressions, often repetitions, etc.' and even expressions that appeared 'all-too-free or otherwise offensive'. Although such similitudes and expressions were allowed in an educational context, they were not always suitable for publication. Students should remember, Thomasius informed Zeidlern, 'that there are many things that can be thought and not suitably said; others that can be said respectably but not respectably written; others again that can be written respectably but not suitably published'.[47]

The place of equality

Thomasius's distinctions between public lectures, private classes and most private classes depended upon the places where he taught. Public lectures were traditionally delivered in the lecture halls of the university. The first lecture hall of the University of Halle was placed next to City Hall in the Weigh House, which, during the early 1690s, also accommodated wedding celebrations, large meetings, travelling comedians and livestock exchanges. Later, the entire building was used for lectures, but the Weigh House still reflected the hierarchical structures of society and university.[48] One engraving from the early eighteenth century depicted the large lecture hall in the Weigh House. Following the traditions of early modern universities, the lecture hall was divided into different spaces according to rank and position (Figure 1).[49] Portraits of patrons decorated the walls and professors were seated upon elevated plateaus above mere students and commoners.

In 1732, one adviser to the Prussian government emphasized the benefits of public lectures. 'When the professors diligently lecture in public and in the public lecture halls', he claimed, 'it adds to the good esteem and good reputation [of the university] among outsiders'. Here, the professors presented themselves to 'the whole world' for 'in public everyone who wants can listen'.[50] Since Thomasius lectured in German, he attracted not only students and local

Figure 1 Engraving of the large lecture hall in the Weigh House in Halle from the beginning of the eighteenth century. Courtesy Det Kongelige Bibliotek, Copenhagen.

scholars but also, as one of his contemporaries remarked, 'common citizens, who wondered about his new teachings'.[51] In such surroundings, Thomasius could not allow himself or his students to forget the rules of decorum.

Private classes were traditionally taught in the professors' own houses. Early modern households did not offer the same privacy as modern homes. The house was still a centre of manufacture and social life. During the sixteenth and seventeenth centuries, however, the upper echelons of European society demarcated spaces, such as the bedroom, the closet and the cabinet, which allowed for various degrees of detachment from the surrounding world.[52] Larger households were increasingly divided into spheres of intimacy and privacy. A similar development, Gadi Algazi has argued, happened within professorial houses. Medieval scholars were, in principle, celibate and did not establish their own households. Early modern professors, on the contrary, surrounded themselves not only with wives and children, but also with servants, assistants and lodging students.[53] Within these large households, though, professors established isolated spaces, such as libraries, studies and laboratories, for contemplation and scholarly work. Here, they not only avoided their extended families but also distanced themselves from other temporal concerns. They even attempted to escape the hierarchies of the traditional institutions of higher learning. One predicament of past scholarship, Thomas Sprat explained in his *History of the Royal Society* in 1667, was that 'the Seats of Knowledge' had been universities and not private laboratories. At university, students were trained to submit to their professors and, Sprat claimed, 'the very inequality of the Titles of *Teachers*, and *Scholars*, does very much suppress, and tame mens Spirits'. Such settings were 'by no means consistent with free Philosophical Consultation'. In contrast, the direct observation of nature in private laboratories 'gives us room to differ, without animosity, and permits us to raise contrary imaginations'.[54]

Thomasius's withdrawal from the public lecture halls served a similar purpose. Inside his house, he and his students escaped hierarchies and indulged in paradoxes, disagreements and free scholarly discourse. They could investigate themselves and the past without concern for the normal conventions of the university and surrounding society. Unlike the members of the Royal Society, they remained within the educational context of the university, but the walls of Thomasius's house protected them from many of the social and cultural demands of that institution. His decision in 1701 to abandon his *collegium privatissimum* and open his private classes to more students was only possible because of his changed living conditions.[55] In 1700, Thomasius acquired and rebuilt a stately residence in Große Ulrichstraße. In the main building, facing the street, he furnished several rooms as private lecture halls. One of these halls was large enough to hold 150 students. Thomasius could here teach a large audience in the same way as his private classes. Simultaneously, Thomasius started delivering public lectures within his private residence, escaping not only the conventions but also the freezing unheated rooms of the Weigh House.[56]

Thomasius and the age of history

The idea that German historical thinking started at the end of the eighteenth century for a long time reduced Thomasius's school to a minor and insignificant episode in 'the prehistory of historicism'.[57] In 1972, Notker Hammerstein reinserted Thomasius's school back into the history of historical scholarship, by emphasizing the significance of his legal philosophy and its enduring influence within German law faculties.[58] However, the best way to understand Thomasius's impact may not be to search for coherent philosophical ideas that lived on in later philosophies of history. Thomasius's works, as Ian Hunter has argued, were weapons in his battle against the confessional state.[59] He cared less about coherence and more about consequences. When he introduced history into the university curriculum, this was because of the effect that historical studies had upon his students and contemporary society. One key result was that it immunized students against overconfidence in philosophical ideas. Thomasius was central to the development of historical scholarship because he created a room for historical scholarship within the university. He offered an alternative definition of academic knowledge and insisted that historical knowledge was not merely auxiliary to theoretical knowledge but independently and equally valuable, as 'the second eye of wisdom'.[60] This definition may have lacked a coherent philosophical justification, but, for a time, it permitted and encouraged the pursuit of historical scholarship within German Enlightenment universities.

Thomasius also created a physical space within the university, where this kind of knowledge could thrive. His transformation of the lecture hall provided a venue where students could explore opinions and arguments that were different from those of their contemporaries and examine their inner selves. The distinction between public and private was no longer just a division between classes that were free of charge and classes that students had to pay for. It was also a distinction between different venues that allowed for different kinds of instruction. For intensive exercises, which aimed at transforming the students, this latter distinction remained important, even after the demise of confessional orthodoxy. Only during the second half of the nineteenth century, with the establishment of large, institutionalized seminars, as discussed in the last chapter of this book, did German history professors gradually abandon the private teaching format.

2

The field

The academic journey as fieldwork

Early Enlightenment scholars did not only search for historical differences in university libraries and bookshops. The confessional authorities of Europe controlled the circulation of dissenting opinions and publishing heterodox ideas could have dire consequences. Several scholars who violated the confessional codes of conduct lost their positions and were forced into exile. Unorthodox books were publicly burned, and radical writers jailed. Even the contemporary intellectual and religious history of Europe was hard to access. To uncover this history, scholars started correspondences with like-minded thinkers, shared clandestine manuscripts and forbidden books and copied one another's notes.[1] Others went even further and travelled across Europe to encounter dissenters and record their thoughts, beliefs and arguments.

Holland was especially suited for such journeys.[2] After the Dutch Revolt against Spanish rule in the sixteenth century, William the Silent had introduced a policy of tolerance of religious dissent.[3] The Calvinist Church dominated, but dissenters were allowed to stay and keep their beliefs. During the seventeenth century, the rights of religious minorities increased. As other European countries simultaneously enforced confessional uniformity within their borders, culminating with Louis XIV's revocation of the Edict of Nantes in 1685 and the exodus of French Protestants, Holland became a place of refuge. Persecuted religious communities, such as Polish and German non-Trinitarian Socinians, French Labadists and English Quakers, resettled here. The country also attracted many intellectuals and scholars, whose writings challenged European religious and political authorities, and produced its own radical thinkers. Around 1700, the most notorious Dutch dissenters were the followers of Baruch Spinoza, whose naturalistic philosophy and biblical criticism were considered as serious threats to the political and religious order.[4] Socinians and Spinozists were also forbidden to publish their ideas in Holland, but, unlike in most of Europe, they were allowed to live there and could be encountered in streets of liberal towns, such as Amsterdam and Rotterdam.

In the spring of 1705, Christoph August Heumann, who recently had acquired his magister degree at the University of Jena, travelled through Northern Germany and Holland, together with his friend, the mathematician Bonifacius Heinrich Ehrenberg. After his return from Holland, Heumann became the most prominent historian of philosophy and scholarship in the Protestant German states. He founded the first journal for the history of philosophy, the *Acta philosophorum* (Acts of the Philosophers) published in Halle between 1715 and 1723. His short 1718 *Conspectus reipublicae literariae* (Overview of the Republic of Letters) served as the standard textbook for the history of scholarship at German universities for most of the eighteenth century. In 1737, he became a professor of theology and the history of scholarship at the newly founded University of Göttingen. In his writings, Heumann advocated a view of history that fitted Thomasius's eclecticism. History, he argued, should deliver a multitude of arguments that the eclectic philosopher could choose from to formulate his own philosophy.[5] Heumann's travel journal from 1705, published in part by Georg Andreas Cassius in 1768, was the notes of a future eclectic historian of philosophy and scholarship.[6] In Holland, he encountered many different viewpoints, which were otherwise not easily available in print, and investigated the accuracy of contemporary historical works about the underground. As a diligent fieldworker, he collected as much information as possible and filled his journal with detailed minutes of conversations with religious and intellectual dissenters. He often recorded exchanges word-by-word and noted questions as well as answers. His journey can be considered as a kind of historical fieldwork, replacing manuscripts and books with oral interviews.

A few similar journals from the early Enlightenment have survived. The authors of these journals were all recent graduates of Protestant German universities and probably all connected to the Thomasius circle in Halle. They normally went together with another young scholar and visited either just Holland or both Holland and England. The most voluminous of these journals is that of the future Jena professor Gottlieb Stolle, who devoted more than a thousand manuscript pages to detailing his encounters in Holland, 1703–4. Other similar journals are those of Johann Burkhard Mencke, 1698–9; Christoph August Lämmermann, 1709–11; Zacharias Conrad von Uffenbach, 1709–11; and Johann Gottlieb Deichsel, 1717–19.[7] These travellers all wrote notes in the same meticulous style as Heumann, and often followed the same routes and visited the same scholars, but their interests differed. Mencke mostly visited academics and probably prepared to inherit his father's position as editor of the most significant academic journal in the Protestant German states, *Acta eruditorum* (Acts of the Learned). Stolle wrote lengthy comments regarding the clothing and manners of academics and about the Spinozist underground. Uffenbach was especially interested in manuscripts, books and curiosity cabinets.[8] Heumann also had his own particular interests. The most extensive notes, which have survived in Cassius's selection, recorded conversations with lay preachers, mystics and religious sectarians. In Holland, Heumann experienced that recent historical works about the underground were not just descriptions of the underground but also interventions in ongoing battles about religion and religious tolerance. The dissenters were not passive objects of investigation but keenly aware of the political importance of the historical works and supplied historians with information and source materials.

Travel guides

Before leaving Jena, Heumann prepared for the journey and studied the Dutch intellectual and religious landscape. His most important source of information, his notes indicate, was Henrich Ludolff Benthem's *Holländischer Kirch- und Schulen-Staat* (Dutch Church and School State) of 1698. Benthem, born in Celle near Hanover, was a Lutheran theologian and future superintendent of Harburg.[9] His book was based upon years of study and two journeys to Holland, in about 1686 and 1693. It contained a comprehensive historical and institutional overview of the Dutch intellectual and religious life, but also offered practical advice to students and academics visiting Holland. Benthem even presented his book as a travel guide and had it printed in a handy *octavo* format, in two volumes, that allowed travellers to bring a copy in their luggage.[10]

The most obvious advantage of Bentham's book was the recommended travel route that ensured that one visited 'the most significant places in these countries, in particular all universities, in the right order'. The route was accompanied by recommendations of sites 'where something remarkable can be seen, or great artists and scholars reside, or where people with unusual opinions in matters of religion can be encountered'. Heumann and Ehrenberger more or less stayed on Bentham's route, as did many other German academic travellers. Heumann also followed Bentham's recommendations concerning interesting scholars and places of knowledge. In connection with Rotterdam, Bentham praised not only the Erasmus statue but also the many libraries in the city and mentioned that 'that of the polite mister Henrici is not among the worst'.[11] Heumann noted this remark in his journal and visited Henrici and his library.[12] On his way back to Jena, Heumann also briefly visited Bentham in Uelzen. Bentham probably also influenced the particular note-taking practices of German academic travellers. He recommended his readers to write down their impressions every night, after returning to their lodgings. To remember the content of academic conversations, however, even diurnal note-taking was not enough. Travellers, Bentham admonished, must therefore always keep a 'small tablet at hand' and 'already in the presence of the learned man write observations down'.[13] Bentham realized that the practice was unusual and therefore recommended readers to ask permission first. But even the restrictions of academic decorum could be circumvented. Uffenbach developed 'a particular skill' to write secretly with a pencil in a notebook hidden in his pocket and 'to record memorable conversations and important relations' without his conversational partners noticing.[14]

Bentham's book was not only a historical and institutional handbook and a travel guide for students and scholars in Holland, but also a contribution to the reconciliation between Lutherans and Calvinists in Brandenburg-Prussia.[15] He dedicated his book to the Elector of Brandenburg Friedrich III, expressing his hope and conviction that the Protestant Churches could be reunited 'through the ties of doctrine and love'. His travel guide therefore also portrayed Calvinist Holland as positively as possible and his route went through an enlightened landscape, in which Northern German scholars would feel at home. Bentham openly admitted that his guided tour was selective, following his own convictions. He wished 'before we fully embark on the journey to show the bad and the good in the United Netherlands so that [the traveller] better can avoid the former and embrace the latter'. Students and young scholars should especially avoid the many sectarians and dissenters, who had found refuge in the country. Benthem praised Dutch liberty and argued 'that so many scholars live in the United Netherlands' because the country 'not only provides well for them, but also allows everyone to speak, write, and live as suits him best'. He was nevertheless critical of the excessive religious freedom in the country. Tolerance and reconciliation between Lutherans and Calvinists should not lead to tolerance of radical dissent and Benthem lamented 'that it is very difficult to combine the large freedom of religion in Holland with the rules of the school of Christ'. In his preface, he expressed a pious hope that his book could serve the 'defense against and extermination of [religious] enthusiasm'.[16]

The German travellers did not always follow Benthem's advice. Heumann was not in Holland to find confirmation of his beliefs, but rather to uncover unknown arguments and ideas and to investigate the claims of recent historical works. His travel journal carefully recorded numerous conversations with Mennonites, Socinians, radical Pietists, Labadists and Quakers. Short remarks in Benthem's book offered clues to how and where one could find members of this religious underground. He briefly mentioned the locations of the Quakers and Mennonites in Amsterdam. Heumann followed these hints and visited both congregations. Benthem also remarked that one could read and buy Quaker writings in Jacob Claus's bookshop in the Prinsenstraat in Amsterdam.[17] Jacob Claus was not only a book dealer; he and his older brother Jan were key figures in the Dutch Quaker community. They had previously lived in England and accompanied William Penn and George Fox during their travels in Holland in 1677 and 1684.[18] Heumann sought out Jan Claus, had a two-hour conversation with him and wrote lengthy notes about the history and faith of the Quakers.

Benthem's book was not Heumann's only guide to the underground. In 1700, the radical Pietist Gottfried Arnold published the second volume of his controversial *Unpartheyische Kirchen- und Ketzerhistorie* (Impartial History of the Church and Heretics), which detailed the history of heresy in the modern age and included comprehensive descriptions of religious sects in Holland. This history was the culmination of Arnold's attempt to rewrite all of church history. He did not just document the beliefs of dissenters but questioned hopes for the unification of the Christian confessions as well as the grand historical narrative of the modern confessional states. In Arnold's counternarrative, the

Holy Roman Empire was not the embodiment of universal Christendom, or the last of the four world monarchies, but an attack on true belief. The early church only remained true to itself as long as it remained heretical and in opposition to secular power. Institutionalized Christianity, especially after Emperor Constantine made it the state religion in the fourth century, primarily served the interests and ambitions of the clergy. The resurrection of the Empire under Charlemagne and the Saxon emperors reinforced the disastrous alliance between the institutionalized church and secular power. The Reformation initially had challenged this alliance, but had been co-opted by the clergy, who again misused faith for their personal benefit and persecuted dissenters, culminating with the bloody religious wars of the sixteenth and seventeenth centuries. Only among heretics, such as those now gathering in Holland, had true faith survived over the centuries. Everywhere and always, he concluded, 'the true Church of Christ' must be 'invisible, hidden, suppressed, and in the desert'.[19] Arnold's book, especially his anticlerical sentiments, resonated with Thomasius, who strongly recommended it to his students as 'the best and most useful book' in the genre, after the Bible.[20] The travel journals, especially those of Heumann and Stolle, frequently referred to Arnold.

The travellers also utilized personal contacts and random encounters in Holland to track down interesting conversational partners. Uffenbach, an ardent bibliophile, sought out local book dealers and asked if 'here among the preachers or others is a connoisseur of studies and books'.[21] The future theologian Heumann instead employed his contacts in the Dutch Lutheran community. When he arrived in a new city, Heumann first visited the Lutheran minister, who often informed him about local controversies and radical dissenters. The Lutheran minister in Rotterdam mentioned the quarrel between Pierre Jurieu and Pierre Bayle; Heumann afterwards visited both. The Lutheran minister in The Hague praised the exemplary life of the radical Pietist Friedrich Breckling, but also condemned his problematic theology. Heumann next visit was to Breckling. The Lutheran minister in Leiden warned Heumann against Thomas Crenius, a pseudonym for Brandenburg philologist Thomas Theodor Crusius, who had immigrated to the city and earned a paltry living as a textbook writer. The minister declared that Crenius 'doesn't attend divine service, doesn't receive the Eucharist, and is a true rabble-rouser, who rejects all our theologians and criticizes everyone'.[22] Heumann immediately went to Crenius.

History as fieldwork

Many of Heumann's conversational partners, even among lay preachers and sectarians, knew the historical literature and had strong opinions about Benthem's and Arnold's descriptions of Dutch religious life. From the dissenters' point of view, the books were not impartial accounts of historical facts, but interventions in an ongoing battle between the Dutch Calvinist majority and different religious minorities.[23] Shortly after Heumann's arrival in Holland, Breckling informed him that Benthem 'on his Dutch journey had enjoyed himself, and often drank a glass of wine with the Reformed, and therefore was persuaded to judge superficially in his book and to pay no attention to the true condition of the Church, which he also did not realize'.[24]

In Holland, Heumann experienced how the production of books was part of the process of interpretation. The dissenters often argued that an author's personal preferences and convictions had influenced the content of a book, but they also pointed to the significance of informers, readers, translators and printers. Benthem did not write much about the Quakers but instead referred readers to Gerard Croese's *Historia Quakeriana* (Quaker History) of 1695.[25] During his long conversation with Jan Claus in Amsterdam, Heumann also asked about this book. Claus reported that Croese had consulted him to find material for the book. Claus had agreed to help and wrote to England to acquire copies of relevant sources, but Croese had disappointed him. He had not allowed the Quakers to read the book before publication and had suppressed the truth, because, Claus claimed, he feared the reaction of the Calvinist clergy. Claus, however, recommended the Latin edition over the German translation, which was even more hostile.[26] The recent publication of the second volume of Arnold's history of heretics stirred emotions among dissenters in Holland. Heumann also asked Jan Claus about Arnold's account of Quaker history. Claus had not yet read it but reported that the book had provoked controversy in the city and that one prominent member of the congregation, Casper Kohlhans, had written a letter to Arnold with grievances. Breckling, on the contrary, complained about German efforts to censor the book and had encouraged leading Pietists, Philipp Jacob Spener and Johann Winckler, to intervene on Arnold's behalf. The Labadist teacher in Franeker, Thomas Varmod, revealed how the community had influenced later editions of Arnold's book. Heumann noted:

> I also asked if Arnold's history [of the Labadists] was accurate and recorded in accordance with the truth. He said that in the beginning Arnold had written many falsehoods, because he had trusted the reports of evil people. However, when his history of heretics was translated into Dutch and should be printed in Amsterdam, the printer, who was their friend, had informed them about this. Then, Arnold also himself had contacted them, and made an appendix, based upon exacter information, and corrected everything: so that now the true history of the Labadists could be found in [Arnold's book].[27]

Heumann explored the Dutch underground, but not the Spinozist thinkers that otherwise attracted much attention. Spinoza and Spinozism were familiar topics in the Thomasius circle and also interested some of the travellers, especially Gottlieb Stolle.[28] But in Heumann's journal the notorious philosopher was only a minor concern. Heumann was also not particularly interested in the controversies over Cartesianism, although Benthem described these over many pages in the second volume of his book.[29] Heumann instead investigated religious ideas and beliefs that were less known in Germany and not easily available in print. He had several conversations about the mystic Jacob Böhme, whose influence upon Dutch religious life Benthem had ignored, but whom Arnold counted among the 'witnesses of truth' and praised as 'highly intelligent and enlightened by God, and placed as a sign and wonder before the scholarly world'.[30] The minutes of some of these conversations even indicate that Heumann had prepared a questionnaire before leaving Jena. Albert Jansen, a shoemaker and Mennonite lay preacher in Emden, had troubles answering these questions and therefore repeated himself:

> I asked what he thought of Jacob Böhme's writings, to which he answered that he sometimes looked into them. However, he could not judge them since they were very unclear and hard to understand. He would also not condemn them, since he did not know if they were condemnable as he did not understand them, and maybe God had granted Böhme a larger light than himself, and he therefore could not understand them. He therefore could not say that he agreed with Böhme, as he did not understand him.[31]

Other travellers were also interested in the religious underground, although no one was as focused as Heumann. Stolle constantly interrogated theologians and lay preachers about Arnold's and Böhme's writings. They also found inspiration and guidance in one another and sometimes repeated the same experiences in Holland. Collected information was not necessarily lost, but often transmitted from person to person. Johann Gottlieb Deichsel visited Uffenbach in Frankfurt am Main in 1718 on his way to Holland and England. Uffenbach was not particularly interested in religious matters, but he nonetheless had followed Benthem's hints and attended the divine services of the Mennonites and Quakers in Amsterdam. He also acquired manuscripts relating to the religious underground. During his visit to Uffenbach's house, Deichel studied this manuscript collection. He was particularly fascinated by Uffenbach's 'beautiful collection of very many Quaker writings, mostly English, which he had bought collected from a Quaker in Rotterdam'. In Holland, Deichsel himself visited the divine services of Quakers, Socinians and Mennonites, and interviewed members of these congregations.[32]

Fieldwork as moral education

Heumann did not visit the Dutch religious dissenters because he shared their beliefs. Late in life, he claimed that as early as 1704, shortly before his journey to Holland, he had adopted the Calvinist interpretation of the Eucharist, which claimed that Christ's body and blood are spiritually, and not physically, present in the wine and bread.[33] In his theological writings, Heumann, like Benthem, defended the reconciliation of Lutherans and Calvinists. He developed a historical-critical method of exegeses, which challenged not only Lutheran orthodoxy, but also the mystical and spiritual theology that filled the pages of his travel journal. In 1716, he divided those who studied the history of philosophy into three groups: eclectic philosophers, who saw the world with their own eyes; sectarians, who saw through the eyes of others; and the last group were 'fantasists and enthusiasts', like Jacob Böhme and other mystics, who 'are dreaming and imagining that they are seeing, although they have closed their eyes'.[34]

However, according to Heumann, the purpose of the history of philosophy and scholarship was not only to provide unknown philosophical ideas but also to serve moral education. Intellectual tolerance, impartiality and open-mindedness were not just abstract principles but had to be personally acquired and demanded practice. The confrontation with the historical plurality of contradictory arguments would develop such epistemic and moral virtues.

Prolonged exercises on the history of philosophy and scholarship, he argued, habituated scholars to 'endure the brightness of paradoxical truths'. Even the history of unsubstantiated arguments, faulty judgements and wrong hypotheses served an educational purpose. The recollection of the mistakes of the past ensured that 'we do not become stubborn in our opinions' and prepared the readers for 'modesty in disputes' and tolerance of disagreements.[35] For such a moral education, no place could be more appropriate than Holland, where travellers could not only investigate the claims in recent historical works, but also encounter the living history of the European religious underground in all its diversity.

In *Discours de la méthode* (Discourse on Method) of 1637, René Descartes compared travelling to history of philosophy and pointed to the alienating effect of both. His readings in school, and the confrontation with the many different and contradictory opinions of past philosophers, had convinced him 'that nothing solid could have been built upon such shaky foundations'. His later travels did not encourage him more, for, he argued, 'so long I merely considered the customs of other men, I found hardly any reason for confidence, for I observed in them almost as much diversity as I had found previously among the opinions of philosophers'. However, his experiences with the strangeness of the past as well as with that of other Europeans still had educational value. Especially his travels had taught Descartes that 'many things which, although seeming very extravagant and ridiculous to us, are nevertheless commonly accepted and approved in other nations; and so I learned not to believe firmly anything of which I had been persuaded only by example or custom'.[36]

Heumann similarly pointed to the parallels between the educational benefits of travelling and those of historical studies. But Heumann's conclusion differed from that of Descartes. The realization of one's human fallibility was not just a step towards a more certain philosophy but the very purpose of such investigations. If the history of philosophy undermined philosophical authorities, Heumann argued, travels through the confessional landscape of Europe was the best antidote to religious intolerance:

So we learn from the history of philosophy that philosophers are human and can make mistakes. . . . He who is inexperienced in the history of philosophy, he binds his entire reason to the authority of one particular philosopher. . . . It is the same as with religion. He who never has set his foot outside of Spain or

Italy, he imagines that Lutherans are cursed heretics and already burning in hell, and he barely believes that they are real human beings. However, when he sees the world and through travels learns to know members of all kinds of religions, then his eyes open. As he before believed that the Lutherans could make mistakes, he now starts to believe that also in the Roman Church the Errare humanum est is more than true.[37]

Philosophy versus history, again

The institutionalization of historical scholarship was not secured with the modernizing programme of Thomasius and his followers. In German academic philosophy, this eclectic and historical programme was short-lived. Descartes's distinction between philosophy and history instead prevailed. In 1703, on the recommendation of Leibniz, Christian Wolff was hired as professor of mathematics at the University of Halle. In the following decades, he introduced a new rationalistic school of Enlightenment philosophy. He was banished to Marburg in 1724, after praising the practical philosophy of the Chinese, but, nonetheless, his school increasingly defined German Enlightenment philosophy.[38] In 1740, when Frederick the Great became King of Prussia, Wolff was called back to Halle. The rise of Wolffianism resulted in a disconnect between the development of university philosophy and the development of historical scholarship. Wolff reinstated a scholastic definition of philosophical knowledge, as theory based upon certain and immutable principles, and of historical knowledge, as auxiliary to theory. Historical knowledge was the bare knowledge of facts, including facts about the natural world, and 'the lowest grade of human knowledge'. Unlike philosophy and mathematics, he explained, 'it does not presuppose any prior knowledge from which as premises it ought to deduce a great labyrinth of proofs. Therefore, there is no type of knowledge which is inferior to common historical knowledge'.[39] Since modern philosophical knowledge was based on secure foundations, concerns for the thoughts of past generations of thinkers were no longer relevant.

Despite the triumph of Wolff, some of the historical works of the early Enlightenment remained influential outside German school philosophy.[40] Heumann's *Conspectus reipublicae literariae* helped establish the history of scholarship as a propaedeutic teaching subject at German universities. The book was republished many times and constantly expanded, even after Heumann's death, and served as a model for several later textbooks. Students would here not only find an overview history of scholarship but also learn about the changeability and temporality of any scholarly and philosophical programme. Historical scholarship also remained important within German law faculties throughout the eighteenth century. The primary interest of scholars within this juridical-historical tradition was not scholarly and philosophical works but legal history and the documents that had shaped this history. These documents could not be found in university libraries, or among exiled philosophers and lay preachers in the Dutch underground, but instead in princely archives.

3

The princely archive

The archives of Rijswijk

During the summer and fall of 1697, diplomats from all over Europe descended upon the small town of Rijswijk in Holland to negotiate a peace after the Nine Years War between Louis XIV's France and the Grand Alliance of European powers.[1] The negotiations were unusually complicated. Many countries had participated in the war and other important matters were on the table as well, including the Glorious Revolution and William of Orange's claim to the British crown, the Spanish succession, and the confessional status of territories in the borderlands between France and the Holy Roman Empire. Apart from the official negotiations in the palace of Rijswijk, representatives also assembled secretly at other locations. Most importantly, two high-ranking and trusted representatives of the French and British monarchs, Marshal Louis-François Boufflers and Hans Willem Bentinck, Earl of Portland, met elsewhere to reach a settlement. One crucial meeting, which probably decided the outcome of the negotiations between France and England, took place in an orchard outside the city gates of Halle, near Brussels, in July 1697.

Among the participants in the German delegation was Johann Peter von Ludewig, the future chancellor of the University of Halle, Thomasius's successor in the faculty of law, and founder of the influential school of *Reichshistorie* (imperial history).[2] In 1697, however, Ludewig was only twenty-nine years old and a newly appointed professor of metaphysics and the art of reasoning. He accompanied the sixteen-year-old crown prince of Schwarzenberg, Adam Franz Karl, and befriended several prominent diplomats, including a delegate of the Habsburg Court in Vienna, Count Johann Friedrich von Seilern and the Swedish mediators Count Carl Bonde and Baron Nils Lillieroot.

In Rijswijk, Ludewig fervently collected eyewitness accounts and written sources. Following the obsessive documenting practices of the early German Enlightenment, discussed in the previous chapter, he interviewed participants for hours and copied every piece of paper from the negotiations that he could find, sometimes, together with a former Halle student, Wilhelm Ludwig von Maskowsky, working in shifts throughout the night if the documents were needed back the next day.[3]

After his return to Halle in 1698, Ludewig offered a new course on the peace negotiations.[4] Instead of just explaining the recent events in Rijswijk, or the complicated politics of the Nine Years War and European dynastic succession, he asked his students to imagine themselves in the situation of future historians, who only had access to written testimonies. Future historians, Ludewig explained, would wonder not only how French armies had resisted the combined forces of the neighbouring states, but also how Louis XIV had managed to gain considerable advantages during the final peace negotiations. To solve the mystery of the French success in Rijswijk, he claimed, one needed to know all the secret meetings and underhand agreements between the various delegates during the long process of negotiation. Even during the negotiations, no one possessed such an overview and the reports that the delegates mailed back to different European courts were not necessarily trustworthy. Even the most recent past – the negotiations that had ended just a few months earlier – was almost inaccessible to the historian. Ludewig had become aware of this because of the unusual insights he had gained about the production of documents in Rijswijk. However, similar problems would emerge for all historical investigations that were based upon archival documents and diplomatic reports. For the young philosophy professor, the peace negotiations therefore offered an opportunity to discuss the epistemology of archival research in general.

Distrust in archives

Ludewig's discussion of the epistemology of archival research added new layers to the sceptical Pyrrhonist critique of history writing and the debate about 'historical belief'. Since the middle of the seventeenth century, several sceptics had questioned if historical actors could be trusted as witnesses. The statesmen and generals, who once were considered ideal historians, were now viewed as offering only partisan and fragmented versions of the past. They were personally invested and therefore described the events to their own advantage. The historian could investigate their moral character, but even if they were honest, their viewpoints would necessarily be limited and only represent one perspective. No general could overview the entire battlefield. No statesman knew everything that happened within the boundaries of his country.[5] These concerns, Ludwig now argued, were equally relevant in relation to archives. Diplomats and bureaucrats had produced many of the documents in archives, and these documents were therefore products of flattery, personal interests and political considerations. They did not become any more credible by being included in an archive, no matter how long they had been lying around. Often such documents would contradict one another, especially if one visited several archives.[6] Ludewig consequently questioned that 'an archive, if it consists of reports from delegates or servants, without exception deserves higher belief' and that 'a historian who bases [his work] upon such an archive is without mistakes'.[7]

The problems did not stop with the untrustworthiness of witnesses and the creators of documents. After the events, archives and archivists further distorted the written record. Archives were not all-inclusive, access was limited and historians were seldom allowed to see the most interesting and sensitive documents. One should therefore apply the critical tools for the evaluation of testimony not only to historians and witnesses but also to archives and archivists. These were no less fallible and Ludewig claimed that he considered 'no archive impartial in domestic matters [and even] less complete'.[8] Most historians, he further complained, did not reflect upon these problems; they rarely visited several archives or compared the contents, and often merely reproduced the documents that were presented to them. Ludewig's solution was to favour those historians who had experienced the events themselves and also collected opposing testimonies from different historical actors and eyewitnesses, as he had done in Rijswijk.[9] This solution, however, was not much of a solution at all. Few events in world history had been documented with a similar diligence and fervour. The solution also demanded that the readers trusted the historian in the field. A few years later, Ludewig's adversary and colleague at the University of Halle, Nikolaus Hieronymus Gundling, questioned if this were possible. In Rijswijk, he claimed, Ludewig did not have access to many important documents from the inner circles of power, and no one should trust reports in gossipy 'fish-market newspapers'.[10]

Ludewig's sceptical discussion of archives and archivists was not unique. Although no other scholar was as scrupulous and empirical as Ludewig, similar thoughts and concerns about archives appear in many contemporary writings on the problem of 'historical belief'.[11] These discussions reflected that historians already were using archives for historical research, but also revealed that the primary purpose of princely archives was not historical research. European courts stored old documents and diplomatic reports for political reasons. The content of an archive and the degree of *fides archivorum* (belief in archives), Gundling explained in his lectures in Halle, depended upon the interests and position of the prince in relation to the topic. The archivist, Gundling declared, 'represents the prince'.[12] German archivists agreed. Throughout the eighteenth century, archival manuals, written by archivists, almost exclusively described archives as tools of state and as repositories of documents relating to the legal and territorial claims of the prince. Archives, according to these manuals, should be partisan. They served, as the head archivist at Plassenburg Philipp Ernst Spieß declared, as 'the bulwark against all claims of hostile neighbors',[13] or, in the words of the Zweibrüchen archivist Georg August Bachmann, as 'the written treasury of a prince'.[14] The most important personal qualities of archivists were therefore not impartiality and honesty, but 'discretion' and 'loyalty'.[15] German scholars could therefore not immediately use archives as a reliable source of information. They first had to transform the princely archive into a place for mediation between past and present.

Trust in documents

During the late seventeenth and eighteenth centuries, as Arnaldo Momigliano pointed out, many antiquarians argued that historical sources included not only testimonies, but also non-literary sources, such as coins, monuments and archaeological evidence, and written sources, such as inscriptions, that could not themselves be considered as testimonies, but rather as remains of the historical event.[16] In connection with the German debates about 'historical belief' and within Thomasius's circle, as Momigliano also noted, such arguments were quite common. German Enlightenment scholars, however, were normally more concerned about distinguishing between different kinds of written sources than about the possible benefits of antiquities. They were especially interested in certain kinds of documents, known in Latin as *diplomata* and in German as *Urkunden*. The conventional English translation would be charters or acts, but German scholars used the word more broadly to describe all official and legally binding documents.[17] In the rest of this book, they will just be referred to as *official documents*.

German princes carefully stored, and guarded, such documents for centuries because of their legal significance within the Holy Roman Empire. The Empire not only played a symbolic role as the embodiment of universal Christendom, as the continuation of the ancient Roman Empire and as the last of the four world monarchies but also offered a practical framework for interactions between the states and cities, even across confessional boundaries. Its legal institutions, the Reichshofrat in Vienna and the Reichskammergericht in Wetzlar, protected longstanding privileges and freedoms, some of which were almost as ancient as the Empire itself. Older official documents remained a central part of the existing legal order, recording these privileges and freedoms. During the seventeenth century, this legal interest resulted in several so-called *bella diplomatica* (document wars), which promoted the development of new critical tools for the evaluation of manuscripts and detection of forgeries, as evidenced by the great works of the Maurist tradition, especially Jean Mabillon's *De re diplomatica* (On Diplomatics) of 1681.[18] Most likely, legal discourse also influenced the discussions about 'historical belief' and 'belief in archives' as much as the writings of antiquarians. Imperial jurists had long distinguished between testimonies and other kinds of non-testimonial evidence, such as a bloody sword found in the hand of an accused murderer. During the late seventeenth century, as Lorraine Daston has shown, these legal distinctions also influenced other European discussions about 'probability' in knowledge-making.[19]

In 1698, the Weimar archivist Tobias Pfanner responded to Ludewig's lecture programme on the epistemology of archival research and emphasized the significance of such distinctions. Ludewig, Pfanner claimed, had disregarded some of the core principles of 'historical belief'. Historical knowledge could never reach perfection and would remain 'fragmented', but scholars could still base historical writings upon archival documents. They should simply remember, Pfanner argued, that the documents were not all 'the same kind' and did not all merit the same 'belief'. He agreed that reports by delegates were normally not trustworthy, but he considered protocols beyond 'doubt'.[20] In his reply to Pfanner, Ludewig questioned the trustworthiness of protocols, but admitted that distinctions were necessary. He also exempted some categories of archival documents from critical scrutiny (granted that they were not forgeries):

> Regarding the belief in archives [one should consider that] all kinds of pieces are in these [archives]. . . . This variation of pieces, that an archive consists of, also varies the belief that one owes to it. . . . I do not doubt any deeds or contracts because these are set up by both sides, collated, and then exchanged with one another's signatures; public privileges and official documents also deserve high belief in so far that those who signed them had the right and might; edicts, rescripts, declarations, bills are always infallible expressions of the will of the prince. . . . Inventory-, acquisition-, tax- and tenure-books seldom have anything in them with which one can make them suspicious . . . only in regard to the other pieces one must employ greater caution.[21]

The discussions about 'historical belief' focused attention on groups of archival documents that escaped the normal problems of testimony and underscored the particular value of these for historical research. Official documents could be considered as remains of historical events or, as Ludewig named his twelve-volume edition of such sources published between 1720 and 1741, as *reliquiae* (relics).[22] The study of these documents therefore granted the historical account credibility and offered an answer to the sceptical challenge. In his lectures on German history, which one of his former students gathered from lecture manuscripts and student notes and published after his death, Ludewig briefly summarized the European discussions about historical Pyrrhonism and explained how his students could avoid the problem of 'doubt':

> But where in history should one really doubt or not? Answer: One investigates what in [history] is called certain and uncertain. That is certain which one can prove from the sources of historical certainties. And these are: 1) Official documents 2) coeval authors; 3) coins; 4) inscriptions and epitaphs; 5) seals; 6) statues; and finally, 7) pictures. Official documents belong among the most distinguished sources. For they are 1) written with the foreknowledge of the prince and 2) flown from the feathers of the most learned men, who

therefore had the best knowledge. 3) They are about official business and therefore cast the greatest light on matters of state.²³

This conviction that document relics reconnected past and present also seem to have influenced his teaching practices. Ludewig rejected traditional lectures and instead involved students in his ongoing work. Visiting his classes, he explained in 1735, was not like reading a book. He did not just read his lecture manuscript aloud, but instead presented his current thoughts on the topic. 'I often, in fervor and profound reflection, come upon thoughts and new truths and their interconnections that otherwise would not have crossed my mind at my writing desk or when alone', he claimed. The student was also not just expected to memorize what he said, but should have 'the pure sources by coeval writers in front of him'.²⁴

History and law

Ludewig may have found a solution to the problem of 'belief in archives' that convinced himself, his students and some of his colleagues, but this does not explain why German princes allowed him to investigate their archives and even to publish some of the content. It was not even obvious if Ludewig's archival work should count as scholarship. In the scholastic definition of knowledge, historical knowledge was only auxiliary to theoretical knowledge. This definition of knowledge was challenged by Thomasius, but it gained new ground with the rise of the rationalistic philosophy of Christian Wolff. Archives only contained local and disparate fragments of the past, which had little or no consequence for theoretical knowledge. In 1739, when the newly founded University of Göttingen considered Ludewig for a chair, one influential education reformer scornfully remarked:

> It doesn't matter that Ludewig has seen into more archives than that in Magdeburg. What can I learn from an archive, apart from particularities about a country that others don't know? This doesn't belong to scholarship, which, of course, is about universals. Otherwise, all archivists should be more learned than other people, although one sees the contrary. It is a mistake ... when one attributes Ludewig's learning and reputation to the archives. Yes, I am quite sure that the inspection of archives has harmed him more than helped him.²⁵

Ludewig was no less dismissive of theoretical knowledge and its dominance over history. Like Thomasius, he rejected the older tradition of *historia magistra vitae*. The attempt to teach 'virtues and vices' through historical examples, he claimed, had resulted in that 'one employed either philosophers in general or theologians for the historical profession'. These were first of all interested in the moral or theological message and therefore started to write history as fiction because 'fables could be thought out much better for moral than what could be found in true histories'. Such history books could be considered as nothing other than 'novels or scholarly lies'. The philosophical and theological dominance over history had been equally devastating for university education. 'One has until now sought the utility of historical classes in morals and ethics', Ludewig claimed in 1719. History education had therefore made 'no one more able or skilled for the state or for matters of lieges and lands or for other functions in the German Empire'.[26]

Ludewig's defence of historical scholarship was instead its usefulness for jurisprudence and political thought. The long history of the Holy Roman Empire not only rendered older documents legally significant but also justified historical research. In all other countries, he claimed, historical research served nothing but 'just knowledge' because 'the state in these has faulted and transformed'. Cumbersome investigations into past 'justice and injustice' were therefore here irrelevant and 'not worth the effort'. This, Ludewig claimed, also explained why most ancient and modern writers on the art of history recommended that the historian should only report 'what has happened', without judgement.[27] Within the Holy Roman Empire, however, things were different. The Empire had remained intact for almost a millennium and built on even older traditions of law.

Ludewig was no believer in the theory of the four world monarchies, but instead emphasized the distinctive German character of the Empire. He did not start the history of the Empire with the Roman Empire or with the coronation of Charlemagne in 800, but instead when Henry the Fowler became Duke of Saxony in 912 and started the Ottonian dynasty of Saxon kings and emperors. The original laws of the Empire were therefore not Roman laws but the ancient German free constitution, which had been 'confirmed and sustained' though many *Reichs-Grund-Gesetze* (imperial fundamental laws) and the modern German states. These laws were more suited to the German states than foreign law, especially Roman law, which now for centuries had corrupted

German jurisprudence. 'Germany', Ludewig claimed, 'would sin against the ashes of its forefathers if it allowed a well-established, reasonable, and free state to be inverted, forged or even overthrown by foreign law'.[28] Ludewig's contemporaries, however, were not aware of their history, had betrayed their heritage and believed in a false continuity between the ancient Roman and the Holy Roman Empire. The task of the historian was to restore and help reinstate German liberties. With the rediscovery of older official documents and their importance for imperial public law, the school of imperial history performed this task.

History between theology and jurisprudence

Together with Gundling, Ludewig established imperial history as a teaching subject at the University of Halle. The programme was soon adopted in law faculties at other German universities. This teaching tradition, as Notker Hammerstein has shown, was primarily oriented towards the practical problems of legal interpretation and framed historical scholarship as a tool of juridical and political thinking.[29] As early as 1720, the future Göttingen law professor Johann Jakob Schmauß celebrated this transformation of historical scholarship. Until the end of the seventeenth century, he explained, history only served moral philosophy and theology and was therefore only used for 'school speeches and sermons'. This had changed with the rethinking of public law, starting with Hermann Conring and culminating with Ludewig's and Gundling's classes on imperial history at the University of Halle. Ludewig especially 'both through his lectures, which he delivered to the studying youth to great use, as well as through his wonderful writings, awoke anew the other universities and scholars, and introduced the right taste in historical scholarship'. So, Schmauß claimed, 'now everyone considers this as an indispensable part of the study of feudal and public law and therefore also intended for the order of jurists more than the other faculties'.[30]

Despite Schmauß's triumphant claims, imperial history had no monopoly on the interpretation of the past. It did not replace older theological frameworks of understanding. Universal histories were still based upon biblical foundations, covering 6,000 years of history since creation, and the theory of the four world monarchies remained a viable explanation for the course of world history.

However, Ludewig and the school of imperial history created new room for historical scholarship within the university as an auxiliary discipline to jurisprudence. Within this juridical framework, empirical investigations of historical documents were independently valuable. This time not because the documents gave access to different opinions and arguments, but because they uncovered a different history of the Holy Roman Empire, which could not be deduced from philosophical principles or biblical revelation. The official documents in princely archives were relics, transporting the past into the present and establishing new continuities and discontinuities. With these relics at hand, the historian could question and reshape the legal and political order.

4

The art cabinet

The battle over antiquarianism

The modern concepts of *Zeitgeist* (spirit of time) and *Kultur* (culture) entered the German academic vocabulary in 1769 in a heated debate over antiquarianism. The originator was Johan Gottfried Herder, who was then still just a young clergyman in Riga. The concepts became core elements in Herder's philosophy of history, which emphasized the incommensurability of cultures and, in the twentieth century, was cast as the beginning of German historicism. This interpretation rejected not only the older ideal of *historia magistra vitae* but also the Enlightenment belief in the political and moral significance of historical differences. It questioned the very idea, central to both of these historiographical ideals, that the present could learn from the past. Herder did not make this turn because the past suddenly seemed irrelevant or new philosophical insights made it impossible to think otherwise, but, on the contrary, in reaction to the transformative potential of the Enlightenment version of history.

During the 1760s, the Halle professor and secret counsellor to Frederick the Great, Christian Adolph Klotz, had launched a programme for a revived antiquarianism, which challenged Protestant puritanical morality and aimed to reinvigorate the paganism and hedonism of the ancients.[1] He not only battled the confessional state, as his early Enlightenment predecessors had done but also questioned whether Christianity should serve as the moral foundation of society and presented a more humane and enjoyable alternative from the distant past. Christianity, according to Klotz, was not the culmination of history but a detour, which had stalled human civilization, destroyed good taste and introduced hypocrisy and intolerance. In his scholarship as well as in his private life, Klotz attempted to revive the past in the present. Together with a small group of scholars and poets, several of whom lived for periods in his house in Halle, he reimagined and relived the ancient world. He and his followers, known as the *Klotzianer*, also informed the rest of the reading public about their ideas and lifestyle in books, printed collections of letters and several journals, including a journal about themselves, entitled *Bibliothek der elenden Scribenten* (Library of Miserable Writers), printed between 1768 and 1770. They here candidly discussed their anticlerical opinions, excessive drinking and libertine adventures, including erotic encounters with other men.

From Riga, Herder retorted with fury. He dedicated two volumes of his *Kritische Wälder* (Critical Forests) to a scalding attack on Klotz. He was not the only contemporary scholar who reacted strongly. In 1768, the professor of antiquities at the Collegium Carolinum in Kassel and later author of *Baron Munchausen*, Rudolf Erich Raspe, wrote a booklet against Klotz. The playwright Gotthold Ephraim Lessing published more than fifty essays attacking Klotz, collected in *Briefe, antiquarischen Inhalts* (Letters of Antiquarian Content) 1768–9.[2] Others contributed to the debate in the many German scholarly journals and magazines of the period. For a few years, Klotz's antiquarian programme was probably the most divisive issue in German academic life. In these debates, the standards of historical scholarship again gained profound moral and political significance. Klotz's most important tool to reconnect with the ancients was a small collection of antiquities, most of which were reproductions. These antiquities, he believed, offered an immediate connection to the distant past. Klotz's opponents not only questioned his moral character but also whether an art cabinet could mediate between past and present. Lessing insisted that ancient art was highly conventional, that it demanded specialist interpretation and that it only revealed a limited part of the ancient worldview. Herder similarly argued that the ancient world had its *Zeitgeist* and *Kultur*, which lost its meaning in the modern world. Any understanding of Antiquity would be limited and demanded a process of hermeneutics. One could not just revive random elements of the past, which challenged the present, in disregard of historical contexts.

Enlightened antiquarianism

The battle over antiquarianism of the 1760s started with the publication of Johann Joachim Winckelmann's *Geschichte der Kunst des Alterthums* (History of the Art of Antiquity) in 1764.³ Winckelmann was a papal librarian and used the vast Roman collections of antiquities to present a comparative art history of the ancient world, which culminated with the beauty and perfection of Greek art. He, moreover, connected this comparative art history to cultural and political history and emphasized the significance of the mild climate and, more controversially, political freedom of ancient Greece.⁴ Klotz was one of the first German scholars to grasp the significance of the work and, shortly after its publication, wrote two glowing and elaborate reviews in Latin and German.⁵ Winckelmann's book, Klotz argued, was not just a history of art but redefined the very purpose and meaning of history as well as art. Art history was not just a chronological account of events, biographies of artists and descriptions of changes in styles but offered lessons to the contemporary world and proved these lessons with the tangible evidence of the material remains of the past.⁶

The publication of Winckelmann's book could not have come at a better time for Klotz. He made his fame during the early 1760s with a series of Latin poems and satires. The most controversial of these writings, *Mores eruditorum* (Manners of the Learned) and *Genius seculi* (Spirit of the Age), ridiculed scholars in the style of other Enlightenment writers, such as Johann Burkhard Mencke in *De charlataneria eruditorum* (On the Charlatanry of the Learned) of 1715 and Lessing in *Der junge Gelehrte* (The Young Scholar) of 1748.⁷ However, Klotz reemphasized the importance of the rediscovery of classical Antiquity for the reform of scholarship. He contrasted the free spirit of the Greeks to the false piety and simple pleasures of the clergy and compared the honesty of ancient writers to his colleagues' vain obsession with academic networks, titles and publication lists. He ridiculed not only the pedantry and otherworldliness of past generations of scholars but also his contemporaries' perfumed fashionable clothing, their lack of knowledge of classical languages and literature and their crass materialistic concerns. The Saxon censorship commission banned Klotz's *Mores eruditorum*, as it had banned Mencke's *De charlataneria eruditorum* half a century before, but this did not harm his academic career. In the following years he received calls from several universities. In 1762, he accepted a position in Göttingen and, in 1765, he was offered another position as professor of oratory in Halle. The change of position to Frederick the Great's Prussia and the discovery of Winckelmann's book together offered him a platform for introducing a new radical version of antiquarianism.

In his satirical works, Klotz had ridiculed conventional antiquarianism as yet another version of academic vanity. Instead of cultivating the spirit and embracing the true virtues of Antiquity, antiquarians merely accumulated ancient objects as an exterior proof of their erudition. In Halle, however, Klotz advocated a revitalized antiquarianism and published a series of books on the topic. To avoid pedantry and move beyond the mere collection of facts and objects, Klotz argued, scholars should cultivate the taste and sense of beauty of their contemporaries. Ancient sculptures and other art objects were particularly suited to this task, but they had been neglected by text-obsessed philologists. To acquire true and useful knowledge of Antiquity, a new kind of academic aesthete was needed. Klotz demanded:

> knowledge of the arts. A teacher of Antiquity knows its history; he is acquainted with the most famous artists and their different styles in different times; he has observed their works with an attentive eye and thereby acquired the skill to judge them; he finds the beautiful, the sublime, the amicable simplicity and noble grace in the Greek works.[8]

Like Winckelmann, Klotz also employed antiquities as a starting point for discussions about broader social developments and emphasized the greatness of Greek art. However, he did not primarily contrast the beauty of Greek art to older ancient cultures, but instead to the barbarism and crudeness of the modern world. The comparative history of art not only proved the superiority of the Greeks over Egyptians and Etruscans but also revealed the destructive influence of Christianity and the shortcomings of Christian Europeans.

Imprints of Antiquity

Klotz's move to Halle in 1765 offered him an opportunity to develop his antiquarian ideas into an educational programme. In his programmatic booklet *Ueber das Studium des Alterthums* (On the Study of Antiquity) published the following year, he declared that his primary purpose was 'to make younger friends acquainted with the utility and beauty of this branch of scholarship' and to attract 'minds that are capable and worthy of this teaching'.[9] In his later works, especially in his work on glyptography – the study of engraved gemstones – he not only emphasized the importance of Antiquity for the German public, but also explained that such outreach would have to be based upon a reform of education and should first be directed towards youth. 'For the correctness of the eye', he explained, 'is not a gift that we receive from nature. Our senses must be elevated through exercise and the power of judgement that is bred [through this exercise]'. The youth was flexible, imaginative and passionate enough to embrace the 'lessons of beauty'. He had written his antiquarian books for 'the teacher who has the noble intention to shape his disciples not just into human beings who escape hunger but also into reasonable people, friends of beauty, connoisseurs of taste, and lead them to the enjoyment of the beautiful and of life itself'.[10]

Klotz's choice of antiquities, primarily coins and engraved gemstones, supported this educational mission. While the statues that Winckelmann had analysed were beautiful, they were far away in Italy and inaccessible to the majority of German scholars and students. Most German universities, including Halle, were located in small towns and did not house museums with larger collections of antiquities. 'So', Klotz asked rhetorically, 'whence the experience of the trained eye? whence the true concept of the important in the arts? whence an observational understanding of the genius and talents of great masters?'[11] Coins and engraved gemstones, however, were much more plentiful than statues, easily transportable and could be imprinted directly on glass, wax, brimstone or plaster. These antiquities offered a unique immediacy. Despite their diminutive size, engraved gemstones could also, Klotz argued, compete in beauty with other antiquities.

Klotz's antiquarian programme would not have been feasible without some innovative new copying techniques of the mid-eighteenth century. He especially relied upon Philipp Daniel Lippert's popular collection of imprints of engraved gemstones and considered his major work on glyptography as a 'commentary' on this collection.[12] Lippert was trained as a glazier, had worked in the porcelain factory in Meißen and later as a drawing teacher and only late in life became extraordinary professor at the Dresden Academy of Art.[13] Lippert's background as a craftsman explains some of his success. He discovered that talc, also used in ceramics, was particularly well suited for copying engraved gemstones, and further developed the technique by experimenting with different materials. These innovations made the imprints much more affordable, durable and accessible. Lippert claimed that the price of his imprints was half that of the fragile imprints on brimstone sold in Italy.[14] The imprints were also aesthetically appealing with their white material and smooth surfaces and, unlike brimstone, did not stink.

Lippert's collections were sold as standard packages, containing thousands of objects. For practicality, they were delivered in wooden boxes that fitted next to the folio volumes on a bookshelf and were bound in leather to look like books. Each volume contained nineteen drawers and around one thousand imprints. The imprints were not divided according to period or provenance, but instead between 'mythological' and 'historical' themes. In each drawer one could find several imprints of the same motives, glued to the bottom next to one another. Lippert produced the first edition in 1753. The most famous edition was his three-volume version, produced between 1755 and 1762. Klotz used the revised and less comprehensive two volumes edition of 1767, *Dactyliothec: Das ist Sammlung geschnittener Steine der Alten* (Dactylotheque: That is Collection of Engraved Stones of the Ancients) which also included a large catalogue in German with detailed descriptions of the content and short summaries of ancient mythology and history.

Lippert acquired imprints from antiquarians across Europe, including Winckelmann, whom he knew from Dresden. German scholars, who could not travel to Italy and otherwise would have no access to large private collections, now had the antiquities directly at hand in their studies. Although isolated in small university towns, they could compare the treasures of Antiquity with an ease that not even Italian scholars could imagine. Lippert's collection made ancient art as available to antiquarians as ancient literature before had been to philologists. The new copying techniques not only made it possible to present many disparate objects together in a book-like container, but also to 'read' these objects as if they were words in a book. Klotz enthusiastically declared:

> This collection makes us owners of the most beautiful works of Antiquity. One becomes the holder of all what those excellent masters created and in our hands is the object of admiration and praise of the most enlightened times. Nothing prevents us from harvesting the desired fruits, which offer acquaintanceship with these treasures. We can observe these imprints, as often and as long as we want; we can study them as the Greek studied the

father of poets and everyone, who wants to comprehend the sublime and the beautiful, should study him.[15]

Studying engraved gemstones as the Greek studied 'the father of poets', Homer, meant that through 'repeated observation' one should familiarize oneself with every detail, and grasp the underlying connection between these details. The student of Antiquity must acquire a new kind of observational skill so that 'his eye rests for a long time at every piece and every part of the whole: his spirit silently traces the intention of the master and seeks to explore his thoughts: he compares, tests, and, from this, draws conclusions'. This observational skill would then allow the observer 'to realize the secrets of art, to reach the wisdom of the artists, to be penetrated by the true concepts of beauty, and to educate his taste in the noblest way'.[16]

Printed etchings and engravings, Klotz claimed, were not suitable for such close observation, because they typically misrepresented the originals and failed to capture their beauty. He remarked about Bernard de Montfaucon's celebrated *L'Antiquité expliquée et representée en figures* (Antiquity Explained and Represented in Figures) printed in Paris in fifteen volumes between 1719 and 1724, that 'the pictures that it contains are badly drawn and even worse engraved'. Klotz also had more principled objections, based upon the Pyrrhonian scepticism of the late seventeenth and early eighteenth centuries. The critique of historical testimonies was especially relevant in connection with printed illustrations. Even the best engravings, such as those by Bernard Picart, were not relics of the past, and using them was like 'borrowing the eyes of other people'. This problem was further enlarged by the sprawling industry in Rome that produced counterfeit antiquities for the Northern European market of collectors. To determine if an engraved gemstone was a forgery required closer inspection and, Klotz argued, one had to reserve judgement about the authenticity 'when one has not seen the stone oneself'. Most scholars and students were also not able to distinguish between the levels of quality of printed engravings and ended as 'the kindhearted people, who patiently listen to travelers and consider all stories as true'. Lippert's imprints, on the contrary, carried the mark of the gems themselves. Viewing and touching these imprints, one no longer depended upon the testimonies or eyes of others but instead embarked oneself upon the journey into the past. With Lippert's collection, Klotz declared, 'the source of good taste is now open'.[17]

Libertine glyptography

The central ideal that ancient, and especially Greek, art should teach contemporaries was love, and its importance for the development of taste, virtue and reason. On the front-page of his book on glyptography, *Ueber den Nutzen und Gebrauch der alten geschnittenen Steine und ihre Abdrücke* (On the Benefits and Use of Ancient Engraved Stones and their Imprints) of 1768, Klotz illustrated the theme with a tiny piece in Lippert's collection. Lippert's catalogue declared that the gem showed Amor as an artist working on the 'head of a philosopher' and offered as interpretation that 'an orderly love makes human beings wise'.[18] Klotz identified the gem as a portrait of Socrates.[19] To the *Klotzianer*, as to many Enlightenment thinkers, the figure of Socrates played a double role.[20] On the one hand, he was the persecuted philosopher and martyr of reason. On the other hand, he was an advocate of homosexual love. For many eighteenth-century scholars, this second image of Socrates was a problem. In *Acta philosophorum*, Christoph August Heumann portrayed Socrates as a model philosopher, but also disputed his homosexuality. He emphasized the importance of Socrates's wife Xantippe, insisted upon their mutual fidelity and strongly opposed the claim that Socrates had a sexual relationship with Alcibiades.[21] With his choice of front-page image, Klotz, on the contrary, emphasized the connection between philosophy and homoerotic love. In his book, he only referred to two Platonic dialogues, *Phaedrus* and *Symposium*, both of which discussed the topic and depicted Socrates as a master of the art of love.

The primary fascination of the *Klotzianer*, however, was probably not with the homosexuality of Socrates, but rather with the idea that eroticism, pleasure and philosophy were closely linked. They celebrated the Dionysian side of Socrates as a way into philosophy. Theirs was the Socrates of the *Symposium*, who resembled Silenus, drank all night and philosophized while enjoying himself with his friends. Socrates, Klotz declared, was a philosopher 'who because he was a human being also strove to think like a human being'.[22] Friedrich Just Riedel, who joined the group in 1767, even assured Klotz, 'The daemon, who always followed Socrates and said his thoughts into his ear, was, this I know for certain, nothing but a small satyr.'[23] In his book on glyptography, Klotz conveyed his message by focusing on specific mythological themes that had already been preselected by Lippert and could be easily compared and analysed. The dominant motive was Amor in all his variations. Another central theme was the cult of Bacchus, which had its own category in Lippert's *Dactyliothec* with altogether 172 imprints. Klotz's love also manifested itself in beautiful bodies and their embraces. Klotz was especially attracted to two motives, Venus in the bath and Leda with the swan, both of which were represented with numerous small imprints in Lippert's collection.

While the naked and bowing Venus provided Klotz with a somewhat passive model of female beauty, Leda and the swan served as an example of the active consummation of love. According to ancient myth, Leda fell in love with Zeus disguised as a swan and willingly engaged in sexual intercourse. The imprints showed the act in many variations, with Leda kissing the swan, pressing it against her body and holding it close to her while standing upright. Klotz considered all the variations appealing, but especially preferred one depiction of Leda lying down with her head back and open mouth, while Amor is pushing the swan in between her legs (Figure 2). This risqué and tiny piece Klotz considered the pinnacle of ancient art. 'I am not afraid of admitting', Klotz declared, 'that I have seen nothing more beautiful, cannot believe anything more beautiful, than this excellent stone, on which Leda lays entirely dissolved by lust. Her eyes, her mouth shows the enjoyment of the pleasure that in this moment entirely pervades her soul. The roguish Amor assists the swan in its purpose'.[24]

Figure 2 Imprint of Leda, the swan and Amor. 1.2 × 1.5 cm. Philipp Daniel Lippert, *Dactyliothecae universalis signorum*, vol. 3 (Leipzig, 1762), plate 1, no. 20. Courtesy Det Kongelige Bibliotek, Copenhagen.

Figure 3 Imprint of Silenus, Amor and satyrs. 5 × 3.7 cm. Philipp Daniel Lippert, *Dactyliothecae universalis signorum*, vol. 1. (Leipzig, 1755), plate 1, no. 165. Courtesy Det Kongelige Bibliotek, Copenhagen.

Klotz also left little doubt that he wished his followers to find a similar joy in bodies, their own as well as those of others. Dwelling upon a series of depictions of beautiful women, including imprints of Amor's wife Psyche revealing her breast and a naked Aurora embracing an equally naked Cephalus, he remarked: 'My young friend will be enchanted by these beauties and the silent wish, once in the love of a similar girl to find his happiness and his satisfaction.' At the end of the book, Klotz recommended three imprints to his reader 'on the explanation of which he can exercise himself'.[25] The common theme of these imprints was the presence of butterflies, which not only signified the immortality of the soul, but also the connections between the body, the soul and the passions. Two of the imprints showed a naked Venus together with Amor and a butterfly. The last, and larger, one showed a scene from a Bacchanalian party (Figure 3) with two butterflies, Amor with a bag of wine, Silenus laying drunk on the ground and naked male and female satyrs who are playing music and dancing.

Radical numismatics

Coins and medals did not offer the same advantages as engraved gemstones. They normally were produced for official purposes, either as means of payment or to commemorate important events, and seldom depicted the risqué and private scenes that so interested Klotz and his followers. Through coins and medals, however, one could trace a continuous artisanal tradition from Antiquity to the present. If the art of engraving gemstones had almost disappeared after Antiquity, the production of coins and medals had remained important. In his works on numismatics, especially his *Beytrag zur Geschichte des Geschmacks und der Kunst aus Münzen* (Contribution to the History of Taste and Art from Coins) of 1767, Klotz could therefore comment upon the entire history of Europe. With the help of coins and medals, he could show not only the excellence of classical art but also 'the rise and decline of taste and the arts'.[26] Such a history could be used to show the damaging effects of Christianity upon European societies.

Klotz probably found inspiration for his numismatic project in Winckelmann's *Geschichte der Kunst des Alterthums*. Winckelmann's book focused upon the rise of Greek art but also discussed its afterlife in Rome, and offered some explanations for its gradual decline after Alexander the Great. The most important reason was the loss of freedom. Under the Roman emperors the artistic tradition could no longer be resurrected for 'the spirit of freedom had receded from the world, and the source of sublime thought and of true glory had disappeared'.[27] Winckelmann hinted that this development was connected to the rise of Christianity, but his book was primarily the history of the triumph of Greek art over older and cruder civilizations. Klotz, on the contrary, wrote very little about older ancient cultures, and instead used the critical tools of comparative art history to expose the depravity and crudity of the moderns, especially after the arrival of Christianity. According to Klotz, art not only needed political freedom but blossomed and declined 'the more or less a people has been educated through taste and the age enlightened through scholarship'. The greatest threat to taste and scholarship was religious superstition. Christianity was not just a symptom of decline, but the most important reason for this decline. The Roman Empire in general was an 'unhappy' time for the arts, but Christianity introduced prudishness, prejudice and hypocrisy. 'The enthusiasm of religion, which brings about unbelievable effects, devastates countries, kills kings', Klotz claimed, 'now damaged the arts much more' than had before 'the wars of barbarians and the fire of Goths'.[28]

He instructed his readers how they could read the rise and decline of taste from minor changes in the fabrication and ornamentation of coins and medals. One indication was the development of technical skills. Another was the use of images. The oldest Greek and Roman coins only had simple images because 'all arts were still in their childhood'. As the arts developed there emerged 'a finer and as if more poetic ornamentation of thoughts and events'. Coins from the Middle Ages, on the contrary, showed 'crucifixes, keys, books, bishop's crosiers, and churches', and thereby revealed 'the force of superstition and a slave-like subservience', illustrating that this period 'was robbed of all scholarship, arts, and understanding'.[29] In Italy, the situation had improved with the Renaissance, in France with the age of Louis XIV and in Germany only recently with Frederick the Great. However, although the technical skill of artisans had grown, the images had still not reached the refinement of the ancients.

Klotz versus *Kultur*

Klotz's libertine and radical writings, not surprisingly, provoked his contemporaries. While generations of German Enlightenment thinkers had critiqued the confessional state, most of them did not question Christianity and Christian morality as such. Those who did were often forced into exile and barred from public positions, including university employment. By the middle of the eighteenth century, confessional disagreements could still have serious consequences. In 1758, a few years before Klotz's arrival, the ageing Christoph August Heumann was fired from the Lutheran University of Göttingen for openly adopting a Calvinist interpretation of the Eucharist.[30] However, the two major opponents of Klotz, Lessing and Herder, did not critique him with arguments from Christian metaphysics or biblical revelation. They instead questioned his scholarly standards and attacked the hidden assumptions of his emancipatory project. Herder even developed his new philosophy of history in reaction to Klotz and, in this connection, introduced the modern concepts of *Zeitgeist* and *Kultur*.

The word *Kultur* was not completely new in the German language or literature.[31] During the first half of the eighteenth century, the word was still primarily used in connection with gardening and agriculture, as in the cultivation of land, but also to describe the cultivation of society, virtues and the human mind. Samuel Pufendorf had employed the word *cultura* in his influential *De jure naturae et gentium* (The Law of Nature and Nations) of 1672 to describe the human inclination and endeavour to rise above the state of nature, and thereby he had given it a place in the legal and philosophical discourse of the eighteenth century.[32] Before Herder, some scholars had also used the word to distinguish one country from another. However, in this debate it began to take on the broader meanings with which we now associate it. Herder insisted that culture was a historical phenomenon and that it defined human existence. It was deeply rooted in its time and shaped by the habits, manners, language and ways of thinking of the people. To Herder, it did not make sense to dream of travelling in time and of escaping one's historical situation as Klotz and his followers wanted.

Herder was initially less critical of Klotz. In his *Ueber die neuere Deutsche Litteratur* (On Recent German Literature) published in Riga in 1767, Herder mentioned Klotz, as the youngest among the Latin poets, and reviewed some of his early philological and satirical writings. Herder did not yet seem aware of Klotz's activities in Halle and his overall conclusion was positive. Klotz had successfully adopted the satirical style of the ancients. His pen could be sharp and his wit provoking, but it was needed. 'In our time', Herder declared (quoting Juvenal), 'it is difficult not to write satire! And in most cases, we give the Klotzian candor our secret and cordial applause.'[33] The *Klotzianer* were equally enthusiastic in return. A reviewer in the first issue of Klotz's *Deutsche Bibliothek der schönen Wissenschaften* (German Library of the Literary and Fine Arts) declared, 'Mr. Herder has shown himself as a thinker, as a connoisseur of the ancients and as a man whose fine taste always is led by the arguments of sound reason.'[34]

However, after the publication of Klotz's anticlerical book on numismatics in 1767, the relationship turned hostile. During the following two years, Herder's dislike of Klotz grew almost obsessive. He often wrote about Klotz in his letters, and his language became more and more abusive. When he first read Klotz's book in the early fall of 1767, he remarked to his Königsberg friend Johann Georg Scheffner that it was 'beautifully written, but poorly thought'. Later Herder's judgement turned moralistic. In November 1768, he again commented on the book in a letter to Scheffner and now claimed, 'I don't know of any more miserable production of our century than his little thing about coins, which nonetheless has been generally praised.' The book revealed 'the poverty of his soul' and that he was an 'unworthy scholar'. Later the same month, he assured the Berlin publisher Friedrich Nicolai that if Klotz 'does not improve himself in his still happy years, he will soon drown in his shallow slime. And since his tone has started to become ever more plebeian, we will soon experience that'. In January 1769, he confessed to his fellow critic Lessing: 'I am ashamed of the judgement of posterity on an age, which worshipped such as man.'[35]

The public could follow Herder's growing dislike of Klotz's through the volumes of his *Kritische Wälder*. Towards the end of the first volume, he criticized Klotz's superficial reading of Homer in his early philological writings. In the second volume, Herder continued this critique and turned to his antiquarian writings. Over many pages, he proved that Klotz had copied parts of his book on numismatics from Joseph Addison's *Dialogues upon the Usefulness of Ancient Medals*, but he also discussed the normative foundations of Klotz's project. It was for this purpose that he introduced his historical understanding of culture. He argued that Klotz's early critical reading of Homer was a product of the arrogance of the eighteenth century and based upon a mistaken idea of historical progress. The scholarship of the modern world might be more advanced than that of Antiquity. Modern human beings might therefore believe themselves to be on a higher 'level of culture', but, in reality, they lived in a completely different world. 'We have', Herder argued, 'not just moved higher up, we have in a certain way moved out of the world, in which Homer composed, wrote, and sang'. Probably with reference to the title of Klotz's satyrical *Genius seculi*, Herder introduced the concept of *Zeitgeist* to emphasize the insurmountable distance between past and present. Over time language changed its meaning, for as 'the way of living and the spirit of the centuries changed, so had also the innate spirit of many words changed'. Even human beings were not the same. Time changed 'the nature of human beings, the manners of characters, the nuances, through which the passions are expressed! A Greek soul certainly was of another form and design than a soul from our century'. Even a scholar who knew all history between Antiquity and the eighteenth century had to be 'extraordinarily cautious' in his judgement. It neither made sense to judge Homer according to the standards of the contemporary world nor to make Homer the standard of all times. Homer had written for his own time and not for 'the critical century that Klotz wants to create in Germany'.[36]

In the third volume, Herder turned his historicizing criticism against Klotz's programme for a revived antiquarianism. For this purpose, he again used the new concepts of *Zeitgeist* and *Kultur*. Only this time, he did not employ the concepts to protect Antiquity from the judgement of the moderns, but to protect the Middle Ages against Klotz's imagined Antiquity. Herder was especially disturbed by Klotz's claim that Medieval coins testified to the barbarism, ignorance and superstition of the period. The Christian symbolism of the Middle Ages neither appealed to Protestant 'culture' nor to the refined taste of the Enlightenment, but the images were the products of contemporary conventions. They bore 'the lead imprint of the spirit of time' and 'the yoke of the century'.[37] Coins did not have the same meaning and function in the Middle Ages as they did to ancients or moderns. They were part of the legal-administrative culture of the Holy Roman Empire.

Herder also emphasized the particularity of the Holy Roman Empire, and its importance for German history, in another chapter in the third volume of *Kritische Wälder*. He here attacked the historian and professor of philosophy, Carl Renatus Hausen, who was one of Klotz's closest associates and for a period lived together with him in his house in Halle. Hausen primarily wrote about recent political history, but, while staying with Klotz, he also employed historical research as a weapon against Christianity. In 1766, he published a draft of German history and, in 1767, a history of German Protestantism, both of which emphasized the dangers of organized religion. Organized religion always resulted in superstition, hypocrisy and intolerance, but Hausen was especially critical of the religious princes, kings and emperors of the Middle Ages, who had reduced Germany to a state of barbarism. By the beginning of the sixteenth century, he argued, art and scholarship had been corrupted, German manners were rude and the German people were 'pious, to a degree of superstition, and yet thereby debauched, lazy, and without attention to the benefits of nature; in short! a dead body, without spirit and without life'.[38] Herder in response argued that German history neither could be written in the style of ancient Greek and Roman historians nor in that of their modern French counterparts. The sources represented another *Zeitgeist* and were closely linked to the legal-administrative history of the Holy Roman Empire. The historian, he claimed, 'must here become a bearer of the shield and arms of the Holy Roman Empire, whether he wants it or not'. A German history, he concluded, 'frankly still has to be written, but in no case according to the Klotzian ideal'.[39]

The *Klotzianer* did not answer these objections, but instead reversed their opinion of Herder and questioned his character as well as his ability and qualifications to make such judgements. A reviewer in one of their journals remarked about Herder's *Kritische Wälder* in 1769: 'Everywhere we encounter a shallow reasoning, overhasty judgement, entirely false observation and in particular a great ignorance of the ancient languages, of which he nonetheless wants to be considered a great connoisseur.'[40] Herder soon after decided to end his quarrels with the *Klotzianer*. In the summer of 1769, he left Riga for France. After arriving, he wrote to Friedrich Nicolai that this move had been necessary to open a new chapter in his life. He had not only started a new life in France but also, as he explained to a friend in Königsberg in November 1769, embarked on the search for a new understanding of history, more important than 'Klotzian letters about nonsense', and tried to grasp 'the formation of people, of times, of laws, of governments, of centuries'.[41] In 1774, he published his *Auch eine Philosophie der Geschichte zur Bildung der Menschheit* (This Too a Philosophy of History for the Formation of Humanity) that many scholars have claimed laid the foundation for modern historicism.

When Herder was cast as the father of historicism in the twentieth century, historians preferred to disregard the role of Klotz in the development of Herder's thought. In 1936, in his work on the origins of historicism, Friedrich Meinecke emphasized the importance of Herder's Riga years, but did not mention Klotz once.[42] Herder, Meinecke reported, was inspired by the songs and folkdances of the Baltic 'original people', Pietist religious ideas as well as his reading of Rousseau and British early romantics. These together convinced Herder about the individuality and incommensurability of national cultures. That Herder developed these ideas in opposition to someone, who challenged such divisions, Meinecke did not consider relevant. The battle over antiquarianism disappeared in a historicist interpretation that considered *Zeitgeist* and *Kultur* as the only relevant contexts. Even in recent works, historians prefer to disregard Klotz or to accept Herder's hostile judgements. In his otherwise detailed account of the early development of Herder's thought, John Zammito only sacrifices a couple of pages on the controversies with Klotz. 'While', Zammito argues, 'Herder's style of thought seemed at this juncture to require some text or author to play off, much of this literary polemic is pointless to modern readers because his targets are so far beneath him and their demolition seems hardly worth the effort'. Klotz was imposing at the time, but, from a modern viewpoint, a 'nonentity'.[43] This reduction of Klotz to a 'nonentity' disguises that Herder's ideas of culture and national development were not just contributions to a philosophical discussion or a reflection of larger changes in the European worldview, but part of a struggle between political and moral ideals. Klotz and his colleagues used history to challenge Christianity. Herder used philosophy of history to revitalize it.

From antiquarianism to archaeology

Klotz died on New Year's Eve 1771, only thirty-three years old. In the following decades, German antiquarian works were considerably less radical and libertine in tone. Klotz's works continued to be read, and some of his arguments for the advantages of numismatics and glyptography remained common in antiquarian circles.[44] However, his highly publicized and rancorous debate with Lessing and Herder made some scholars doubtful about the promises of reviving classical Antiquity. The battle over antiquarianism contributed to two different, but related, developments that over time would change the German relationship to the past. On the one hand, it inspired the rise of a new philosophy of history that emphasized the incommensurability of past and present. The past was not only radically different from present but also impossible to revive in the contemporary world. Works and worldviews of historical actors must be understood in the particular contexts of their unique historical period, its *Zeitgeist* and *Kultur*.

On the other hand, the battle over antiquarianism further promoted a specialized approach to historical scholarship. A prominent example is the Göttingen professor Christian Gottlob Heyne. Heyne arrived in Göttingen in 1763, before Klotz's departure in 1765. He later became personally acquainted with Herder and read his *Kritische Wälder*.[45] In the summer of 1767, he started teaching classes on 'archaeology' and for this purpose employed Lippert's collection of imprints. As the many surviving student notes testify, the course focused narrowly upon aesthetics and techniques of art.[46] Heyne explicitly rejected the political and moral readings of recent years.[47] He also increasingly distinguished archaeology not only from the work of amateurs and older forms of antiquarianism but also from other historical disciplines. Archaeology, as he explained to his students in 1789, should only study 'pictorial works as beautiful artworks'.[48] Herder's new philosophy of history insisted the sources could only be understood in the context of their historical period. The new specialized approach to historical scholarship, advocated by Heyne, instead argued that scholars had to interpret sources together with similar kinds of sources. The viewpoints of the different historical disciplines, their methodologies and working practices, increasingly divided the past into multiple pasts, each of which only could be accessed by specialists within that discipline.[49]

5

The study

The gravestone

Around New Year 1770, a local clergyman in Quedlinburg in the Harz named Georg Christoph Hallensleben went for a short stroll outside the city walls to the nearby village of Münzenberg. On his way, he noticed a remarkable medieval gravestone, which had been used in the construction of one of the Münzenberg houses, a former guesthouse, and now had been exposed by a mudslide. The clergyman, who had strong antiquarian interests, studied the stone in the sharp light of the afternoon sun and was soon convinced that he had discovered the gravestone of Henry the Fowler, the founder of the Ottonian dynasty of Saxon kings and emperors, who, according to local legend, had been buried in Quedlinburg after his death in 936. Hallensleben immediately reported to the authorities and, on 27 January 1770, a Hamburg paper publicized the story. It praised his 'inquiring eyes' and claimed that the finding was 'a very remarkable discovery' that 'sends a great light into history and enlightens many dark points about which history writers could never agree'.[1]

Two days later, another paper in Halle published an anonymous retort, which questioned that the gravestone belonged to Henry and concluded that even if the discovery 'was correct, which it is not and cannot be, then it would truly be useless, or at least an insignificant trifle, for history'.[2] Hallensleben's discovery threatened to become yet another frontline in the ongoing battle over antiquarianism, which had been unleashed with Klotz move to Halle a few years before in 1765, as discussed in the previous chapter. While Klotz and his opponents primarily wrote about classical ancient art, and not German medieval gravestones, both disputes concerned the importance of antiquities for the understanding of history as well as the role of amateurs and connoisseurs in such discussions.

The controversy about the Münzenberg gravestone, however, did not continue long. Johann Christoph Gatterer, who was a professor of history at the University of Göttingen, quickly intervened in the debate. He produced a balanced report, which argued for the historical value of the gravestone, but, at the same time, proved that it could not have belonged to Henry the Fowler.[3] In the report, Gatterer did not base his scholarly authority upon an intimate knowledge of medieval antiquities and monuments. He also did not claim special insights into the history of Quedlinburg or the biography of Henry the Fowler. Instead, Gatterer based his conclusions about the

Figure 4 Reproduction of the gravestone in Johann Christoph Gatterer, *Praktische Diplomatik* (Göttingen, 1799), 146. Courtesy Det Kongelige Bibliotek, Copenhagen.

gravestone upon his knowledge of *Diplomatik* (diplomatics), the art of reading and assessing historical official documents. The debates surrounding Klotz, from the viewpoint of his opponents, had emphasized the need for specialized and technical art criticism. The discussion about the gravestone evidenced that political history depended no less on specialized and technical expertise (Figure 4).

The statesman and the historian

Gatterer was a central figure in the professionalization and institutionalization of modern historical scholarship. In 1757, he became the second person to occupy the chair of history at the University of Göttingen, and afterwards he worked tirelessly to unify the growing community of historical scholars. In 1764, he created the world's first institute for specialized historical research, the Königliche Institut der historischen Wissenschaften zu Göttingen. In the following years, he launched two specialized journals for historical research, *Allgemeine historische Bibliothek* (General Historical Library), published from 1767 to 1771, and its continuation *Historische Journal* (Historical Journal), published from 1772 to 1781. He also produced numerous textbooks, especially in technical auxiliary sciences, such as diplomatics, heraldry and genealogy. Through these efforts, Gatterer hoped, as Martin Gierl has shown, to transform historical research into a 'more precise' kind of scholarship.[4]

Gatterer emphasized how his academic approach to the past distinguished him and his contemporaries from earlier generations of historians. In 1768, he compared himself to the great Augustan historian, Livy. Apart from their sanguine temperaments, promoting 'a certain lightness and liveliness' of expression, Gatterer found few similarities. If he should publish a new history of ancient Rome, a 'modernized Livy', this book would not be the work of a pagan Roman but that of a citizen of an enlightened Protestant German-speaking state.[5] Almost two millennia had passed, and each of them had their *Standort* (place) and their *Gesichtspunct* (viewpoint). Their approaches to historical scholarship and interpretations of Roman history would therefore be very different. The temporal distance between the world of the Roman Empire and that of the Holy Roman Empire, however, was not the most important difference between him and Livy:

> The greatest difference between Livy and me probably expresses itself in regard to the way of life. I am no statesman, like him; I am a scholar, a professor; I know the larger world more from books than from experience. ... I have since my youth studied the history and constitution of all known people from the most ancient times to our day and for more than 14 years the calling – for which I thank providence – have committed me even more to this kind of knowledge. ... I do not deny that everywhere, despite all efforts to the contrary, the professor and the study come to sight. The way of life into which one has been habituated, cannot be completely denied.[6]

While the ancients often were better writers than contemporary scholars, the standardized methods of inquiry and instruction opened a more dependable road to the past. His academic background, Gatterer even claimed, granted him a better overview and understanding of political history than Livy. The most reliable historian was not the statesman who had experienced the events, but the academic who knew modern research techniques and viewed the past from the objectifying distance of the professorial study. The point of Gatterer's concepts of *Standort* and *Gesichtspunct* was not to introduce a new philosophy of history or, as Herder a few years earlier, to claim that the past and the present were incommensurable. The concepts instead emphasized that knowledge of the past demanded specialized expertise. Modern historians could have a better understanding of past events than the historical actors themselves, if only he had access to enough sources and had acquired the necessary skills to interpret these sources.

In 1770, Gatterer used the Münzenberg gravestone dispute to showcase the strength of modern research techniques and to illustrate that the professional historian did not have to rely upon the testimony of past eyewitnesses. Unlike the other participants in the dispute, Gatterer ignored the written testimonies about Quedlinburg history and Henry the Fowler's death and burial. Without any signs of irony, he even questioned whether the recent newspaper reports about Hallensleben's discovery were trustworthy. The dates of publication were suspiciously close, so maybe someone in Quedlinburg was just trying to ridicule the clergyman and his passion for antiquities. But this, Gatterer declared, did not belong 'to the essence of the dispute'.[7] What mattered was only the evidence and conclusions that could be derived from the gravestone itself.

Linnean graphics

In Göttingen, Gatterer continued the tradition of Ludewig and the school of imperial history. He taught diplomatics to future imperial jurists, and wrote expert opinions for court cases, but also argued for the importance of official documents for historical research.[8] In his plan for the Königliche Institut der historischen Wissenschaften zu Göttingen, he insisted that no one could become a member who did not already know or was willing to learn the art of diplomatics.[9] Gatterer also developed an almost mechanical procedure for the reading of documents, which should remove any 'doubt' about their age and authenticity. Following Gatterer's directions, one should start with *Graphik* or *Graphica* (graphics), including not only the style and form of writing but also the material conditions of these sources, such as if they were written on parchment or paper, the size and location of wormholes and the colour and composition of the ink. In each case, Gatterer carefully listed the known variations. For the analysis of the script, he had even developed a *Linnaeismus Graphicus* (Linnaean Graphic), where different forms and shapes of letters had been divided according to Linnaean categories, replacing the Swedish botanist's three realms of nature – animals, plants and minerals – with the four realms of script – artificial realm, including inscriptions and letters on works of art; the book realm, describing the scripts used in book manuscripts; the notary realm, covering the writings of public officials; and the private realm. In later versions, he reduced this to three realms by collapsing notary and private realms into the *Urkundenschrift-Gebiet* or *regnum diplomaticum* (official document realm). Like Linnaeus, Gatterer further subdivided these realms into class, order, series, genus and species.[10] Unlike Linneaus's natural classification system, however, Gatterer's system placed scripts, within typological categories, in chronological series. The primary function of the system was not to uncover an immutable structure, but to determine the historical and geographical origins of particular scripts. After analysing 'graphics', one should move on to *Semiotik* or *Semiotica* (semiotics), which included the interpretation of seals, symbols and monograms. Finally, one turned to the *Formelkunde* or *Ars formularia* (art of formulas), which analysed the standardized vocabulary, language and composition of documents. Gatterer also sorted these symbolic representations and formulas into different

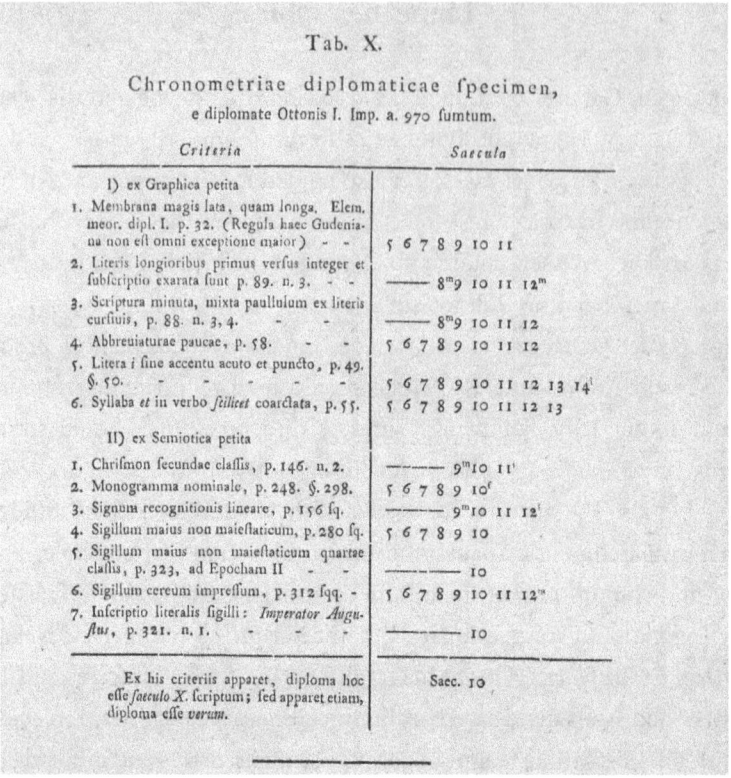

Figure 5 A table illustrating that a document, attested by Emperor Otto I in 970, can only be from the tenth century and can be considered 'true'. Gatterer reaches this conclusion solely on the basis of 'graphic' and 'semiotic' traits. Johann Christoph Gatterer, *Praktische Diplomatik* (Göttingen, 1799), tab. X. Courtesy Det Kongelige Bibliotek, Copenhagen.

typological categories and subdivided them into geographical and historical sequences. By comparing different traits, one could identify the likely place of origin and age of a document and thereby also decide its authenticity (Figure 5).

When Gatterer decided the case of the supposed gravestone of Henry the Fowler, he based his authority upon his mastery of this mechanic method for analysing legal and official documents. The script of the gravestone belonged in the 'artificial realm' of inscriptions, but Gatterer wrote with the authority of the historian who specialized in archival documents, especially documents relating to the legal-administrative history of the Holy Roman Empire. He named his report *diplomatisches Gutachten* (diplomatic expert opinion) and *diplomatisches Responsum* (diplomatic response) like the opinions he wrote for court cases and only quoted diplomatic reference works. The characteristics of the gravestone were similar to those of official documents and its origin could therefore be decided by following the steps of his diplomatic method, proceeding from 'graphics' to 'semiotics' to 'the art of formulas'. Already his investigation of 'graphics' revealed that the style of the letters was 'neogothic' and, in his Linnaean taxonomy of script, belonged to the *Genus Thulemarium*. The gravestone therefore must have been made in the thirteenth century or later. Moving to 'semiotics', Gatterer compared the gravestone to the engravings in Anton Ulrich von Erath's *Codex diplomaticus Quedlinburgensis* (Diplomatic Codex of Quedlinburg) of 1764 and thereby determined that the coast of arms belonged to the Hoym noble family. He further argued that the iconography was that of a knight rather than of a king. So, in different ways, Gatterer proved that the gravestone must be that of the knight Friedrich von Hoym and not that of the founder of the Holy Roman Empire, Henry the Fowler.

The problem of reproduction

Some eighteenth-century scholars argued that the use of non-testimonial evidence did not necessarily solve the problem of 'historical belief'. Archival sources and ancient monuments were unique and often not easily accessible. One therefore relied upon the skill and credibility of other historians and editors, who were not always trustworthy. In effect, the testimonies of the eyewitnesses had only been replaced by the testimonies of the historians. 'Everywhere', Gatterer lamented about the low quality of German source editions, 'it is teeming with errors. Some originate from uneducated reading, therefore from ignorance, others from carelessness, many also from an unauthorized and presumed freedom to improve the text of the writer'.[11] In the case of the Münzenberg gravestone, Gatterer nonetheless relied upon two drawings that had been sent to him in Göttingen, as well as Hallensleben's detailed description.[12] Gatterer knew that such second-hand descriptions of ancient artefacts often were not more reliable than source editions. This had been emphasized in connection with the controversies about antiquarianism, especially Klotz's discussions about reproductions of artefacts in print. Gatterer wrote much less about antiquities than Klotz, but, in his methodological writings, he expressed similar concerns about reproductions and warned against judging 'a statue of Hercules [or] a coin of Emperor Augustus, if one does not have the original'.[13]

Like Klotz, Gatterer attempted to find practical solutions to the problem of reproduction. Klotz thought he had solved the problem through imprints of engraved stones, because these were produced immediately from the ancient artefacts themselves. Gatterer did not revert to technological solutions but instead argued that official documents could solve the problem. Because they were formulaic and written in a standardized language, one could determine their authenticity on the basis of copies. 'The formulas', Gatterer explained, 'always betray the forger, and indeed in most cases even more reliably than the attributes of the original solely according to graphics and semiotics'. Official documents therefore possessed 'as if double the truth of coins and other antiquities'. And, he concluded, 'from this follows that diplomatic proofs are capable of more evidence than all other kinds of historical proofs; it also follows from this that the history writer is obliged to prefer diplomatic proofs, as often as they can be had, before all other kinds of proofs'.[14] By treating the Münzenberg gravestone as an official document and drawing upon his experience of diplomatics, he acquired a similar advantage in regard to antiquities.

The credibility of the historian

Still, reproductions were not enough. Gatterer repeatedly emphasized the importance of experience and embodied skills. While he praised Hallensleben for his antiquarian zeal, he concluded with the comment that 'the explanation and judgment of such antiquities' required more than just 'good, generous will'.[15] In 1766, Lessing had emphasized that proper understanding of art demanded not only access to art but also specialized skills and a particular scholarly character. One should not just enjoy the immediacy of art, as the *Liebhaber* (connoisseur) or know the general principles of aesthetics, as the philosopher, but, through the study of the conventions of different art forms and time periods, become a *Kunstrichter* (art critic).[16] Lessing's problem with Klotz was not least that he claimed to be an art critic, and even held a professorial chair, but nonetheless behaved and argued like a connoisseur. Hallensleben similarly behaved like a connoisseur, drew his conclusions from his immediate experiences and had little understanding of the larger context of his findings.

Gatterer's credibility, on the contrary, rested on his expert knowledge of auxiliary sciences and great familiarity with official documents. Many contemporaries noted how Gatterer's scholarly character supported his style of inquiry. The Swedish scholar Johan Hinric Lidén visited Göttingen for a year during the 1760s and participated in Gatterer's class on diplomatics. In his travel journal, Lidén noted how the preoccupation with official documents coloured almost everything about the professor. At his first visit to Gatterer's house, Lidén observed that he had a 'philosophical, yes entirely document-like appearance' and that they talked about 'nothing but official documents and manuscripts'. Later, after a meeting of the Königliche Institut der historischen Wissenschaften, which also took place in his house, Lidén remarked that Gatterer had been criticized for producing officially looking diplomas for local students, who attended as 'observers' and that the institute could change its name to the Institutum Diplomaticum. During class, Lidén marvelled at Gatterer's large collection of documents and noticed that while Gatterer lectured over the principles of his textbooks, 'he always has original official documents at hand'.[17] In 1775, one booklet, preparing law students for the University of Göttingen, similarly, and somewhat sarcastically, described Gatterer's course on diplomatics through the peculiar scholarly character of Gatterer:

> Diplomatics, the branch of scholarship of how to read, judge and use official documents, can be learned nowhere better than with Gatterer. No scholar can easily collect as many official documents as him, no one cuts as many diplomatic writings, no one is the Linneaus of diplomatics like him. His German diligence, his large knowledge of history, of heraldics, makes the study easier for him. He has an amazing amount of original and printed official documents, monograms, chrisms, seals of all kinds, and playfully one learns this branch of scholarship with him. One learns to understand his textbook masterpiece and to love this branch of scholarship, which so many avoid, with delight. Old documents that we drag out of dusty archives, old seals that we tear out of the hands of the needlewomen, are as beloved by us as gold and with the greatest delight we ruin our eyes on obscure, unreadable script.[18]

Gatterer's credibility also relied upon his personal collection of such material. In his house on Alleestraße in Göttingen, he had gathered, in the words of one of his colleagues, 'all kinds of paper and other writing materials, also entire collections of alphabets, chancellor-emblems, monograms, seals and entire official documents, partly originals, partly also drawings and engravings'.[19] He also had borrowed several documents from the state archives and bought many more himself. These documents he used for his classes on diplomatics, as his students reported, but they also served as evidence for his theories. References to these unique documents often appeared in his diplomatic reports, including in the one about the Münzenberg gravestone. To support his claim about the coat of arms, he not only referred to printed seals but also informed his readers: 'I have separated this series of seals for my diplomatic cabinet and show them here publicly (at the gathering of the Historical Institute) for additional assurance.'[20]

Disciplinarity between jurisprudence and philosophy

At the end of the nineteenth century, some German historians still considered Gatterer as a founder of their discipline. When German historiography became associated with Herder and historicism, he, like Klotz, disappeared in the background.[21] During the 1970s, however, historians restored Gatterer to the history of German historiography, most importantly Peter Hanns Reill in his *The German Enlightenment and the Rise of Historicism* of 1975.[22] Reill emphasized a series of essays that Gatterer wrote during the late 1760s. His essay on Livy, demarcating modern scholars from ancient statesmen, was one of them. Gatterer also wrote about the epistemology of history, proposed a plan for the writing of German history and discussed the importance of literary style. According to Reill, these essays made Gatterer a major representative of a German school of 'pragmatic history', which reacted against contemporary philosophical histories and laid the foundation for the rise of historicism.

Gatterer's short period of essay writing may have been motivated by more immediate concerns. The primary purpose was probably to secure a territory for historical scholarship within the University of Göttingen as well as within the German academic landscape at large. When planning the Königliche Institut der historischen Wissenschaften, Gatterer had great plans for a network of such institutes across German universities. But, as Martin Gierl has shown, after the establishment of the institute in 1764, Gatterer encountered fierce opposition from the Königliche Sozietät der Wissenschaften in Göttingen.[23] The Society disliked the competition for government funding and for the designation as *königlich* (royal), lobbied for university intervention and thwarted his plans to call the institute an academy as well as to include natural history. Gatterer's sudden interests in the theory of history may have reflected these conflicts and the need to justify his position.

In 1767, in an overview of German historiography, Gatterer dated the beginning of modern German history writing to Ludewig and Gundling. These historians, he claimed, 'showed through their writings, and even more through their lectures, that much more belonged to our history of the fatherland than just the history of emperors'. Hereby they had 'become founders of a very large historical sect, which one could call the juridical'. While the juridical approach to the past opened up new fields of history, the 'sect' also threatened to limit history to 'bread studies' and 'one now almost only considers imperial history as an aid to German public law'[24] Historical knowledge might no longer be auxiliary to theoretical knowledge, but it had just submitted to jurisprudence instead. To liberate historical scholarship, Gatterer again turned to the traditional scholastic definition of knowledge, as presented in the epistemology of the Halle philosopher Christian Wolff. Like Wolff, Gatterer distinguished between philosophical, mathematical and historical forms of knowledge. He described the theoretical knowledge of mathematics and philosophy as *wissenschaftliche Evidenz* (scholarly evidence), whereas historical knowledge only consisted of facts or 'evidence of individual things'. To become an independent *Wissenschaft* (branch of scholarship), historical scholarship had to prove that it could also deliver theoretical knowledge. 'One rightfully demands from a branch of scholarship', Gatterer argued with a Wolffian formulation, that 'everything in it is made certain or in the proper sense can be demonstrated, that is, that all concepts that belong to a branch of scholarship can be derived from its main concepts'. Pragmatic history, Gatterer claimed, could approach this ideal by undercovering a 'system' under the individual facts and events. 'A system of events in history and a system of concepts in a proper branch of scholarship', he explained, 'have a large similarity to one another' and were 'both the business of a philosophical spirit'.[25] In his eagerness to elevate history to an independent discipline, Gatterer even revived the old rhetorical ideal of *historia magistra vitae*. The historian should narrate the past 'where it is most instructive, that is, religion and superstition, virtue and vices, political prudence and mistakes of governing, wisdom and folly, in one word, everything, should be uncovered under the transparent veil of events'. Then, he argued, history would again become 'a teacher of humankind'.[26]

Gatterer's Wolffian and Ciceronian arguments should probably not be considered as a beginning of modern historicism, but rather as an example of the problems of establishing a new discipline. Gatterer was convinced that history should be an independent branch of scholarship, but he had to resort to older philosophical definitions of knowledge to justify this conviction. These philosophical definitions, however, did little justice to the actual working practices of historians. Gatterer's theoretical essays, as already Reill noted, had almost no relation to his historical works. His strengths were not philosophical ingenuity, rhetorical clarity or literary imagination. Even his books on universal history were conservative and offered few daring conclusions or new grand narratives. In the first issue of *Historische Journal*, published in September 1772, after his conflicts with Königliche Sozietät der Wissenschaften had been settled, Gatterer also reversed his opinion on the matter of philosophical, rhetorical and literary history writing. In the introduction, he recalled his demand for narrative history and complained that he now after five years had more than enough. German historical scholarship was now full of imitators of the British and French traditions of conjectural and philosophical history, 'little Humes, little Robertsons, little German Voltaires'. 'These insects', Gatterer declared, 'we will persecute without mercy wherever we find them; they can be harmful, like all insects'. Narrative could be an addition, but the 'essence of history' was 'pure clean truth'.[27] Historical scholarship should limit the harmful influence of philosophy and defend the unique German sense of the past.

Gatterer's contemporaries also did not celebrate him for his contributions to the philosophy of history. He was known for his technical skills and command of auxiliary sciences of history, such as diplomatics, genealogy and heraldics. These qualifications, and not his Wolffian epistemology, gave him the authority to decide what counted as historical knowledge. He exemplified a new kind of specialized scholar with unique control over the relationship between past and present. The present did not have immediate access to the past but needed the mediation of the specialist. The specialist could mediate because of his access to sources and command of particular research techniques to interpret these sources. These techniques could be standardized and taught through textbooks and exercises, ensuring disciplinary coherence and independence.

6

The state archive

The revolution

The Holy Roman Empire was dissolved in 1806 after Napoleon's invasion. Almost a thousand years of historical continuity had been broken. After the fall of Napoleon in 1814, the European states, under the leadership of the Austrian statesman Prince Klemens von Metternich, reestablished order at the Congress of Vienna. The Congress did not reinstate the Empire but instead gathered most of the German states in a weak confederation and secured peace across the continent through censorship and repressive control. This new order was unstable. After the July Revolution in France in 1830, a wave of revolutionary fervour swept across Europe. During a short period of time, the Belgians declared their independence from Holland and the Poles rebelled against their Russian oppressors. Civil war broke out between clericals and liberals in Spain and Portugal. Unrest spread throughout Italy and the German states, momentarily threatening Austro-Prussian domination within the German confederation and Austrian hegemony on the Italian Peninsula. Liberal advocates for constitutional rule found new hope and captured new momentum across the continent. The July Revolution not only dethroned the Bourbons but also unsettled the European status quo of the Congress of Vienna.[1] A new age of revolutions and extremes was on the rise.

The young historian Leopold Ranke, residing in Venice during the late summer and fall of 1830, was terrified. Although never a revolutionary, Ranke had sympathized with the liberal and democratic cause during the 1810s and 1820s. Now, he saw only destruction and disorder. In his letters, he grieved that he suddenly found himself in 'decisive opposition to public opinion'. He worried that the 'plebes' would seize Germany before his homecoming, and he could not accept a government of 'journeymen and street urchins'. He considered the 'incessant blabbering about governing' a threat to European peace, described the new revolutionary spirit as 'a kind of contagion' and foresaw a 'horrible catastrophe' and 'most unhappy times'.[2] Arriving safely in Berlin in March 1831, Ranke discussed with colleagues, friends and allies how their historical studies could serve as a bulwark against the horrors of revolution. His publisher, Friedrich Perthes, expressed their sentiments in December 1830, in a letter to Friedrich von Gentz at Metternich's Court in Vienna. Perthes predicted the 'breakup of the closely-knit Europe' as 'one little people after another are agitated to elect princes, who are not grounded upon divine right' and proposed an intellectual counter-offensive:

> It is due time to protect public opinion from new corruption – one can restrain the newspapers, and that is justified, but no force can halt the deluge of pamphlets, public leaflets, and all kinds of writings – the division of Germany and the character of our literature and book-trade spoil every preventative measure against these. The only defense against the lie is to let the truth be heard – it still has power. . . . In times where everything is questioned, everyone, who values right and truth, must at every moment do what he can in his position.[3]

Ranke's first publication after the July Revolution was a small booklet, *Ueber die Verschwörung gegen Venedig im Jahre 1618* (On the Conspiracy Against Venice in the Year of 1618), on a mercenary plot to plunder the city.[4] The book, written in Venice between August and December 1830 and printed in Berlin in the summer of 1831, summarized some of his recent findings in the archives of Austria and Italy. On the surface, it had no connection to contemporary politics. However, the book announced an important shift in the development of the modern historical discipline. During the 1830s, Ranke established his reputation as the leading German historian.[5] He founded the *Historisch-politische Zeitschrift* (Historical-Political Journal), together with Perthes, in 1832. In the mid-1830s, he began teaching his famous exercises at the University of Berlin, which, at the end of the century, garnered him the reputation as the father of the historical discipline. Ranke's book about Venice contributed to this shift. It delivered an example of how historians ought to work and helped establish the archive as the key site for the production of historical knowledge. It showed how the historian's command of the archive, rather than any philosophical theory of knowledge, defined and justified the historical discipline as an independent branch of scholarship.

Archival and universal history

During the second half of the eighteenth century, German historians still struggled to justify their new discipline. The scholastic definition of knowledge as certain, deducible and based upon universal laws and principles had not yet lost its influence. Johann Christoph Gatterer's embrace of Wolffian epistemology during the 1760s, discussed in the previous chapter, illustrates this need for philosophical justifications. The influence of French and British Enlightenment philosophical histories only further emphasized the importance of philosophical overview.[6] At the beginning of the nineteenth century, historians continued to express anxieties about the independent value of their craft. Even Barthold Georg Niebuhr, who inspired Ranke in his use of critical methods, shared this sentiment. In 1811, in the introduction to his celebrated lectures on Roman history at the University of Berlin, Niebuhr condemned the *philologische Halbkenntniß* (philological pseudo-knowledge) of specialized academics, who neither appreciated the eternal value of Antiquity nor considered the contemporary significance of their research. The ideal academic not only knew sources and historical particularities but also searched for divine *Allwissenheit* (omniscience).[7] In the early 1830s, Ranke still had to explain to his students in Berlin that historical scholarship did not rely upon philosophical justifications and that historiography and philosophy had different and competing goals.[8]

During the 1830s, however, Ranke convinced many of his contemporaries that historiography was independently purposeful. Historical research based upon primary sources was not an aid or a supplement to theological and philosophical universal histories but the only proper way to engage with the past. The strong reactions of Ranke's contemporaries testify to the newness of his approach.[9] In 1847, Karl August Varnhagen von Ense, a pillar of Berlin's intellectual community who during the 1820s had been a friend and supporter of Ranke, condemned not only Ranke's new politics but also his 'delusion that the essence of history is located in those materials that he is the first to open and use'.[10] In 1841, another critical observer, writing in the left-Hegelian *Hallische Jahrbücher* (Halle Yearbooks), noted that Ranke has not only more than any other of our historians reverted to the archive, the handwritten records and documents; but he also loves to create primarily, yes exclusively, from these. . . . Only within these, he thinks, one can find thorough and secure knowledge; only from these, one can learn the true and original interrelationship between the events and their ultimate causes.[11]

The clearest example of Ranke's new approach to history, the critic claimed, was his 1831 booklet about the conspiracy against Venice.

Discovering the archive

Ranke's first book, *Geschichten der romanischen und germanischen Völker* (Histories of the Roman and Germanic People), published in 1824, with his famous demand that the historian should show 'what actually happened', was not based upon archival research. He wrote the book as a high school teacher in Frankfurt Oder and had not yet had the opportunity to visit archives himself. His book therefore relied upon printed works. However, the book ended with a discussion about the possibility of uncovering new archival material. Despite a century of archival research, even German history, Ranke claimed, remained in darkness. To uncover this history, one needed a new kind of historian, who resembled the ancient historian exploring foreign countries, but visited archives rather than battlefields. Ranke concluded:

> Here would be required a man, who, furnished with enough knowledge, plenty of recommendations, and good health, crisscrossed all parts of Germany, and sought out the rest of a world, half vanished and so nearby. We hunt for unknown weeds as far as into the deserts of Libya. Should the life of our ancestors not be worthy of the same eagerness in our own country?[12]

Ranke may have felt that the archival research of the last century was insufficient because he was looking for different kinds of sources. He was not primarily interested in official documents, but rather in testimonies that offered reliable accounts of the events. For eighteenth-century historians, such as Ludewig and Gatterer, official documents had offered a solution to the challenge of historical Pyrrhonism because they were not testimonial but relics of the events. However, these documents only offered a very limited view of the past. Historians with broader interests still relied upon testimonies to write their works. To ensure 'historical belief', they then instead assessed the moral character of the authors, following procedures, similar to those Thomasius had recommended to his students in Halle.[13] The critical appendix to Ranke's 1824 book was an elaborate exercise in this kind of character assessment.[14] His way to know the past was to familiarize himself as intimately as possible with the authors of his sources. Few accounts survived his scrutiny. Early modern historians could not be trusted, and Ranke concluded 'that their information is neither sufficient nor authentic; that we remain in darkness as long as we follow them straightforward'. The rare exception was the sixteenth-century Roman physician Paolo Giovio, who remained largely unpartisan, reported the 'facts' and even wrote 'bitter truths' about his patrons. He had collected 'a large treasure of the best and most original reports' and based his writings upon information 'from the mouth of the most distinguished participants and other eyewitnesses'.[15] To uncover other reliable witnesses, like Giovio, who reported immediately and honestly from the events, Ranke had to enter the archives.

Shortly after his arrival in Berlin, in the spring of 1825, he uncovered a collection of forty-eight manuscript volumes in the Königliche Bibliothek. The volumes contained reports written by early modern Venetian diplomats about the politics and lives of other European countries.[16] Reading through these volumes, Ranke became convinced that he had finally uncovered 'immediate history'.[17] Already by the summer of 1825, he was planning an ambitious book, based upon these diplomatic reports, which would redefine European history from the Reformation to the French Revolution.[18] This book never materialized, but, in 1827, his work with the Venetian sources resulted in *Fürsten und Völker von Süd-Europa* (The Princes and People of Southern Europe), which carried the programmatic subtitle: 'Primarily from unpublished diplomatic reports'. To uncover more reports and expand his work on Southern Europe, Ranke travelled to Austria in the early fall of 1827. Initially, he had only planned a short archival visit to Vienna, but, mesmerized by the treasures of foreign archives, he refused to return to his teaching duties at the University of Berlin and repeatedly begged for extensions of his leave – at one point, inciting rumours in Berlin that he had converted to Catholicism.[19] Ranke finally returned in late March 1831, after more than three years in German, Austrian and Italian archives. Before leaving Berlin, Ranke had imagined what the foreign archives would be like. 'How rich this archive must have been!' he exclaimed about Venice in *Fürsten und Völker von Süd-Europa*.[20] However, the daily archival work was unlike anything he could have anticipated. Apart from his intensive work with the forty-eight manuscript volumes in the Royal Library, Ranke had little archival experience. Only during his journey through Austria and Italy did Ranke fully convince himself that historiography and archival research were inseparable. In the archives, he learnt to view human history as a history of documents.

A history of documents

By Ranke's standards, *Ueber die Verschwörung gegen Venedig* was a brief book. It contained only 141 short pages of analysis, followed by a 48-page appendix of documents from the Venetian archive. Not only this appendix but also the composition and rhetorical style of the book revealed Ranke's turn to the archive. The reader was not immediately presented with 'what actually happened' in 1618. Only on page 98 did he tell the story of the French mercenary Jacques Pierre who conspired with a group of fellow mercenaries in Venetian service to attack and plunder the city, possibly aided by the Spanish viceroy of Naples, Pedro Téllez-Girón, Duke of Osuna.[21] The drama of Ranke's book was not the drama of 1618 but the drama of Ranke's struggle with his sources. It recounted his investigations, his gathering of evidence and his recording of testimonies from more or less reliable witnesses. The intention was not primarily to present an account of past events, but to explain to the reader how Ranke had uncovered these events. The main character in this story was not the deceitful Jacques Pierre, betraying the Venetian republic, but the heroic Leopold Ranke, facing the deceits of past historians of Venice. The first programmatic words of the book read:

> The investigation, on which I venture, poses more than one difficulty. The authors, whom it concerns, often make unintended, and sometimes even deliberate, errors; many of the documents, which are presented to us, are not authentic; the actors themselves are faced with false as well as well-founded indictments. As I strive to recognize undeceived the authentic, and to discern the true course of these matters, it is my wish, to lead the reader out of this labyrinth and to a pure and satisfactory conviction.[22]

Ranke began the book with 'the first reports' emerging in chronicles, letters and printed pamphlets, shortly after the conspiracy had been exposed. He emphasized the context of these writings – when, where and by whom they were written and read – not the context of the conspiracy itself. He also chose not yet to deal with documents that only were known to the Venetian authorities. Ranke then turned to historiography. The first part of the history of historiography described pro-Venetian and anti-Spanish interpretations. Ranke discussed the official Venetian history of the events, written by Battista Nani half a century later, and inspected the seventeenth-century Savoyan historian Abbé de St. Real, his sources and his Venetian imitators. The second part of the historiography described what Ranke called the 'opposition'. He especially focused upon two recent histories by the Prussian diplomat Jean Pierre de Chambrier and the French historian Pierre Daru.[23] The conclusion Ranke drew from his historiographical readings was that none of the previous accounts of the events of 1618 were trustworthy. Some of these accounts, he admonished, could not even be labelled as history. To reach this verdict, Ranke pointed to disagreement between the texts and inconsistencies within the texts.

Ranke most dramatic display of this comparative technique was his exposure of a collection of false documents, reproduced in an anonymous manuscript entitled *Sommario della congiura contra la citta di Venetia* (Summary of the Conspiracy Against the City of Venice).[24] This summary, which could be found in Paris and several Italian libraries, had heavily influenced St. Real, and, through him, many later historians. It was, more or less, the basis of the pro-Venetian interpretative tradition. Ranke found several names and dates in the summary that were inconsistent with those in other contemporary documents. Some of the names had also been misplaced or misspelled. These small inconsistencies led Ranke to a daring conclusion: Not only was the summary mistaken – its mistakes descended from a much larger forgery. The presumed documents in the summary were forgeries that had been produced and sold for profit. With the authoritative voice of the archival researcher, Ranke finished his detailed critique:

> This large fraud points us to a school of forgers, who, to sell what they did not have, instead produced something that was in demand. For good money, these people sold documents, which would have been invaluable if they had been authentic, from the earliest times of the Republic to the houses of the most revered nobles; they even imitated the worm holes of such old paper. However, [the forgery] was not done flawlessly.[25]

More than a third of the way into the book, Ranke ended his historiographical overview with a sad conclusion: 'After so many efforts, we are still almost standing where one stood immediately after May 1618.'[26] He had not learnt anything from two centuries' cumulative literature, but instead, he had proven an important point: the archive was the only proper site for the production of historical knowledge. An author who did not have an intimate and personal knowledge of the archival documents would only reproduce tradition or expose his own fantasies. He would not write history. Historiography could not be separated from the collecting of historical evidence. History only came into being through the archive. Shortly after his return to Berlin in 1831, Ranke clarified his position to his students. In an introductory lecture on universal history, Ranke distinguished undocumented history from the rest of history. Unlike philosophical historians, who allowed for conjectures and speculations about the entire history of humankind, Ranke insisted that only written records could keep the past alive:

> In and for itself, history embraces the life of humankind through all times. However, all too much of this is lost or unknown, . . . Some of what has been described is lost, some has never been described – all this is draped with death; only those, whom history considers, are not entirely dead, their essence and existence still act, when they are understood: with the loss of memory the actual death emerges. Fortunate, where documentary traces still remain. At least these can be considered. But when not? For example, in the earliest history? I think that this should be excluded from history, for good reasons, as it contradicts its principle, which is documentary research.[27]

Entering the archive

The culmination of Ranke's 1831 book was his description of the great Venetian archive, which, during the 1810s and 1820s had been gathered in the former convent of Santa Maria Gloriosa dei Frari, after negotiations with French and Austrian authorities and squabbles between local archivists.[28] Ranke opened with a guided tour and engaged the reader in what Steven Shapin and Simon Schaffer call 'virtual witnessing'.[29] The historian's work in libraries and archives was inherently solitary, but Ranke invited the reader to visualize the archive and imagine himself in Ranke's place. He not only listed the many documents that one could find on the shelves but also described the building, the rooms, the light falling through the windows and the coolness of the air in August. Ranke compared this tour through the archives with that of the ordinary tourist through the streets of Venice. While the tourist sensed, the historian and his readers witnessed. The city's palaces, churches and market squares made the visitor remember the past, but only the documents in archives could truly mediate between past and present. Ranke claimed,

> if one wants to proceed from these loose inklings to a view of past existence, if one wants to become acquainted with the inner driving forces, which provided this being with constancy, then one must move to these [archival] rooms and seek advice in the vellum treasures. Only that part of life, which has been stored in writings, can once again be clearly understood.[30]

Allowing his readers to witness the research process, Ranke diminished their spatial distance from the Italian archive and concealed their dependence upon his personal credibility. With Ranke's book in hand, the reader could enter the Frari from anywhere in the world. In his description, the archive had no doors or opening hours. No other users inhabited it. No restrictive librarians or archivists were standing between the researcher and his sources. Ranke and his virtual visitor strolled freely through the rooms and explored the documents as they appeared in front of them. They had few problems finding documents or understanding them. History immediately presented itself to them, even before they had started reading. 'Already by the sizes of diverse sections of these papers', Ranke explained, 'we again recognize some ways of life of the Venetians'. The archival work was also not disturbed by considerations of the outside world. Although placed in Venice, the Frari escaped place. Personal, financial or political concerns did not influence Ranke's choice of topics or sources. Inside the archive, the historian's only allegiances were to God, truth and the silenced and otherwise dead voices of the past. 'God doesn't want', Ranke assured, 'that I should hide or gloss over some act of violence, regardless of if the rulers or their opponents have committed [this act of violence]. Only the defense of those, who no longer can defend themselves, to bring the truth into daylight, I will always consider one of the most important duties of history'.[31]

The archival self

The printed description did not, however, tell the whole truth about Ranke's work. In his letters, Ranke reported how he disciplined himself for the work in the archives, discussing how he structured his day and planned his diet according to the needs of archival research.[32] More importantly, the letters reveal how the many hours in the archives changed his understanding of himself as a historian and as a human being. Ranke's style of letter writing was confessional and anecdotal.[33] His letters resembled the sentimental travelogues of German romantics. Ranke replaced English landscapes, Italian castle-ruins and rosy-cheeked millers' daughters with early modern diplomatic reports, but imitated the sentiment. For the romantics, Nicholas Jardine argues, '[t]he most authentic reunion with nature requires not the discursive exercise of the mind, but immediate engagement: the innocent gaze of the child (Novalis), the sensitivity of the nervously disordered (Schubert), the absorption of the artist-genius lost in the work of creation (Schelling).'[34] Much the same could be said of Ranke's reunion with the sources. While Ranke's 1831 book emphasized the visual immediacy of the past within the archive, his letters contained the entire register of romantic emotions and experiences.

To his brother Heinrich, a Lutheran minister, Ranke described how his studies catapulted him between desperation and joy; how, at times, he felt the presence of God among the fragments he studied, and, at other times, he sensed nothing but hopelessness and confusion.[35] With his friend Heinrich Ritter, Ranke discussed his erotic experiences inside as well as outside the archives. While detailing an encounter with a scantily clad young Czech woman with whom he shared his overcoat during a stroll outside Prague, he suddenly interrupted himself: 'I am terrified that I am more long-winded about this than about all the manuscripts.' Later, rhapsodizing about the Italian collections in Vienna, he declared: 'Here I have splendid and sweet lovers' trysts with the object of my desire, which is a beautiful Italian woman. And I hope we bring forth a Romano-Germanic wonder-child.' Sometimes, Ranke compared himself to a romantic explorer. He saw his future as 'a Columbus of Venetian history'. Later, he lowered his ambitions to 'becoming if not a Columbus than a kind of Cook for the many beautiful, unknown islands of world history'.[36] At other times, employing a metaphor especially popular among German romantics, Ranke compared the archives to mines. In Vienna, shortly before leaving for Italy, Ranke slipped the following note into one of the archival packets: 'I compare this library to a mine. However, the prince brings it together. Benevolent overseers ensure that it is a pleasure to work here. To each one belongs what he hauls out and, in the end, the purest gold is still here. L. Ranke, Professor in Berlin.'[37]

Historical research demanded a character assessment of the authors of sources. The daily emotional involvement and confrontation with these writers, however, also transformed the historian's character. Ranke increasingly viewed his life from the perspective of the archive. After a year abroad, he confessed to his brother: 'I have now become a gatherer. . . . Sometimes I feel the need to gather myself.' In the summer of 1829, he started to doubt if anywhere in this world could be considered his 'home'. By the summer of 1830, he had learnt to overcome this feeling of homesickness – this time longing for Rome and not Germany – through more archival research. After more than two years abroad, archival research had become his entire existence. To historical research, Ranke wrote to his brother, 'I have been called, to this I have also been born, here is my sufferings and my joys, my life and my destiny is defined through this!' His life, he wrote to Ritter, had 'no other purpose'.[38]

Accessing the archive

Ranke's letters from Italy and Austria also reveal some of the practical problems of archival research. His book's description of the open and transparent Venetian archive had little to do with Ranke's actual experiences. During the journey, Ranke used considerable time and energy gaining access to archives. Once inside, many documents remained inaccessible and had to be released one at a time. Ranke's favourite sources were diplomatic reports, which were normally confidential. Civil servants did not save secret notes, encrypted documents and diplomatic correspondences to aid visiting historians. Openness reduced the value of the archive as an administrative tool and possibly damaged the administration. The centralization of archives during the eighteenth and early nineteenth centuries, such as the Viennese Haus-, Hof- und Staatsarchivs in 1749, the French Archives Nationales after 1789, the reorganized Prussian Staatsarchiv after 1810 and the Venetian Frari archive after 1815, did not necessarily result in more transparency. The centralization of archives primarily served the consolidation of power of the modern bureaucratic state.[39] The French National Assembly in 1794 declared the new national archives 'the central depository for the entire Republic' and made access a right of all citizens, but, in practice, access remained limited and a public reading room was not installed before 1847.[40] The old monarchies of Europe did not share the French democratic sentiment and were even less inclined to allow the public to inspect their secrets.

As early as 1818, the Prussian minister of culture, Karl vom Stein zum Altenstein, recognized this problem for historical research and proposed that the Prussian archives be divided between documents vital to contemporary politics and those 'which merely can be attributed a historical value'. The political section of the archives, Altenstein argued, 'can, according to its nature, only be accessible to few' and, therefore, 'fruitful use [of the archives] for scholarship has until now not been feasible'. The Prussian chancellor, Karl August von Hardenberg, rejected his minister's proposal, since 'a borderline between the two sections cannot be drawn with accuracy'.[41] A division of the archives would not only harm the government but also historians and philologists, who would lose access to documents in the political section. Hardenberg only made documents from before 1500 immediately accessible to historians. The borders between political and scholarly documents were no less blurry in Austria and Italy. In Vienna, no guidelines for the use of the archives existed, and the central administration determined questions of access on an individual basis. During the first decades of the nineteenth century, the administration was extremely cautious and, for periods, the archives were almost completely closed to scholars. Access to documents from secret government archives, such as diplomatic reports, Metternich dictated in 1818, demanded government authorization. Without such authorization 'nothing shall be released from the archive . . . not even when the content seems entirely harmless'.[42] Even when access had been granted, the director of the archive carefully examined archival packets for compromising material before showing them to visitors.[43] In Italy, where many documents were within private collections or scattered between small city-states, the diplomatic game over archival access became even more complicated.[44]

When Ranke reached his first destination, Vienna, in late September 1827, he wrote to Bettina von Arnim: 'You know what I have to search for next: Libraries and archives, and the persons who can pave my way to these.' During the rest of his journey, he carefully cultivated contacts with civil servants, noble families and other dignitaries who could open archival doors. Already before leaving Berlin, Ranke obtained letters of recommendation from Prussian officials. Later, Prussian diplomats in Vienna and Florence interceded on his behalf. When he discovered Alexander von Humboldt's popularity in Italy, he wrote to friends in Germany to secure himself a letter from the scientist.[45] Ranke's most vital contacts were at the Viennese Court. Friedrich von Gentz especially proved an invaluable ally. Gentz was one of the intellectual fore-figures of the European reaction.[46] He had been secretary to the Congress of Vienna and was one of the chief architects of the Carlsbad Decrees of 1819, which limited the freedom of press and universities. More important, Gentz was a close associate of Prince Metternich. In Vienna, a Prussian diplomat on 28 September 1827, applied on behalf of Ranke for archival access, but the director of the archive, Josef Knechtl, initially recommended that the administration should deny him access, since he was a foreigner and it would be impossible to properly censor the large Italian collections. Only after Gentz's personal intervention, and a meeting with Metternich, could Ranke enter the archive, on 13 October, despite the director's complaints.[47] A few months later, Ranke explained to Varnhagen how this was negotiated:

> Concerning the archive, everything appeared to fail. Baron von Maltzahn, who occupies himself with this matter, after some time called me to him and read me a letter, as utterly negative as ever possible, from the State Chancellery: 'Too recent history. Rules. A stranger to the archive'.... Fortunately, however, a man was interested in the matter, who had the inclination and capability: Mr. von Gentz. He also called me to him, and indeed to the Prince ... that [Metternich] knew my situation and appeared to think much good of me, impressed me considerably. The matter was immediately decided ... The next day, I gave Gentz a slip of paper, without heading or signature, only with a more detailed description of what I was searching for. This [slip] was delivered to the archive.[48]

Parts of the Italian collections in the Viennese archive remained inaccessible and demanded new authorizations. To continue his work, Ranke developed an intimate relationship with Gentz. On 9 December 1827, he wrote to Ritter about his frequent meetings with Gentz since their first encounter in October: 'Not seldom I visit him after dinner and always find him well-disposed and as helpful as then.'[49] According to Knechtl, Ranke's archival privileges were unprecedented, even among Austrian historians.⁵⁰ In Italy, Ranke likewise encountered problems with access. The Frari proved especially troublesome. When Ranke first arrived in Venice in October 1828, he was allowed to peep into the archive, but not to read his treasured diplomatic reports. 'With agony', Ranke wrote to his publisher on 12 October, 'I have spotted my treasure, the final reports, from a distance; little protected, without bindings or order, held together with strings, and nonetheless not to be reached immediately.' Since Venice was under Austrian control, Ranke wrote to Gentz on 17 October. The distance from Vienna, however, made it impossible for Gentz personally to oversee Ranke's work at informal meetings. On 9 January 1829, Ranke complained that, despite Metternich's support, 'even now no definite decision has followed as these matters not only pass through different ministries, but also are sent here for assessment and must be returned to Vienna'.⁵¹ The same year, however, the Austrian government bypassed the local archivists and granted Ranke an unusually generous authorization to see all documents dating before the French Revolution.⁵²

Ranke's romantic relationship with his sources, and his new self-identification as archival researcher, made him feel increasingly passionate about his patrons at the Viennese Court. After their first meeting in the fall of 1827, Ranke praised Metternich's 'fresh, spirited, stately personality' and confessed to Varnhagen: 'Do you know what I thought when I left? That, in the end, the effort to acquaint oneself with those people who are in the highest places and estates normally pays off. Honestly, I am for now somewhat bought.'⁵³ A year later, in January 1829, while his case was pending between Venice and Vienna, he had forgotten his reservations and critical distance, and declared to an Austrian friend: 'I truly venerate your Prince Metternich. It is surely most noble that he offhandedly has permitted my access to the final reports of this archive.' After finally entering the Venetian archive, in August 1830, he considered his 'obligations to the Austrian government' as 'extraordinary'.⁵⁴ Immersed in his work with the Venetian final reports, and probably writing on his book about the Venetian conspiracy, he thankfully wrote to Gentz on 26 September 1830:

> when a human being, whoever he is, achieves what he honestly and eagerly wishes for, and what is necessary for the realization of the purpose of his life, then he feels very obliged to those, whom he can thank for this. I simply

consider it the result of your recommendation to His Highness Prince Metternich that everything goes well, and without significant difficulties, with my current endeavors in Venice, as before in Vienna. . . . In the archive, I have consequently been received as a good friend.[55]

In his 1831 book, Ranke also expressed his gratitude for 'the extraordinary favor with which both of the two great German governments [the Prussian and the Austrian] have honored me undeservingly'.[56] However, Metternich and Gentz's favours were probably not given without reason and certainly not the result of unconditional love for academic freedom. Ranke also knew that Vienna expected some guarantees, especially considering the recent eruption of revolutionary passions across Europe. On 26 September 1830, in his thankful letter to Gentz, Ranke assured him that 'Even if I had had the hatred against Austria of a Frenchman from the extreme left, it would be hard for me to bring forth anything from this material, which could harm your cause in public opinion.' He even considered publishing some of the documents he had uncovered since, 'the nature of these sources corresponds with my own loyalty towards a country, which has treated me with such extraordinary liberality'.[57]

Action and reaction in the archive

In the fall of 1832, the poet Heinrich Heine, who had befriended Ranke during a visit to Venice in 1828, distinguished between the new political Ranke, writing openly in support of the Prussian government and his previous identity as 'a quaint talent for cutting out small historical figurines and gluing them picturesquely next to one another, a good spirit, as cozy as mutton with turnip from Teltow, an innocent human being'.[58] However, Ranke's figurines were not entirely innocuous. Ranke's archival research practices helped connect his historiographical reaction to the broader political reaction. Political figures like Friedrich von Gentz and Prince Metternich controlled access to the archives. Before a single archival packet had been opened, political concerns had coloured the outcome. Ranke denied that political considerations would make him ignore inconvenient evidence, but, in his letters to Gentz, he recognized the value and significance of their shared political outlook and even offered to publish material that supported the Viennese position in the heated political climate of his day.

Inside the archive, Ranke's work was limited by political decisions beyond his control. Diplomats and higher civil servants had produced most of the documents that fascinated him. The documents had been saved, and collected in archives, because the authorities needed them for future reference. During the early nineteenth century, as the centralization of archives and high-level government involvement in questions about archival access testify, archives were considered of crucial political importance. The interests and concerns of civil servants determined the limits of Ranke's historical work. Especially considering Ranke's strong personal identification with his sources, his books were necessarily written from the viewpoint of the state. The state archive as the site for the production of historical knowledge also determined the content of that knowledge. In 1841, the *Hallische Jahrbücher* remarked:

> It often happens that progress and life completely escapes both the administration and the diplomacy, and that historic moments also only can be encountered where one does not encounter the government and its archive. . . . In his studies as well as in his life, Ranke has had so much commerce with diplomats that he himself completely has become a diplomat and sees everything through the eyes of a diplomat. He . . . has been called an 'Austrian historian,' and it is impossible to deny, that his view of states and people and their development is very Austrian: nothing is permitted to happen from below, but everything must be made and controlled from the top in utter secrecy.[59]

Ranke's new history 'from the top' did share some important characteristics with history writing of the Enlightenment. The dissolution of the Holy Roman Empire in 1806 had disrupted the long legal tradition that had sustained the school of imperial history. At the beginning of the eighteenth century, Ludewig had claimed that the unbroken tradition of German public law made historical scholarship much more relevant here than in other countries, where it no longer determined questions of 'justice and injustice' and therefore was 'not worth the effort'.[60] With the end of the Holy Roman Empire, German specialists in imperial law had become equally irrelevant. Centuries of scholarship, Robert von Mohl summarized in 1856, lost 'with the fall of the Empire its primary meaning, namely its practical application'. The 'book collection' of such an expert 'largely became wastepaper; his scholarship a breadless art'.[61] Ranke did not revive the Holy Roman Empire, or the school of imperial history, but he did re-establish continuity.[62] Hence after 1840, as John

Toews documents, Ranke's historical works proved an important component in the anti-revolutionary identity politics of the Prussian regime of Friedrich Wilhelm IV.[63] In 1841, Ranke was even appointed official historiographer of the Prussian state.

In February 1831, in the same letter in which he first proposed his book on the Venetian conspiracy to his publisher, Ranke emphasized how sound German scholarship could serve as a counterweight to the radicalized 'French' voices in the newspapers. In Germany, he found 'so much love to calm development' that a violent revolution was preventable. The Germans, he assured, 'are not like the French. Our mind is not reflected in the newspapers.... We must face them upon their field in open battle and not let the world keep the misapprehension that we are German Frenchmen. However, even without this, I have confidence that we will endure, if we do not abandon ourselves'.[64] In 1832, in the editorial introduction to his *Historisch-politische Zeitschrift*, which focused on the Restoration and the July Revolution, Ranke openly allied himself, and the emerging historical discipline, with the Prussian bureaucracy committed to gradual, controlled reform. 'True politics', Ranke explained, 'does not abandon its past for a possibly deceitful promise; it aims at calm progress, a gradual secure development; it keeps with its line'. In his own time, Ranke complained, 'the extremists set the tone'. The historian should limit the destructive effects of 'political theories', support the existing order and prove both liberal revolutionaries and conservative counter-revolutionaries wrong. Proper history underscored continuity as well as gradual progress. 'Nothing is more urgent', Ranke emphasized, 'than to keep in memory the distinction between regular progress and impatient destructive change, between reasonable perseverance and one-sided defense for what's outdated and now lifeless'.[65]

The July Revolution and its European aftermath, as Ranke recognized, proved that ideas were powerful and that civil servants did not control the course of history. Since the Congress of Vienna, which had gathered European states around Metternich's post-revolutionary order, governments had toiled together to secure the status quo. Despite these united efforts, most of the continent was suddenly gripped by revolutionary fervour. At this crucial point in European history, Ranke introduced a new model for the production of historical knowledge that favoured the viewpoints of civil servants and administrators and emphasized historical continuities. Late in his life, Ranke even claimed that his works would not have been possible if the revolutions had succeeded. Objective history and revolutionary politics were incompatible:

> Among the events that we have experienced, one recognizes the defeat of the revolutionary forces, which make the regular development of world history impossible. Had these [revolutionary forces] sustained their position, then one could not have talked of further advancement of the historical forces, not even of an unpartisan view of these [historical forces]. A world history, in the objective sense, would have become impossible.[66]

The politics of the historical discipline

The revolutions of 1789, 1830 and 1848 did sustain their positions and lay the foundations for the constitutional states of modern Europe. Yet the Ranke school survived and adjusted to the needs and demands of the civil servants and administrators of these new constitutional states. While Metternich's European order slowly crumbled, Ranke's model for historical research grew stronger and, at the end of the nineteenth century, became the standard for the historical discipline, even within countries with revolutionary pasts such as France and the United States.[67] Ranke himself came to embody what it meant to be a historian. Some rebelled against his example, but, for generations, no historian could just ignore him. As late as 1962, Georg G. Iggers noted in an influential article that 'the history of German and American historical thought not only can but must be organized around the issue of the acceptance or rejection of Ranke'. Iggers continued to argue that there existed two different images of Ranke in America and Germany. American historians, because of their ignorance of German philosophy, solely considered Ranke the farther of the 'scientific school' of history, focused on facts and detached from morals and politics.[68] German historians, on the other hand, associated Ranke's work with German idealism and historicism. In 1968, in *The German Conception of History*, Iggers himself presented modern German historiography as a unique product of idealism and historicism, inspired by Herder and given academic form by Ranke and Wilhelm von Humboldt. The particularity of German historiography was not its critical methods and working practices, but rather shared 'theoretical convictions in regard to the nature of history and the character of political power'.[69] This interpretation has since become the standard view of Ranke's legacy. Ranke's historical works, John Toews summarized in 2004, 'now appear as forms of constructive storytelling informed by the desires and purposes emerging from his time, culture, and personal situation'.[70]

Reducing Ranke's historical research to a product of idealism, historicism and cultural context, however, also hides the significance of his scholarship. Ranke's writings were not so influential because they reflected common thinking at the time. Those who wanted a theory that emphasized the importance of the state could have found it in the works of many of his contemporaries. They would have not had to read about an obscure conspiracy in seventeenth-century Venice and search for the message between the lines. However, unlike contemporary theoretical work, Ranke's writings offered an argument for why the historical discipline should be considered independently valuable and not reduced to an auxiliary discipline to theology, philosophy or jurisprudence. Similar developments towards disciplinary autonomy happened across the university during this period, but Ranke delivered the necessary justification for historians.[71] If chemists were chemists because of their unique command of the laboratory, historians were historians because they knew their way around archives.

There was no contradiction between these scholarly accomplishments and Ranke's political engagement. Ranke's model of research was political because it produced reliable knowledge about the past. He proved that history was independently valuable by serving a political purpose. For Ranke, the distinction between past and present as well as the insights into contingencies of historical development disproved traditionalists as well as radicals. Historical scholarship questioned whether it was possible to return to the old order of the Holy Roman Empire as well as if such an order, lasting for a thousand years, had ever existed. Simultaneously, he challenged philosophical theories, which insisted upon the necessity of revolutionary ruptures. This view of the past benefitted contemporary rulers, such as Prince Metternich and King Friedrich Wilhelm IV, who supported Ranke's work. However, the model did not depend upon the worldviews of the Austrian and Prussian states and later proved equally useful for constitutional and democratic governments across the world.

7

The seminar

Exercising character

Students who during the 1860s wanted the best and most scholarly history education in the world knew where to go: a modern three-storey townhouse, built in neoclassical style, on Bahnhofstraße 8, just outside the old city gates of Göttingen, where the medievalist Georg Waitz lived.[1] Among his contemporaries, Waitz was known as the most objective, impartial and careful historian of his generation. He was considered the principal progeny of Ranke and the foremost authority on historical and philological source criticism. Historians, who advocated a more literary and public style of history writing, described Waitz as an extreme example of a school of historiography that sacrificed imagination and political engagement for academic purity. For others, he was a hero and the primary example of a new kind of academic historian, who, in a time of division, was not blinded by religious and political partisanship. In Göttingen, he attracted not only Protestant Northern German students but also Jews and Catholics as well as many foreign students.[2]

Once or twice a week, in the evening from six and eight, he gathered these students in a small reading group or, as such classes were called, *Übungen* (exercises).[3] The group, consisting of about a dozen students, would sit together around a large round table by the couch in his study. Normally one student would present a paper and afterwards Waitz and the other students commented. Waitz was not the most inspiring lecturer and even his devoted disciples admitted that he lacked 'pedagogical talent' and 'the Socratic gift' for seeing and unlocking the inner potential of each student.[4] But the few students who were allowed to enter the study nonetheless considered the exercises a life-changing experience. They agreed with their contemporaries that Waitz was unusually impartial, critical and careful, but insisted that this did not make his research and teaching less relevant. Waitz's scholarly attitude, on the contrary, was the key to his moral significance. The significance, moreover, was conveyed to the students through his style of teaching. As the French historian Gabriel Monod later explained:

> One left these lessons not just better instructed, not just with clearer ideas and a better ordered mind, but also with love and respect for truth and scholarship, with understanding for the price that they cost and with resolution to work for them. One sensed that Mr. Waitz put his entire soul into this informal and direct teaching, that he wanted to accomplish a moral as well as an intellectual work, that he wanted to form men as well as scholars, that he gave the best of himself.[5]

Waitz and his students often described the intensive meetings in Göttingen as a direct continuation of Leopold Ranke's famous exercises on the medieval Saxon kings and emperors, which he offered at the University of Berlin during the 1830s. The primary purpose of both Ranke's and Waitz's exercises was not to teach history, understood as a well-established body of knowledge about the past, but rather to prepare students to investigate the past. This demanded that the students acquired methodological skills, but also that they changed personally and morally. This acquirement of skills and moral character was tested and exercised by doing scholarly work. So the students in Waitz's exercises did not merely read historiographical works or listen to lectures but also wrote independent research papers and engaged in reciprocal scholarly critique. The most important outcome, however, was not the papers themselves but the personal transformation that the process of research and critique resulted in. Waitz's lessons, as Monod reported, aimed at forming 'men as well as scholars'.[6]

Institutionalizing the discipline

In some important ways, Waitz was behind his time. During the second half of the nineteenth century, German higher education changed dramatically. An increasing number of students entered university, from about twelve thousand in 1860 to about sixty thousand in 1914, and, in response, professors institutionalized and standardized instruction.[7] One important aspect of this transformation was the introduction of new textbooks on the methods, practices and techniques of research.[8] German professors standardized and formalized older oral and tacit educational traditions and made these available in print to a much larger student audience. Equally important was the proliferation of institutionalized seminars, where students had access to source editions, journals, supervision and exercises, and sometimes also had their own workspace. Such seminars had already been introduced at German universities during the eighteenth century, when they primarily served the education of clergymen and secondary school teachers in philology.[9] During the second half of the nineteenth century, they were introduced in all disciplines and at all German universities.[10] The main purpose of these seminars remained vocational training, but they also taught research methodology.[11]

When late-nineteenth-century scholars celebrated German universities as the model of modern history education, they normally had these institutionalized seminars in mind. German universities published detailed descriptions of the seminars, their organization, architecture, the sources and books in the libraries and the format of the exercises. Foreign scholars travelled to Germany to investigate the institution. In 1881, the Belgian historian Paul Fredericq visited several German universities – Berlin, Halle, Leipzig and Göttingen – to observe modern historical education. Fredericq published his travel notes in a Belgian educational journal in 1882 and later in a collected volume, together with similar observations from Holland, Belgium, Britain and France.[12] These notes were also translated into English and published in Herbert Baxter Adams's *Johns Hopkins University Studies in Historical and Political Science*. In 1885, the Danish historian Kristian Erslev similarly visited the exercises of several Berlin professors to document their teaching style and later inquired about the teaching style at other German seminars.[13] Many scholars around the world described their seminars as copies of German seminars. In 1883, G. Stanley Hall collected and published several detailed descriptions of American historical seminars, many of which mentioned German inspirations.[14]

Not everyone, however, agreed that the institutionalized seminars were the best way to secure the unity of teaching and research. Ranke never taught in a seminar and the University of Berlin was one of the last major German universities to introduce a historical seminar. Waitz detested and resisted the development and complained that the seminars taught 'method, but not the spirit and art of history writing'.[15] He, according to one colleague, remained 'marvelously unchanged' and loudly complained about the many new graduates and compared German universities to 'dissertation factories'[16] History professors, Waitz admonished, now had 'the task to warn, yes to scare away, rather than to attract, those who want to dedicate themselves to the study of history'.[17] For students who cherished the coming of a more egalitarian and meritocratic age, Waitz was hardly the man of the day. One critical observer barked at 'the sacrosanct solemnity of Waitz's room' and the cultish seclusion and uniformity of his disciples. 'Waitz', he claimed, 'was worshipped by his students, untouchable to the highest degree, already his surroundings hallowed, his word an oracle, which one spread with a secretive whisper'.[18] Despite Ranke's and Waitz's opposition to the institutionalized seminars, however, many advocates of institutionalization emphasized the importance of tradition from Ranke as well as the central role of Waitz within the Ranke school. During the second half of the nineteenth century, they claimed, the seminars adopted Ranke's and Waitz's research and teaching methods.

Ranke's exercises

When late-nineteenth-century historians celebrated Ranke as the founder of the historical discipline, they seldom referred to his first published monograph of 1824, or the introductory remark that the historian should show 'what actually happened'. They instead pointed to his teaching practices in Berlin and especially his exercises on the history of the Saxon kings and emperors, which started with an 1834 prize competition on Henry the Fowler. Ranke arranged for the publication of his students' papers in *Jahrbücher des Deutschen Reichs unter dem Sächsischen Hause* (Yearbooks of the German Empire under the Saxon House), which appeared over a period of three years from 1837 to 1840. In his introduction to the first issue, written by Waitz, Ranke emphasized that the yearbooks should be considered as the product of an educational experiment. All students, he argued, should be divided into two major groups, each needing different kinds of education. The largest group consisted of those who studied for personal edification or for vocational training and only needed to attend lectures. For a smaller group of students, who felt an 'inner calling' to research, lectures were not enough. These students needed 'a closer introduction to actual academic matters' and 'guidance to individual activity'. The training for independent academic work, Ranke admitted, had 'for a fairly long time' been offered in seminars and exercises. But, in Ranke's personal experience, students tended to work too independently. Even if they discovered something new, they ended up with 'dispersed papers', which were not suitable for publication.[19] Ranke therefore coordinated their efforts and focused upon one century of German history, after Henry the Fowler was elected as King of East Francia, or 'Germany', in 919.

Waitz did not enroll his students in collaborative research, as Ranke had done, but his intention was still that the exercises should result in publishable scholarly works. Many of the papers appeared as articles in *Forschungen zur deutschen Geschichte* (Research on German History), which Waitz edited, and in other scholarly journals. Some were published as monographs.[20] Both in style and content the works of Waitz's students resembled Ranke's yearbooks. They primarily concerned medieval political and legal history and usually followed a chronological order, some noting the year in the margins and with bold print. They constantly referred to their sources in the text as well as in numerous critical footnotes. Ranke, as Anthony Grafton noted, was rather economical with footnotes in his own books, but in the works of his students, he expected an extensive critical apparatus.[21] Waitz demanded a similar carefulness. His students' works often contained appendices with printed sources and further critical discussions. A couple of works, which were defended as doctoral dissertations, carried the programmatic subtitle 'critically investigated'.[22]

Historians past and present

One important lesson of the Ranke school was that any study of the sources had to start with a study of the authors. An important part of this investigation, as discussed in the previous chapter, was an assessment of moral character. His students learned this methodology in the exercises. During the first exercises on Henry the Fowler, Ranke pointed out to his students that the *Chronicon Corbejense* (Corvey Chronicle), which concerned the history of the imperial Abby of Corvey and was considered a credible contemporary source, may have been written later and collected from several untrustworthy sources.[23] Together with Siegfried Hirsch, Waitz investigated the case. In the third volume of the yearbooks, they published their findings and concluded that the chronicle was not reliable. Parts of it had been copied from later sources and many of its claims did not concur with other contemporaries. Following Ranke's critical approach, Hirsch and Waitz did not just reject the chronicle, but continued and pursued the real author. This did not serve their investigations into the history of Henry the Fowler and his time, since they had already proven that the chronicle was not authentic, and may have been an educational exercise.

The most plausible author, they argued, was the erudite and otherwise respected theologian and antiquarian Johann Friedrich Falcke, who published several authoritative works on the history of the imperial Abby of Corvey during the 1740s and 1750s. Falcke first discovered the manuscript, which supposedly had been lost, and informed the Abby about its existence.[24] However, Hirsch and Waitz claimed, he was familiar enough with medieval sources to know that it was a fake. His erudition revealed his complicity and, they argued, most likely he had written the chronicle himself. This theory would later be disproven, but their detailed investigations, nonetheless, offer interesting insights into the critical and educational practices of the early Ranke school.[25] To reconstruct how and why Falcke had written the chronicle, they not only discussed his ideas about medieval history but also examined his personality. They based this assessment upon historical writings rather than upon the known facts about his life. When defending himself against opponents, Falcke's tone was 'hard' and 'passionate'. He trusted his own bold and random conjectures, 'lightheaded, arrogant, and without true justification' and ignored evidence that contradicted his assumptions. The probable reason for the falsification, they argued, was Falcke's self-confidence. He had convinced himself that he was correct but could not find sufficient evidence. What started as bold conjectures ended as a forgery. This judgement of Falcke could seem brutal, but to 'solve the riddle of the chronicle' Hirsch and Waitz had to 'sacrifice the piety for a name to the duty of historical critique'.[26]

Waitz's students followed similar critical procedures when studying the Middle Ages and further emphasized the importance of the moral character of past historians. Even if no information was available about the author, this character revealed itself in the writing. Waitz's students often connected the character of a writer to moral and epistemic virtues and vices. In his dissertation on the twelfth-century chronicle of Henry of Livonia, Hermann Hildebrand argued that Henry possessed several personal qualities. Hildebrand not only attempted to understand Henry's background and motivations to write but also included a chapter on his 'trustworthiness'. Henry, Hildebrand argued, based the account of the events of his time upon personal experiences as well as those of contemporary eyewitnesses. To know his credibility, it was therefore only necessary to determine his 'carefulness', 'accurateness', and 'love of truth'. Hildebrand afterwards listed several strengths in Henry's account, which were connected to these virtues. Most important, while Henry's viewpoint coloured his account, this 'viewpoint had in itself no influence upon the transmission of the facts'. He had never invented 'actual untruths' about his enemies or positive stories about his friends.[27] A much harsher judgement can be found in Karl Wittich's treatment of Richer of Reims. If Henry of Livonia embodied virtues, Richer exemplified vices:

> every page testifies to his carelessness, his vanity, alongside this a remarkable addiction to pragmaticizing, in his own way to decorate the content of his dry, often fragmented and abstruse, sources, then further a nearly laughable liking for the outer form, often imitated from the ancients. How in love of this [form], the truth is even intentionally sacrificed, how he instead of telling what has happened – if only according to his opinion – he wants to invent and to interest: so, we may indeed just consider his work as a kind of historical novel.[28]

Waitz did not lecture his students on the historian's virtues and vices but instead taught them to appreciate virtues such as carefulness, accurateness and love of truth, and to detest vices such as carelessness, vanity and love of form, through his performance as a teacher and engagement with their papers. Several students emphasized that they could not have written these papers without Waitz's help. The monographs were often dedicated to Waitz, for example 'in grateful veneration' or to the 'highly venerated teacher'.[29] Others contained longer, remarkably similar, praises of Waitz, which normally thanked him for his 'supportive participation', acknowledged their profound debts and ensured their unending loyalty.[30] When Waitz's former students described the educational experience in Göttingen, they also often emphasized the parallels between the methods of instruction and Waitz's personal character. Monod remembered how Waitz listened attentively to the presentation and then started pulling out small pieces of paper, one after another, filled with microscopic hand-written notes, from the pocket of his vest, and 'examined every point of the paper with meticulous rigour, combined with a larger respect for the thought and work of another'.[31] His teaching style exhibited the carefulness and restraint necessary for proper historical research. The training should prevent students from extending their judgement too far, or beyond the sources, and teach them academic humility. Ludwig Weiland, who also studied in Göttingen during the 1860s, similarly claimed that Waitz 'influenced his pupils, as the example of the faithful father influences his sons. The confident calm and cool objectivity, with which he handled and treated every question, retained the pupils, to themselves unknowingly, from preferring their conjectures to findings created from the sources [and] drove the conviction into them that there is a boundary to our knowledge'.[32] According to the students, Waitz's way of teaching exemplified how they should investigate a strange and almost inaccessible past. They learned how to regiment themselves and their writings not just by mirroring themselves in writers of the past – and discussing their conclusions about these writers with their fellow students – but also by following the example of Waitz as a teacher.

Institutionalized exercises

During the second half of the nineteenth century, practical exercises were increasingly offered in institutionalized seminars. The first historical seminar had been founded in 1832 in Königsberg and similar institutions were opening fast at other German universities.[33] Even at the forefront of historical research and within the Ranke school, scholars embraced the seminar institution. At Ranke's University of Berlin, Johann Gustav Droysen in 1860 complained that the university lacked a seminar and therefore was falling behind.[34] In 1882, one of Ranke's former students, Julius Weizsäcker, again proposed a Berlin seminar and reported to the ministry that 'The reason that such wishes for the historical branches of scholarship only appear so late is not that there is no pressing need or that there has not been [a pressing need] for a long time'.[35] The new seminars sometimes received considerable financial and institutional support. The University of Leipzig probably housed the most impressive historical seminar. The seminar occupied the entire third floor of a university building. The director, Carl von Noorden, had a study and each student had a desk with a lockable drawer and gas lighting. The students could also consult a well-stocked working library with atlases and encyclopaedias as well as geographical, palaeographical and epigraphical materials.

The institutionalized seminars were not as exclusive as Ranke's and Waitz's exercises. They were not just intended for a small group of future researchers. They should accommodate the growing number of students at German universities and satisfy the increasing demand for teachers at German secondary schools. When the Berlin seminar finally opened in January 1885, Weizsäcker accepted forty-two new students.[36] The students in the seminars were often at the beginning of their studies and had not received any philological or historical training beforehand. One could not expect them to seek out unknown medieval manuscripts in foreign archives before writing their papers. One brochure for new students in Noorden's Leipzig seminar, probably from the early 1880s, declared that the practical exercises 'at our university primarily are taught so that they are understandable by themselves for those who have no other qualifications than a high school degree'.[37] The brochure further recommended students to attend courses that would be helpful in their future work. Those who wanted to become teachers in German secondary schools should not give 'excessive attention' to auxiliary sciences and did not have to attend many exercises. They should, according to the brochure, 'apart from schooling in the principal historical methods, acquire certain and broad historical knowledge'.[38]

In the seminars, German professors therefore had to rethink their teaching practices. The Leipzig seminar also here set an example. One of the teachers in Leipzig was Wilhelm Arndt. As a student in Göttingen, Arndt participated in Waitz's exercises. In 1861, he defended his dissertation on medieval history and, like several of Waitz's former students, went to work at the *Monumenta Germaniae Historica* (Historical Monuments of Germany). At the twenty-fifth anniversary of Waitz's exercises, Arndt dedicated a book to his old teacher and sentimentally described his time in Göttingen as 'a sunshine, which still throws its warming rays into my life'.[39] However, when Arndt in 1876 became an extraordinary professor of the auxiliary sciences of history in Leipzig, he did not continue Waitz's style of teaching. He instead taught in Noorden's historical seminar and there developed a new kind of practical exercises. Unlike Ranke and Waitz, Arndt did not expect that the students prepared beforehand, but instead at the start of each session presented a question, which they could answer solely with the printed source editions in the seminar library.⁴⁰ He changed the theme and question every week and tried to convey an overview of medieval history. The students also were not supposed to write or to present papers during the semester but only to participate in the discussions. Noorden's exercises in Leipzig seem to have resembled Arndt's. He did not expect his students to write independent papers, but instead asked them all the same questions and based his exercises upon printed sources in the seminar library.⁴¹ When Kristian Erslev in 1885 visited the newly established Berlin seminar, he noted that Weizsäcker based his exercises upon exemplary quotes from sources, which he handed out to students in hectograph copies at the beginning of class. Instead of having the students work through the material themselves, he asked questions directly and only demanded 'a couple of words as answer'.⁴² The purpose was no longer to transform the students, or to penetrate into a distant and unknown past, but to teach source criticism and historical methodology.

The morals and politics of the historical discipline

Already at beginning of the Enlightenment, as discussed in the first chapter of this book, Thomasius had confronted students with examples from the past to help them examine their inner selves. Waitz in a similar way used historical examples, but instead of the great historical figures whom Thomasius selected, he employed the scribes and chroniclers, who had reported about those figures. This served not only a moral purpose but also an epistemological purpose. The connection to earlier writers gave access to an otherwise distant past. The regimentation of the students' selves secured proper interpretation. The acquirement of these moral and epistemic virtues also secured the relevance of the past. Historical scholarship, according to Waitz, had to be rigorous to be truly political. The past informed the present, but only if the historian uncovered the past itself. Historical scholarship wanted to present, he explained, 'the true meaning of things, their value for life, and the development of humankind, of peoples, of states, or of the smaller circle'. But, he continued, 'it will only solve its assignment worthily, when it approaches it soberly and calmly, clear eyed and unprejudiced, when it realizes that there are limits to its knowledge'.⁴³

Waitz's academic rigour also did not prevent him from engaging politically. For a short period, he even served as a member of the Frankfurt National Assembly, which drafted a new constitution for a united Germany. He employed his studies of medieval history to argue for German reunification, to defend his native Schleswig-Holstein against the Danish monarch, and, not least, to come to terms with the collapse of the Holy Roman Empire.[44] In his monumental *Deutsche Verfassungsgeschichte* (German Constitutional History), published in eight volumes between 1844 and 1878, he offered a version of medieval German history, which did not rest upon the dynastic history of the Holy Roman Empire, as Ranke had preferred. He instead traced the longer and continuous history of the German tribes, starting with the earliest surviving sources. The earliest German history had once helped Enlightenment scholars imagine a Holy Roman Empire without the confessional state. Now this history helped Waitz and his contemporaries imagine a Germany without the Holy Roman Empire. 'The German Empire has fallen', Waitz declared in a speech at the University of Kiel in 1843, and 'like in the times of Tacitus, [the German people] is shattered in many kinds of reigns, many a territory has been lost to the neighbors, and at more than one border German national character has great difficulties surviving'. The distant past, however, also gave hopes for the future. The German tribes had existed before the Holy Roman Empire and they could be united once more in a different way. 'Seeing this future', he argued, 'it is easy to think about the past without pain and bitterness'.[45]

During the late nineteenth century and early twentieth century historians started questioning if historical scholarship could and should engage with the past and the present simultaneously. Since the Ranke school and the historical discipline seemed almost inseparable, they invented, what Peter Novick has called, 'the myth of Leopold von Ranke as value-free investigator, interested only in "the facts"'.[46] The primary problem with this myth is not the claim that Ranke and his followers wanted to show 'what actually happened'. They did. The problem is instead that the recasting hid the moral and political purpose of the project. Ranke and his followers did not just work to institutionalize the historical discipline, but also to improve themselves, their students and the world they lived in. Historical scholarship was a modernizing project. The idea that historical scholarship constituted such as project had motivated scholars throughout the eighteenth and nineteenth centuries. It had survived religious persecution, philosophical relativism, disciplinary specialization, revolutionary ruptures and the ideals of objectivity and scientific history. Only in the hostile environment of the modern university, with its bureaucratic routines, standardized formats of teaching and research, and institutional divisions of labour, did historians stop believing in this project.

Epilogue
The purpose of historiography

The politics of historiography

The age of history never really ended. The historical profession has expanded beyond what its eighteenth-century founders ever could have imagined. Even the triumphant historical guild of late-nineteenth-century Germany pales in comparison to the size of the profession today. Across the globe hundreds of thousands of people are investigating the past, and disseminating knowledge about the past, as their primary occupation. Their work is made available to billions through education, exhibits, books and articles, and an ever-increasing number of historical documentaries, series and movies. The methods and worldviews of historical scholarship have become a foundation of modern society. It is not the only possible way of understanding the modern world, as early-twentieth-century German historicists claimed, but it is a powerful tool among others, and one firmly rooted in the institutions of modern society.

Historical scholarship is far from neutral. It favours some ways of viewing the world at the expense of others. It enables particular kinds of politics. During the last century, following Herbert Butterfield's 1931 *The Whig Interpretation of History*, theorists and historians have repeatedly pointed to the political biases of modern history writing. Some, such as Hayden White, have depicted all of modern history writing as a tool of political ideologies. However, historiography is not most powerful when it allies with ideologies. These can do without the past or invent a past that suits them. Their advocates don't care much for the cumbersome work of historians, unless it serves their purpose. The Nazi dreams of the revival of a German Empire and claims to the medieval roots of this Empire during the 1930s and 1940s, in utter disregard for centuries of careful historical research, may serve as the clearest example.

If historiography only confirmed contemporary ideologies, we would not need it and it would not change anything.

Historical scholarship did not become a force in the modern world because it served ideologies but, on the contrary, because of its ability to reveal and undermine ideological assumptions. From the early Enlightenment, as shown in this book, German scholars used the past to challenge viewpoints that otherwise seemed universal and immutable and to question contemporary institutions, politics and moral standards. Their challenges and questions served the interests of rulers and administrators, who therefore supported the expansion of the historical profession, but the challenges and questions partly emerged from historical research itself. It is not possible, as Butterfield and many of his contemporaries tried, to distinguish between true historians who merely studied 'the past for the sake of the past' and tainted and politicizing historians who studied 'the past for the sake of the present'.[1] Historiography was not least political, and serving contemporary political interests, when it emphasized the differences between past and present. Historians challenged and questioned the present by uncovering a different past and by confronting themselves, their students and their contemporaries with the differences. The power of historiography is the power of anachronism.

Historiography without politics

The scholars discussed in this book were fully aware of the moral and political significance of historical research. They studied the past because it mattered in the present. In the late nineteenth and early twentieth century, this changed. Historians increasingly rejected the relevance of past, its values and ideas, to the contemporary world. German historicism helped justify this rejection, especially with the claim that each time period had an internally coherent worldview and that its values and ideas could only be explained with reference to this worldview. However, the emergence of a new professional identity of historians was probably more important for the rejection of the relevance of the past. In 1932, the church historian Karl Heussi summarized the debates about the 'crisis of historicism' and pointed to the industrialization of historical research as a possible explanation. The working habits that sustained German historical scholarship also caused its problems. Historians were not indulging in discussions about the philosophy of history, relativism and historicism, but seemed to have forgotten such discussions altogether. 'Entire human lives', Heussi noted, 'are sacrificed to the bare hoarding and ransacking of ever new masses of material'. Historical research had become its own purpose and 'with zeal and the feeling of acting according to duty, the researcher gives himself to this service of history for the sake of history: l'histoire pour l'histoire'.[2]

This development was not unique to the historical discipline. Across the university, professors and students increasingly embraced a vocational ideal and insisted upon the importance of disciplinary specialization and value-free research.[3] Modern scholarship, as the German sociologist Max Weber famously declared in 1918, 'is a "vocation" organized in special disciplines in the service of self-clarification and knowledge of interrelated facts. It is not the gift of grace of seers and prophets dispensing sacred values and revelations'.[4] Moral and political education was no longer the responsibility of professors but, as Julie E. Reuben has shown in her discussions of the North American situation, either irrelevant to universities or outsourced to the student affairs office.[5] The historical discipline did not abandon its moral and political purpose because of some fundamental shift in the historical worldview, as Reinhart Koselleck and others have suggested, but rather because all other disciplines did as well. The German 'crisis of historicism' may merely be a symptom of this larger institutional transformation. The development was also not unique to German historians and similar arguments surfaced in other parts of the world. Butterfield also insisted that history 'is concerned with the processes of life rather than with the meaning or purpose or goal of life'.[6]

The purpose of the history of historiography

The insistence that historiography should be value-free re-emphasized the difference between ideology and historiography. The claim also hid the conflict and, so, the moral and political import. However, the transformative power of historical scholarship does not depend upon the recognition of historians. It changes the world by uncovering the past. Since the beginning of the twentieth century, historians have continued challenging universal and immutable viewpoints and questioning contemporary institutions, politics and moral standards. The constant expansion of the profession and conquest of new territories also brought challenges and questions to these fields. The most dramatic example may have been the application of modern European historical scholarship to non-European histories and sources. The problem with this application was not just 'historicism' and its tendency to place some people in the 'waiting room' of history, as Dipesh Chakrabarty has argued.[7] Equally challenging was the introduction of the critical methods and working practices, which historians still defend, even when they are sceptical about historical progress and the superiority of Europeans. Just like these critical methods and working practices once shattered the theory of the four world monarchies and robbed the Holy Roman Empire of its unique role in world history, they now destroyed local mythologies and chronologies around the world, one after another.[8] Acknowledging this hidden moral and political history of modern historiography may be valuable. Historical scholarship should not only challenge and question other viewpoints, but also those of the profession. The way we view the past is not simply a result of the validity of our methods. These methods may be valid and lead us closer to the past. However, other ways of viewing the past were, and continue to be, possible. We cannot fully understand today's battles over the past, from Islamic Ottoman revisionism, to the revival of Hindu histories of India, to the new historical identity politics of Europe and North America, if we fail to recognize the moral and political significance of historical scholarship. The global success of the historical profession, its methods and ways of viewing the past, has turned history into a major political battlefield of the twenty-first century.

The point here is neither that modern historiography is inherently bad nor that it would be better to let Islamic revisionists, Hindu nationalists or European white supremacists write the history of the world. The point is instead that modern historiography was a choice and a choice that served particular political interests and promoted particular moral values. It was not a choice that was taken lightly. It demanded effort, endless hours of work and considerable financial and institutional support. It is a choice that can be unmade again, if we no longer find it worthwhile. Governments could close the archives, universities could decide not to hire history professors, and television stations and streaming services could stop caring about the evidentiary basis for the stories that they tell about the past. In some ways, this is already happening, and such a future is not unthinkable. The disappearance of modern historical scholarship would not mean the end of history writing.

Humankind has always told stories about its past and, most likely, will continue to do so in the future. These will just be other kinds of stories, like the story of the four world monarchies that, not so long ago, to many Europeans seemed the most reasonable explanation of world history. The disappearance, however, would result in the demise of a vision of modernity, which has shaped us and our societies over the last three centuries. We should be aware of this choice.

Notes

Acknowledgements

1 Copyright © International Society for Intellectual History, reprinted by permission of Informa UK Limited, trading as Taylor & Francis Group, www.tandfonline.com on behalf of International Society for Intellectual History.
2 Copyright © 2013 Kasper Risbjerg Eskildsen. DOI: 10.1177/0952695113496094

Introduction

1 Rüdiger vom Bruch, 'Mommsen und Harnack: Die Geburt von Big Science aus den Geisteswissenschaften', in *Theodor Mommsen. Wissenschaft und Politik im 19. Jahrhundert*, ed. Alexander Demandt, Andreas Goltz and Heinrich Schlange-Schöningen (Berlin: De Gruyter, 2005), 121–41. Also, Carlos Spoerhase, 'Big Humanities: "Größe" und "Großforschung" als Kategorien geisteswissenschaftlicher Selbstbeobachtung', *Geschichte der Germanistik* 37/38 (2010): 9–27, and Torsten Kahlert, '"Große Projekte": Mommsens Traum und der Diskurs um Big Science und Großforschung', in *Wissenskulturen: Bedingungen wissenschaftlicher Innovation*, ed. Harald Müller and Florian Eßer (Kassel: Kassel University Press, 2012), 67–86.
2 Hans Proesler, *Das Problem einer Entwicklungsgeschichte des historischen Sinnes* (Berlin: Ebering, 1920), 8.
3 Hayden White, *Metahistory: The Historical Imagination in Nineteenth Century Europe* (Baltimore: Johns Hopkins University Press, 1972), 73.
4 Reinhart Koselleck, *Vergangener Zukunft: Zur Semantik geschichtlicher Zeiten* (Frankfurt am Main: Suhrkamp, 1979). Also, for recent discussions, see Chris Lorenz and Berber Bevernage, eds., *Breaking Up Time: Negotiating the Borders between Present, Past and Future* (Göttingen: Vandenhoeck und Ruprecht, 2013).
5 Historical knowledge, or *historia*, did not only include knowledge about the human past but also other kinds of empirical knowledge about the world,

see Arno Seifert, *Cognitio historica: Die Geschichte als Namengeberin der frühneuzeitlichen Emperie* (Berlin: Duncker und Humblot, 1976) and Gianna Pomata and Nancy Siraisi, eds., *Historia: Empiricism and Erudition in Early Modern Europe* (Cambridge: MIT Press, 2005). Also, on the importance of the concept of *historia* for early modern historiography and history education, Per Landgren, *Det aristoteliska historiebegreppet: Historieteori i renässansens Europa och Sverige* (Gothenburg: Acta Universitatis Gothoburgensis, 2008).

6   Emil Clemens Scherer, *Geschichte und Kirchengeschichte an den deutschen Universitäten: Ihre Anfänge im Zeitalter des Historismus und ihre Ausbildung zu selbständigen Disziplinen* (Freiburg im Breisgau: Herder, 1927), Johann Engel, 'Die deutschen Universitäten und die Geschichtswissenschaft', *Historische Zeitschrift* 189, no. 1 (1959): 223–378, and Stefan Fisch, 'Auf dem Weg zur Aufklärungshistorie: Prozesse des Wandels in der protestantischen Historiographie', *Geschichte und Gesellschaft* 23, no. 1 (1997): 115–33.

7   Georg H. Nadel, 'Philosophy of History before Historicism', *History and Theory* 3, no. 3 (1964): 291–315, and Rüdiger Landfester, *Historia magistra vitæ: Untersuchungen zur humanistischen Geschichtstheorie des 14. bis 16. Jahrhunderts* (Geneva: Droz, 1972). Also, and more broadly, Anthony Grafton, *What Was History? The Art of History in Early Modern Europe* (Cambridge: Cambridge University Press, 2007).

8   Notker Hammerstein, *Jus und Historie: Ein Beitrag zur Geschichte des historischen Denkens an deutschen Universitäten im späten 17. und 18. Jahrhundert* (Göttingen: Vandenhoeck und Ruprecht, 1972) and Konrad Jarausch, 'The Institutionalization of History in 18th-Century Germany', in *Aufklärung und Geschichte: Studien zur deutschen Geschichtswissenschaft im 18. Jahrhundert*, ed. Hans Erich Bödeker, Georg G. Iggers, Jonathan B. Knudsen and Peter Hanns Reill (Göttingen: Vandenhock und Ruprecht, 1986), 26–48. Also, Horst Walter Blanke and Dirk Fleischer, eds., *Theoretiker der deutschen Aufklärungshistorie*, vol. 1 (Stuttgart: Frommann-Holzboog, 1990), 19–102. For a list of history chairs at German universities, 103–23.

9   Steven Shapin and Simon Schaffer, *Leviathan and the Air-Pump: Hobbes, Boyle, and the Experimental Life* (1985; Princeton: Princeton University Press, 1989) and, linking law, history and natural philosophy, Barbara J. Shapiro, *A Culture of Fact: England 1550–1720* (Ithaca: Cornell University Press, 2000). Also, on the social sciences, Mary Poovey, *A History of the Modern Facts: Problems of Knowledge in the Sciences of Wealth and Society* (Chicago: Chicago University Press, 1998).

10 Christian Thomasius, *Introductio ad philosophiam aulicam* (Leipzig, 1688).
11 Constantin Fasolt, *The Limits of History* (Chicago: University of Chicago Press, 2004), esp. 3–39.
12 For a recent overview, Markus Völkel, 'The "Historical Consciousness" of the Holy Roman Empire of the German Nation (Sixteenth to Eighteenth Century)', in *The Holy Roman Empire 1495–1806*, ed. R. J. W. Evans, Michael Schnaich and Peter H. Wilson (Oxford: Oxford University Press, 2011), 323–45.
13 Markus Völkel, 'German Historical Writing from the Reformation to the Enlightenment', in *The Oxford History of Historical Writing*, ed. Daniel Wolf, vol. 3 (Oxford: Oxford University Press, 2012), 324–46, on p. 326.
14 T. J. Hochstrasser, *Natural Law Theories in the Early Enlightenment* (Cambridge: Cambridge University Press, 2000).
15 For an overview, Hugh Trevor-Roper, *History and the Enlightenment* (New Haven: Yale University Press, 2010), esp. 1–16.
16 Peter Hanns Reill, *The German Enlightenment and the Rise of Historicism* (Berkeley: University of California Press, 1975), Helmut Zedelmaier, *Der Anfang der Geschichte: Studien zur Ursprungsdebatte im 18. Jahrhundert* (Hamburg: Meiner, 2003), and Avi Lifschitz, *Language and Enlightenment: The Berlin Debates of the Eighteenth Century* (Oxford: Oxford University Press, 2012).
17 Heinrich von Sybel, 'Ueber den Stand der neueren deutschen Geschichtschreibung', in idem, *Kleine historische Schriften* (Munich, 1863), 343–59, on p. 355.
18 Ignaz von Döllinger, *Die Universitäten sonst und jetzt* (Munich, 1867), 37.
19 Especially Wilhelm Dilthey, *Einleitung in die Geisteswissenschaften: Versuch einer Grundlegung für das Studium der Gesellschaft und der Geschichte* (Leipzig, 1883) and *Aufbau der geschichtlichen Welt in den Geisteswissenschaften* (Berlin: Königliche Akademie der Wissenschaften, 1910). For a recent discussion, Julian Hamann, 'Boundary Work Between Two Cultures: Demarcating the Modern Geisteswissenschaften', *History of Humanities* 3, no. 1 (2018): 27–38.
20 Also, Herman Paul and Adriaan van Veldhuizen, eds., *Historicism: A Travelling Concept* (London: Bloomsbury, 2020).
21 Ernst Troeltsch, *Der Historismus und seine Probleme* (Tübingen: J. C. B. Mohr, 1922), 9–10.
22 Karl Mannheim, 'Historismus', in idem, *Wissenssoziologie: Auswahl aus dem Werk*, ed. Kurt H. Wolff (1964; Neuwied am Rhein: Luchterhand, 1970), 246–307, on 247–8.

23 Troeltsch, *Der Historismus*, 2 and 4–6.
24 Ernst Troeltsch, 'Die Krisis des Historismus', in idem, *Kritische Gesamtausgabe*, vol. 15: *Schriften zur Politik und Kulturphilosophie (1918–1923)* (Berlin: Walter de Gruyter, 2002), 437–55, on 451.
25 Troeltsch, *Der Historismus*, 18.
26 Friedrich Meinecke, *Die Entstehung des Historismus*, 2 vols. (Munich: Oldenbourg, 1936), vol. 1, 1–2, 4–5 and 6, and vol. 2, 307–25.
27 Georg G. Iggers, *The German Conception of History: The National Tradition of Historical Thought from Herder to the Present* (Middletown, CT: Wesleyan University Press, 1968), 30 and 36.
28 White, *Metahistory*, 431–2.
29 For example, Friedrich Jaeger and Jörn Rüsen, *Geschichte des Historismus: Eine Einführung* (Munich: C. H. Beck, 1992), Jörn Rüsen, *Konfigurationen des Historismus: Studien zur deutschen Wissenschaftskultur* (Frankfurt am Main: Suhrkamp, 1993), and Frederick C. Beiser, *The German Historicist Tradition* (Oxford: Oxford University Press, 2011).
30 Reinhart Koselleck, 'Einleitung', in *Geschichtliche Grundbegriffe*, ed. Otto Brunner, Werner Conze and Reinhart Koselleck, vol. 1 (Stuttgart: Ernst Klett Verlag, 1972), xiii–xxvii. Also, for a recent discussion and overview, Daniel Fulda, 'Sattelzeit: Karriere und Problematik eines kulturwissenschaftlichen Zentralbegriffs', in *Sattelzeit: Historiographiegeschichtliche Revisionen*, ed. Elisabeth Décultot and Daniel Fulda (Berlin: De Gruyter, 2016), 1–16.
31 Christian Meier, Odilo Engels, Günter Horst and Reinhart Koselleck, 'Geschichte, Historie', in *Geschichtliche Grundbegriffe*, ed. Otto Brunner, Werner Conze and Reinhart Koselleck, vol. 2 (Stuttgart: Ernst Klett Verlag, 1975), 593–718. Also, for a critical discussion, Jan Marco Sawilla, '"Geschichte": En Produkt der deutschen Aufklärung? Eine Kritik an Reinhart Kosellecks Begriff des Kollektivsingulars "Geschichte"', *Zeitschrift für Historische Forschung* 31, no. 3 (2004): 381–428.
32 Peter Fritzsche, *Stranded in the Present: Modern Time and the Melancholy of History* (Cambridge: Harvard University Press, 2004), esp. 11–54.
33 François Hartog, *Regimes of Historicity: Presentism and Experiences of Time*, trans. Saskia Brown (New York: Columbia University Press, 2015), 11.
34 Karl Popper, *The Poverty of Historicism* (London: Routledge, 1957).
35 Steven Shapin, 'Why the Public Ought to Understand Science-in-the-Making', *Public Understanding of Science* 1, no. 1 (1992), 27–30, on 28. Also, Bruno Latour, *Science in Action: How to Follow Scientists and Engineers Through Society* (Cambridge: Harvard University Press, 1987).

36 Patricia M. Mazón, *Gender and the Modern Research University: The Admission of Women to German Higher Education, 1865-1914* (Stanford: Stanford University Press, 2003), esp. 115-151. Also, Katharina Rowold, *The Educated Woman: Minds, Bodies, and Women's Higher Education in Britain, Germany, and Spain, 186-1914* (London: Routledge, 2010), 69-151.

37 On sites of knowledge production, also David Livingstone, *Putting Science in Its Place: Geographies of Scientific Knowledge* (Chicago: University of Chicago Press, 2003), Nicholas Jardine, *The Scenes of Inquiry: On the Reality of Questions in the Sciences* (Oxford: Oxford University Press, 2000), esp. 274-87, Adi Ophir and Steven Shapin, 'The Place of Knowledge: A Methodological Survey', *Science in Context* 4, no. 1 (1991): 3-21, and Steven Shapin, 'Placing the View from Nowhere: Historical and Sociological Problems in the Location of Science', *Transactions of the Institute of British Geographers* 23, no. 1 (1998): 5-12.

38 Johann Gustav Droysen, *Grundriss der Historik* (Leipzig, 1868), 79-80.

39 Robert E. Kohler, 'Place and Practice in Field Biology', *History of Science* 40, no. 2 (2002): 189-210, on 192. Also, *Landscapes and Labscapes: Exploring the Field-Lab Boundary* (Chicago: University of Chicago Press, 2002), and, with Henrika Kuklick, 'Introduction', *Osiris* 11 (1996): 1-14.

40 For an overview, Daniel Garber, 'Philosophia, Historia, Mathematica: Shifting Sands in the Disciplinary Geography of the Seventeenth Century', in *Scientia in Early Modern Philosophy: Seventeenth-Century Thinkers on Demonstrative Knowledge from First Principles*, ed. Tom Sorell, G.A.J Rogers and Jill Kraye (Dordrecht: Springer, 2010), 1-17.

Chapter 1

1 Hans-Jürgen Engfer, 'Christian Thomasius: Erste Proklamation und erste Krise der Aufklärung in Deutschland', in *Christian Thomasius 1655-1728: Interpretation zu Werk und Wirkung*, ed. Werner Schneiders (Hamburg: Meiner, 1989), 21-36.

2 Christian Polycarp Leporin, *Germania literata vivens, oder das jetzt lebende gelehrte Deutschland* (Quedlinburg, 1724), 162.

3 Anonymous, 'Wohlmeinendes Gutachten über Herrn Thomas bißherige Art zu schreiben', in Christian Thomasius, *Allerhand bißher publicirte kleine teutsche Schrifften mit Fleiß colligiret und zusammen getragen: Nebst etlichen Beylagen und einer Vorrede* (Halle, 1701), 271-340, on 316-7.

4 Siegfried Bentzen, *Christianus minime christianus, oder das Eben-Bild Christian Thomasii* (Ratzeburg, 1692), 1–2.
5 Christian Thomasius, *Discours welcher Gestalt man denen Frantzosen in gemeinen Leben und Wandel nachahmen solle?* (n.p., n.d.), 3.
6 Also, Thomasius, *Introductio ad philosophiam aulicam*, preface, unpag.
7 Thomasius, *Discours*, 12 and 35–6.
8 Heinz Schilling, 'Die Konfessionalisierung im Reich: Religiöser und gesellschaftlicher Wandel in Deutschland zwischen 1555 und 1620', *Historische Zeitschrift* 246, no. 1 (1988): 1–45, and Ute Lotz-Heumann and Matthias Pohlig, 'Confessionalization and Literature in the Empire, 1555–1700', *Central European History* 40, no. 1 (2007): 35–61. Also, on the role of universities, Ian Hunter, 'The University Philosopher in Early Modern Germany', in *The Philosopher in Early Modern Europe: The Nature of a Contested Identity*, ed. Conal Condren, Stephen Gaukroger and Ian Hunter (Cambridge: Cambridge University Press, 2006), 35–65.
9 Also, on the importance of confessional disagreements for Thomasius's educational thinking, see Thomas Ahnert, *Religion and the Origins of the German Enlightenment: Faith and the Reform of Learning in the Thought of Christian Thomasius* (Rochester: University of Rochester Press, 2006) and Ian Hunter, *The Secularisation of the Confessional State: The Political Thought of Christian Thomasius* (Cambridge: Cambridge University Press, 2007).
10 Frank Grunert, 'Zur Aufgeklärten Kritik am theokratischen Absolutismus: Der Streit zwischen Hector Gottfried Masius und Christian Thomasius über Ursprung und Begründung der summa potestas', in *Christian Thomasius (1655–1728): Neue Forschungen im Kontext der Frühaufklärung*, ed. Friedrich Vollhardt (Tübingen: Niemeyer, 1997), 51–78.
11 Gustav Wustmann, 'Verbotene Bücher', in idem, *Aus Leipzigs Vergangenheit: Gesammelte Aufsätze*, vol. 1 (Leipzig, 1885), 194–235, on 197–202.
12 Christian Thomasius, *Einleitung zu der Vernunfft-Lehre, worinnen durch eine leichte/ und allen vernünfftigen Menschen/ waserley Standes oder Geschlechts sie seyn/ verständliche Manier der Weg gezeiget wird/ ohne die Syllogisticâ das wahre/ wahrscheinliche und falsche von einander zu entscheiden/ und neue Warheiten zu erfinden* (Halle, 1691), dedication, unpag. Also, Werner Schneiders, 'Nicht "plump", nicht "säuisch", nicht "sauertöpfisch": Zu Thomasius' Idee einer Philosophie für alle', in *Die Philosophie und die Belles-Lettres*, ed. Martin Fontius and Werner Schneiders (Berlin: Akademie Verlag, 1997), 11–20, and Helmut Holzhey, 'Initiert Thomasius einen neuen Philosophentypus?', in *Christian Thomasius 1655–1728: Interpretation zu Werk und Wirkung*, ed. Werner Schneiders (Hamburg: Meiner, 1989), 37–51.

13 Anonymous, 'Philosophe', in *Le Dictionnaire de l'Académie françoise, dédié au Roy*, vol. 2 (Paris, 1694), 229. Also, on different ideals of the philosopher in early modern Europe, Conal Condren, Stephen Gaukroger and Ian Hunter, eds., *The Philosopher in Early Modern Europe: The Nature of a Contested Identity* (Cambridge: Cambridge University Press, 2006).

14 On ancient philosophy as a 'way of life', see Pierre Hadot, *Qu'est-ce que la philosophie antique?* (Paris: Gallimard, 1995).

15 Matthew L. Jones, *The Good Life in the Scientific Revolution: Descartes, Pascal, Leibniz, and the Cultivation of Virtue* (Chicago: University of Chicago Press, 2006), 6.

16 Also, Ulrich Johannes Schneider, 'Eclecticism and the History of Philosophy', and Martin Mulsow, 'Gundling versus Buddeus: Competing Models of the History of Philosophy', in *History and the Disciplines. The Reclassification of Knowledge in Early Modern Europe*, ed. Donald R. Kelley (Rochester: University of Rochester Press, 1997), 83–101 and 103–26.

17 Horst Dreitzel, 'Zur Entwicklung und Eigenart der "eklektischen Philosophie"', *Zeitschrift für historische Forschung* 18 (1991): 281–343, esp. 324–30. Also, Michael Albrect, 'Thomasius – kein Eklektiker?' in *Christian Thomasius 1655–1728: Interpretation zu Werk und Wirkung*, ed. Werner Schneiders (Hamburg: Meiner, 1989), 73–94, and *Eklektik: Eine Begriffsgeschichte mit Hinweisen auf die Philosophie- und Wissenschaftsgeschichte* (Stuttgart: Frommann-Holzboog, 1994), 398–416.

18 Christian Thomasius, *Höchstnötige Cautelen welche ein Studiosus Juris, der sich zu Erlernung der Rechts-Gelahrheit auff eine kluge und geschickte Weise vorbereiten will/ zu beobachten hat* (Halle, 1713), 106–7.

19 Ibid., 84, 83, and 82.

20 Ibid., 93.

21 William Clark, *Academic Charisma and the Origins of the Research University* (Chicago: University of Chicago Press, 2006), 45–50 and 62–6.

22 Christian Thomasius, 'Kurtzer Entwurff/ was auff der Chur-Brandenburgischen Friedrichs Universität zu Halle Christian Thomas/ JCtus und P.P. voriges Jahr gelesen/ und küfftig für Lectiones und Collegia zu halten besonnen sey. Publicirt 1694. am Sonntag Cantate', in idem, *Allerhand bißher publicirte kleine teutsche Schrifften mit Fleiß colligiret und zusammen getragen; Nebst etlichen Beylagen und einer Vorrede* (Halle, 1701), 631–54, on 650.

23 Thomasius, *Einleitung zu der Vernunfft-Lehre*, 21.

24 Christian Thomasius, 'Mein Anno 1689. Herrn M. August Herman Francken ertheiltes Responsum Juris', in idem, *Vernünfftige und Christliche aber nicht*

Scheinheilige Thomasischen Gedancken und Erinnerungen uber allerhand Gemischte Philosophische und Juristische Händel, vol. 2 (Halle, 1724), 352–492, on 353.

25 Christian Thomasius, 'Summarische Erzehlung von der Verjagung des Autoris aus seinem Vaterlande', in idem, *Vernünfftige und Christliche aber nicht Scheinheilige Thomasischen Gedancken und Erinnerungen uber allerhand Gemischte Philosophische und Juristische Händel*, vol. 2 (Halle, 1724), 44–201, on 63.

26 Christian Thomasius, *Briefwechsel: Historisch-kritische Edition*, ed. Frank Grunert, Matthias Hambrock, and Martin Kühnel, vol. 1 (Berlin: De Gruyter, 2017), 170.

27 Philipp Jakob Spener, *Pia desideria: oder herzliches Verlangen nach Gottgefälliger Besserung der wahren Evangelischen Kirchen* (1675; Frankfurt am Main, 1680), 144.

28 Also, Clark, *Academic Charisma*, 143–58.

29 Georg Wilhelm von Raumer, 'Christian Thomasius und die Entstehung der Universität Halle', in *Neues Allgemeines Archiv für Geschichtskunde des Preußichen Staates*, ed. Leopold von Ledebur, vol. 1 (Berlin, 1836), 185–95, quotes on 188 and 190.

30 For Thomasius's theory of temperaments and morality, Christian Thomasius, *Von der Arzeney wieder die unvernünfftige Liebe, und der zuvor nöthigen Erkäntnß sein Selbst. Oder: Ausübung der Sitten Lehre* (Halle, 1696). Also, on medicine and philosophy in Halle, Carsten Zelle, ed. *'Vernünftige Ärtze': Hallesche Psychomediziner und die Anfänge der Anthropologie der deutschsprachigen Frühaufklärung* (Tübingen: Max Niemeyer Verlag, 2001).

31 Raumer, 'Christian Thomasius', 193–4.

32 Thomasius, *Höchstnötige Cautelen*, 107.

33 Christian Thomasius, *Kurtzer Entwurff der politischen Klugheit* (Frankfurt am Main, 1728), 39–40.

34 On Pyrrhonism, Anton M. Matytsin, *The Spectre of Skepticism in the Age of Enlightenment* (Baltimore: Johns Hopkins University Press, 2016). On historical Pyrrhonism, see also Meta Scheele, *Wissen und Glaube in der Geschichtswissenschaft: Studien zum historischen Pyrrhonismus in Frankreich und Deutschland* (Heidelberg: Carl Winters Universitätsbuchhandlung, 1930), esp. 81–131, Markus Völkel, *'Pyrrhonismus historicus' und 'fides historica': Die Entwicklung der deutschen historischen Methodologie under dem Geschichtspunkt der historischen Skepsis* (Frankfurt am Main: Peter Lang, 1987), esp. 110–202, and Gisela Schlüter, ed., *Historischer Pyrrhonismus* special issue of *Das Achtzehnte Jahrhundert* 31, no. 2 (2007).

35 Thomasius, *Höchstnötige Cautelen*, 98 and 105.
36 Raumer, 'Christian Thomasius', 191 and 190.
37 Thomasius, 'Summarische Erzehlung', 118–9.
38 Spener, *Pia desideria*, 146.
39 Thomasius, *Einleitung zu der Vernunfft-Lehre*, frontpage.
40 Raumer, 'Christian Thomasius', 192.
41 Christian Thomasius, *Summarischer Entwurf der Grundlehren, die einem Studio Juris zu wissen/ und auff Universitäten zu lernen nöthig sind* (Halle, 1699), 40 and preface, unpag.
42 Thomasius, *Cautelen*, 135.
43 Zacharias Conrad von Uffenbach, *Merkwürdige Reisen durch Niedersachsen Holland und Engelland*, vol. 1 (Frankfurt am Main, 1753), xlviii–xlix.
44 Theodor Wotschke, 'Eine Kollektenreise von Leipzig nach Wolfenbüttel im Jahre 1721', *Thüringisch-Sächsische Zeitschrift für Geschichte und Kunst* 16, no. 1 (1927): 79–94, on 85.
45 Christian Thomasius, 'Erinnerung wegen derer über den dritten Theil seiner Grund-Lehren/ bißher gehaltenen Lectionum privatissimarum und deren Verwandelung in Lectiones privatas', in idem, *Außerlesene und in deutsch noch nie gedruckte Schrifften*, vol. 2 (Halle, 1714), 193–220.
46 Christian Thomasius, 'Erinnerung wegen zweyer Collegiorum über den ersten Theil seiner Grund-Lehren', in idem, *Außerlesene und in deutsch noch nie gedruckte Schrifften*, vol. 2 (Halle, 1714), 253–84, quotes on 261–2.
47 Christian Thomasius, *Dreyfache Rettung des Rechts Evangelischer Fürsten in Kirchen-Sachen*, ed. Johann Gottfried Zeidlern (Frankfurt am Main, 1701), preface, unpag.
48 Johann Christoph von Dreyhaupt, *Pagus neletici et nudzici, oder ausführliche diplomatisch-historische Beschreibung des zum ehemaligen Primat und Ertz-Stifft, nunmehr aber durch den westphälischen Friedens-Schluss secularisirten Hertzogthum Magdeburg gehörigen Saal-Creÿses, und aller darinnen befindlichen Städte, Schlösser, Aemter*, vol. 2 (Halle, 1755), 5 and 36–7.
49 Clark, *Academic Charisma*, 77–8.
50 Johann Christoph Hoffbauer, *Geschichte der Universität zu Halle bis zum Jahre 1805* (Halle, 1805), 179–80, note c.
51 Dreyhaupt, *Pagus neletici et nudzici*, vol. 2, 5.
52 Norbert Elias, *Die höfische Gesellschaft. Untersuchungen zur Soziologie des Königtums und der höfischen Aristokratie* (1969; Frankfurt am Main: Suhrkamp, 1997), 68–101. Also, Michael McKeon, *The Secret History of Domesticity: Public, Private, and the Division of Knowledge* (Baltimore: Johns Hopkins University Press, 2005).

53 Gadi Algazi, 'Scholars in Households: Refiguring the Learned Habitus, 1480–1550', *Science in Context* 16, no. 1/2 (2003): 9–42.
54 Thomas Sprat, *The History of the Royal-Society of London for the Improving of Natural Knowledge* (London, 1667), 68 and 56. Also, Steven Shapin, 'The House of Experiment in Seventeenth-Century England', *Isis* 79, no. 3 (1988): 373–404, and '"The Mind is Its Own Place": Science and Solitude in Seventeenth-Century England', *Science in Context* 4, no. 1 (1990): 191–218.
55 Thomasius, 'Erinnerung wegen derer', 195. Also Erich Neuß, '"Christian Thomasius" Beziehungen zur Stadt Halle', in *Christian Thomasius: Leben und Lebenswerk*, ed. Max Fleischmann (Halle: Niemeyer, 1931), 453–78, esp. 463–74.
56 Thomasius, 'Erinnerung wegen derer', 209.
57 The phrase from Ulrich Muhlack, *Geschichtswissenschaft im Humanismus und in der Aufklärung: Die Vorgeschichte des Historismus* (Munich: Beck, 1991).
58 Hammerstein, *Jus und Historie*.
59 Hunter, *The Secularisation*.
60 Thomasius, *Höchstnötige Cautelen*, 93.

Chapter 2

1 Also, on the 'precarity' of underground knowledge, Martin Mulsow, *Prekäres Wissen: Eine andere Ideengeschichte der Frühen Neuzeit* (Franfurt am Main: Suhrkamp, 2012).
2 On German academic travellers to Holland, see Heinz Schneppen, *Niederländische Universitäten und deutsches Geistesleben: Von der Gründung der Universität Leiden bis ins späte 18. Jahrhundert* (Münster: Aschendorffsche Verlagsbuchhandlung, 1960) and Julia Bientjes, *Holland und der Holländer im Urteil deutscher Reisender 1400–1800* (Gronningen: J. B. Wolters, 1967).
3 Christinane Berkvens-Stevelinck, Jonathan Israel and G.H.M. Posthumus Meyjes, eds., *The Emergence of Tolerance in the Dutch Republic* (Brill: Leiden, 1997).
4 On the Spinozist underground, see Jonathan Israel, *Radical Enlightenment: Philosophy and the Making of Modernity 1650–1750* (Oxford: Oxford University Press, 2001) and *Enlightenment Contested: Philosophy, Modernity, and the Emancipation of Man 1670–1752* (Oxford: Oxford University Press, 2006). Also, Wien van Bunge, *The Early Enlightenment in the Dutch Republic, 1650–1750* (Leiden: Brill, 2003) and Michiel Wielema, *The March of the Libertines: Spinozists and the Dutch Reformed Church* (1660–1750) (Hilversum: Uitgeverij Verloren, 2004).

5   On Heumann and his works, see also Martin Mulsow, Kasper Risbjerg Eskildsen, and Helmut Zedelmaier, eds., *Christoph August Heumann (1681–1764): Gelehrte Praxis zwischen christlichem Humanismus und Aufklärung* (Stuttgart: Franz Steiner Verlag, 2017).

6   Georg Andreas Cassius, *Ausführliche Lebensbeschreibung des um die gelehrte Welt Hochverdienten D. Christoph August Heumanns* (Kassel, 1768), 32–137.

7   Gottlieb Stolle, *Eine Reise durch die Gelehrtenrepublik: Reisejournal 1703/1704*, ed. Martin Mulsow (Stuttgart: Franz Steiner Verlag, forthcoming), page numbers refer to pages in the manuscript, Johann Burkhard Mencke, *Das Holländische Journal 1698–1699: (Ms. Germ. oct. 82 der Staatsbibliothek Berlin)*, ed. Hubert Laeven (Hildesheim: Olms, 2005), Christoph August Lämmermann, 'Literarische Anekdoten, die Elzevirische Buchdruckerey in Leiden, und die beiden dasigen Gelehrten, Herm. Boerhave und Thom. Crenius', *Historisch-litterarisch-bibliographisches Magazin* 3, no. 6 (1792): 99–109, Uffenbach, *Merkwürdige Reisen*, and Johann Gottlieb Deichsel, 'Reise durch Deutschland nach Holland und England in den Jahren 1717–1719', *Johann Bernoulli's Archiv zur neuern Geschichte, Geographie, Natur- und Menschenkenntniß* 3 (1786): 137–88, and 7 (1787): 151–212.

8   Also, Hubert Laeven, 'Einleitung', in Mencke, *Das Holländische Journal*, 9–29, Martin Mulsow, *Die unanständige Gelehrtenrepublik: Wissen, Libertinage und Kommunikation in der Frühen Neuzeit* (Stuttgart: J. B. Metzler, 2007), 67–86, and Konrad Franke, 'Zacharias Conrad von Uffenbach als Handschriftensammler: Ein Beitrag zur Kulturgeschichte des 18. Jahrhunderts', *Börsenblatt für den Deutschen Buchhandel – Franfurter Ausgabe* 51 (29 July 1965): 1235–338.

9   Hermann Kniggen, 'Lebens-Lauf des Wohlseeligen Herrn General-Superintendenten', in Henrich Ludolph Benthem, *Vorstellung und Betrachtung der Schrifften der alten Kirchen-Lehrer von der Wahrheit und Göttlichkeit Christlicher Religion* (Hamburg, 1727), unpag.

10 On the preparations for the journey, see also Uffenbach, *Merkwürdige Reisen*, vol. 1, xlii and cxii.

11 Henrich Ludolff Benthem, *Holländischer Kirch- und Schulen Staat*, vol. 1 (Merseburg, 1698), 24, 27 and 121.

12 Cassius, *Ausführliche Lebensbeschreibung*, 47.

13 Henrich Ludolff Benthem, *Engeländischer Kirch- und Schulen-Staat* (Lüneburg, 1694), preface, unpag. On travelling and note-taking, also Wolff Bernhard von Tschirnhauß auf Hackenau, *Getreuer Hofmeister auf Academien und Reisen* (Hanover, 1727), esp. 124–7, and Andreas Hartmann, 'Reisen und Aufschreiben', in *Reisekultur: Von Pilgerfahrt zum modernen Tourismus*, ed. Hermann Bausinger, Klaus Beyrer, and Gottfried Korff (Munich: C. H. Beck, 1991), 152–9.

14 Uffenbach, *Merkwürdige Reisen*, vol. 1, lii.
15 Benthem also supported this effort in several of his writings, for example [Henrich Ludolph Benthem], *Pacifici Verini ohnmaßgebliches Bedencken, ob und wie die heutiges Tages gesuchte Vereinigung derer, welche die ohnveränderte Augspurgische Confession angenommen, mit den übrigen diene zum Wohlstande der Kirche Christi* (n. p., 1700).
16 Benthem, *Holländischer Kirch- und Schulen-Staat*, vol. 1, dedication, 2, vol. 2, 169, vol. 1, 6 and preface, unpag.
17 Ibid., 52–3 and 621.
18 J. Z. Kannegieter, *Geschiedenis van de vroegere quakergemeenschap te Amsterdam 1656 tot begin negentiende eeuw* (Amsterdam: Scheltema en Holkema, 1971), 135–54 and 206–8.
19 Gottfried Arnold, *Unpartheyische Kirchen- und Ketzer-Historie*, vol. 2 (1700; Frankfurt am Main, 1729), 1178.
20 Christian Thomasius, 'Erinnerung wegen zweyer Collegiorum über den vierdten Theil seiner Grund-Lehren', in idem, *Außerlesene und in deutsch noch nie gedruckte Schrifften*, vol. 2 (Halle, 1714), 221–52, on 227. Also, Ahnert, *Religion*, 59–64.
21 Uffenbach, *Merkwürdige Reisen*, vol. 2, 271.
22 Cassius, *Ausführliche Lebensbeschreibung*, 64.
23 Also, on these conflicts, Jonathan Israel, *The Dutch Republic: Its Rise, Greatness, and Fall, 1477–1806* (Oxford: Clarendon Press, 1995), 637–76 and 1019–37, and John Marshall, *John Locke, Toleration and Early Enlightenment Culture: Religious Intolerance and Arguments for Religious Toleration in Early Modern and 'Early Enlightenment' Europe* (Cambridge: Cambridge University Press, 2006), 138–93.
24 Cassius, *Ausführliche Lebensbeschreibung*, 64.
25 Benthem, *Holländischer Kirch- und Schulen-Staat*, vol. 1, 623. Also, William I. Hull, *William Sewel of Amsterdam 1654–1720: The First Quaker Historian of Quakerism* (Philadelphia: Paterson and White Company, 1933), 115–44.
26 Cassius, *Ausführliche Lebensbeschreibung*, 92–4.
27 Ibid., 105. Also, Stolle, *Eine Reise*, 268–9 and 373–5.
28 Ibid., 325–7, 343–4, 348–54, 357–64, 650 and 734–7.
29 Benthem, *Holländischer Kirch- und Schulen-Staat*, vol. 2, 55–116.
30 Arnold, *Unpartheyische Kirchen- und Ketzer-Historie*, vol. 2, 1094.
31 Cassius, *Ausführliche Lebensbeschreibung*, 129.
32 Deichsel, 'Reise', 3 (1786): 182–3, and 7 (1787): 154–5, 165 and 187–8.

33 Christoph August Heumann, *Erweiß daß die Lehre der Reformirten Kirche von dem Heil. Abendmahle die rechte und wahre sey* (Eisleben, 1764), 78. Also, Inge Mager, 'Die theologische Lehrfreiheit in Göttingen und ihre Grenzen: Der Abendmahlskonflikt um Christian August Heumann', in *Theologie in Göttingen: Eine Vorlesungsreihe*, ed. B. Moeller (Göttingen: Vandenhoeck und Ruprecht, 1987), 41–57, Walter Sparn, 'Philosophische Historie und dogmatische Heterodoxie: Der Fall des Exegeten Christoph August Heumann', in *Historische Kritik und biblischer Kanon in der deutschen Aufklärung*, ed. Henning Graf Reventlow, Walter Sparn, and John Woodbridge (Wiesbaden: Harrassowitz, 1988), 171–92, and Sicco Lehmann-Brauns, *Weisheit der Weltgeschichte: Philosophiegeschichte zwischen Barock und Aufklärung* (Tübingen: Max Niemeyer Verlag, 2004), 359–71.

34 Christoph August Heumann, 'Der Einleitung zur Historia Philosophica. Sechstes Capitel von dem Ingenio Philosophico', *Acta philosophorum, das ist: Gründl. Nachrichten aus der Historia Philosophica, nebst beygefügten Urtheilen von denen dahin gehörigen alten und neuen Büchern* 1, no. 4 (1716): 567–670, on 582.

35 Christoph August Heumann, 'Der Einleitung zur Historia Philosophica. Das 1. Capitel/ von deren Nutzbarkeit', *Acta philosophorum, das ist: Gründl. Nachrichten aus der Historia Philosophica, nebst beygefügten Urtheilen von denen dahin gehörigen alten und neuen Büchern* 1, no. 1 (1715): 1–63, on 26 and 32–3. Also, Merio Scattola, "Historia literaria" als "Historia pragmatic": Die pragmatische Bedeutung der Geschichtsschreibung im intellektuellen Unternehmen der Gelehrtengeschichte', in *Historia literaria: Neuordnung des Wissens im 17. und 18. Jahrhundert*, ed. Frank Grunert und Friedrich Vollhardt (Berlin: Akademie Verlag, 2007), 37–63.

36 René Descartes, 'Discourse on the Method of Rightly Conducting One's Reason and Seeking Truth in the Sciences', in idem, *The Philosophical Writings*, ed. and trans. John Cottingham, Robert Stoothoff, and Dugald Murdoch, vol. 1 (Cambridge: Cambridge University Press, 1985), 111–51, on 115–6.

37 Heumann, 'Der Einleitung zur Historia Philosophica. Das 1. Capitel', 20–1.

38 On German academic philosophy during the Enlightenment, Max Wundt, *Die deutsche Schulphilosophie im Zeitalter der Aufklärung* (Tübingen: Mohr, 1945). Also, on the school of Christian Wolff, Hans-Martin Gerlach, ed., *Christian Wolff: Seine Schule und seine Gegner* (Hamburg: Meiner, 2001).

39 Christian Wolff, *Preliminary Discourse on Philosophy in General*, trans. Richard J. Blackwell (Indianapolis: Bobbs-Merrill, 1963), 13.

40 Also, on the split between Thomasius and Wolff in the German Enlightenment, see Ian Hunter, *Rival Enlightenments: Civil and Metaphysical Philosophy in Early Modern Germany* (Cambridge: Cambridge University Press, 2001).

Chapter 3

1 Heinz Durchhardt, Matthias Schnettger and Martin Vogt, eds., *Der Friede von Rijswijk 1697* (Mainz: Philipp von Zabern, 1998).
2 Notker Hammerstein, 'Reichs-Historie', in *Aufklärung und Geschichte: Studien zur deutschen Geschichtswissenschaft im 18. Jahrhundert*, ed. Hans Erich Bödeker, Georg G. Iggers, Jonathan B. Knudsen and Peter Hanns Reill (Göttingen: Vandenhoeck und Ruprecht, 1986), 82–104, and Michael Stolleis, *Geschichte des öffentlichen Rechts in Deutschland*, vol. 1 (Munich: C. H. Beck, 1988), 302–4.
3 Johann Peter von Ludewig, 'Zulängliche Antwort auf die liederlige Zunöthigung Herrn Tobias Pfanners', in idem, *Gesamte kleine teutsche Schriften* (Halle, 1705), 358–409, on 368–70, 'Praefatio' in idem, *Opuscula miscella* (Halle, 1720), 13–36, on 17–8, and 'Auswertiger Todes-Fall des Heßischen Cantzlers, Wilhelm Ludewigs von Maskowsky', in idem, *Gelehrte Anzeigen, in alle Wissenschaften, so wol geistlicher als weltlicher, alter und neuer Sachen*, vol. 1 (Halle, 1743), 337–9.
4 Johann Peter von Ludewig, 'Uber die Riswikische Friedens-Handlung und dessen Instrumentum wird der Studirenden Jugend ein collegium eröffnet. Anno 1698', in idem, *Gesamte kleine teutsche Schriften* (Halle, 1705), 321–35.
5 Jan Marco Sawilla, 'Das Zeugnis des Historiographen. Anwesenheit und gestufte Plausibilität in der Geschichtsschreibung der Frühen Neuzeit', in *Zeugnis und Zeugenschaft: Perspektiven aus der Vormoderne*, ed. Wolfram Drews and Heike Schlie (Munich: Wilhelm Fink, 2011), 311–35.
6 Johann Peter von Ludewig, 'Gebrauch und Mißbrauch der Zeitungen/ bey Eröffnung eines collegii geführet. Anno 1700', in idem, *Gesamte kleine teutsche Schriften* (Halle, 1705), 80–111, on 83–4, 'Uber die Riswikische', 324–6, and 'Zulängliche Antwort', 375–87.
7 Ludewig, 'Zulängliche Antwort', 373.
8 Ludewig, 'Gebrauch und Mißbrauch', 84.
9 Ludewig, 'Uber die Riswikische', 324–5, and 'Zulängliche Antwort', 387–90 and 394–6.
10 Nikolaus Hieronymus Gundling, *Ausfürlicher und vollständiger Discours über dessen Abriß einer Rechten Reichs-Historie* (Frankfurt am Main, 1732), 33.
11 For an overview, see Friedrick Wilhelm Bierling, *Commentatio de pyrrhonismo historico* (Leipzig, 1724), 227–34 and 323–6.
12 Gundling, *Ausfürlicher und vollständiger Discours*, 32. Also, for a critique of naïve uses of archival documents, 'Vorbericht zu denen Winter-lectionen', in

idem, *Sammlung kleiner teutscher Schriften*, vol. 1 (Halle, 1737), 94–142, on 108–11.
13 Philipp Ernst Spieß, *Von Archiven* (Halle, 1777), 5.
14 Georg August Bachmann, *Ueber Archive deren Natur und Eigenschaften: Einrichtung und Benutzung* (Amberg, 1801), 2.
15 Spieß, *Von Archiven*, 9, and Bachmann, *Ueber Archive*, 12–38.
16 Arnaldo Momigliano, 'Ancient History and the Antiquarian', *Journal of the Warburg and Courtauld Institutes* 13, no. 3/4 (1950): 285–315. Also, for recent discussions, Peter N. Miller, ed., *Momigliano and Antiquarianism: Foundations of the Modern Cultural Sciences* (Toronto: University of Toronto Press, 2007), and, concerning the question of historical evidence, Markus Völkel, 'Historischer Pyrrhonismus und Antiquarismus-Konzeption bei Arnaldo Momigliano', *Das Achtzehnte Jahrhundert* 31, no. 2 (2007): 179–90.
17 For some later definitions, see Johann Christoph Gatterer, *Elementa artis diplomaticae universalis* (Göttingen, 1765), 5, *Handbuch der Universalhistorie nach ihrem gesamten Umfange*, vol. 1 (Göttingen, 1765), 30, and *Abriss der Diplomatik* (Göttingen, 1798), 1. Also, Johann Christoph Adelung, 'Die Urkunde', *Grammatisch-kritisches Wörterbuch der Hochdeutschen Mundart*, vol. 4 (Leipzig, 1801), 963–4.
18 Carlrichard Brühl, 'Die Entwicklung der diplomatischen Methode im Zusammenhang mit dem Erkennen von Fälschungen', in *Fälschungen im Mittelalter: Internationale Kongreß der Monumenta Germaniae Historica*, ed. Detlev Jasper, vol. 2 (Hannover: Hahnsche Buchhandlung, 1988), 11–27, esp. 18–22.
19 Lorraine Daston, *Classical Probability in the Enlightenment* (Princeton: Princeton University Press, 1988), 39–47.
20 Tobias Pfanner, 'Bedencken von dem principio fidei historicae zumahlen wie selbiges auf denen Gesandtschaffts- und andern Acten gegründet', in Johann Peter von Ludewig, *Gesamte kleine teutsche Schriften* (Halle, 1705), 336–57, on 339, 344 and 347–8. Also, Völkel, *'Pyrrhonismus historicus' und 'Fides historica'*, 191–5.
21 Ludewig, 'Zulängliche Antwort', 374–5.
22 Johann Peter von Ludewig, *Reliquiae manuscriptorum omnis aevi*, 12 vols. (Frankfurt am Main, 1720–41).
23 Johann Peter von Ludewig, *Erläuterte Germania Princeps, das ist: Historisch-Politisch- und Rechtliche Anmerckungen über desselben Teutsche Fürsten-Staaten*, ed. H. von Finsterwald (Frankfurt am Main, 1744), 13.
24 Johann Peter von Ludewig, *Rechtliche Erleuterung der Reichs-Historie von erstem Ursprung biß 1734* (Halle, 1735), cxvi and cxiv.

25 Johann Daniel Gruber, 'Hofrath J. D. Gruber an Gerl. Adolf von Münchhausen über den Zustand und die Blüthe der deutschen Universitäten', in *Die Gründung der Universität Göttingen: Entwürfe, Berichte und Briefe der Zeitgenossen*, ed. E. F. Rössler (Göttingen, 1855), 458–67, on 460.

26 Johann Peter von Ludewig, *Vollständige Erläuterung der Güldenen Bulle*, vol. 2 (Frankfurt am Main, 1719), 1463–4 and 1473.

27 Ludewig, *Rechtliche Erleuterung*, xci and xciii–xciv. Also, *Vollständige Erläuterung der Güldenen Bulle*, vol. 2, 1465–8.

28 Ludewig, *Rechtliche Erleuterung*, xci and cii. Also, on the concept of fundamental law in Early Modern Europe, Martyn P. Thompson, 'The History of Fundamental Law in Political Thought from the French Wars of Religion to the American Revolution', *The American Historical Review* 91, no. 5 (1986): 1103–28, especially on German Imperial history, 1121–4.

29 Hammerstein, *Jus und Historie* and 'Reichs-Historie'.

30 Johann Jacob Schmauß, *Kurzer Begriff der Reichs-Historie* (Leipzig, 1729), preface to first edition, 9–10.

Chapter 4

1 Almost everything written about Klotz since the eighteenth century has been negative and only because of his role as an opponent to others. For a brief description of his life and works, see Conrad Bursian, 'Klotz, Christian Adolph', in *Allgemeine Deutsche Biographie*, vol. 16 (Leipzig, 1882), 228–31. Bursian's conclusion that Klotz died at thirty-three years old 'too late rather than too early' is characteristic of the secondary literature, ibid., 230. For a recent discussion of the Klotz and his followers, see also Hans-Joachim Kertscher, '"Klotz und die Klotzianer" als Autoren des halleschen Gebauer-Verlags', in idem, *Literatur und Kultur in Zeitalter der Aufklärung: Aufsätze zum geselligen Leben in einer deutschen Universitätsstadt* (Hamburg: Kovac, 2007), 381–96.

2 Johann Gottfried Herder, *Kritische Wälder: oder einige Betrachtungen über die Wissenschaft und Kunst der Schönen*, 3 vols. (Riga, 1769), Rudolf Erich Raspe, *Anmerkungen über die neueste Schrift des Hernn Geheimden Rath Klotz in Halle vom Nutzen und Gebrauch der geschnittenen Steine und ihrer Abdrücke* (Cassel, 1768), and Gotthold Ephraim Lessing, *Briefe, antiquarischen Inhalts*, 2 vols. (Berlin, 1768–9).

3 Johann Joachim Winckelmann, *Geschichte der Kunst des Alterthums*, 2 vols. (Dresden, 1764).

4 On Winckelmann and his German reception, see Carl Justi, *Winckelmann und seine Zeitgenossen*, 3 vols. (Cologne: Phaidon, 1956) and Katherine Harloe, *Winckelmann and the Invention of Antiquity: History and Aesthetics in the Age of Altertumswissenschaft* (Oxford: Oxford University Press, 2013).

5 Christian Adolph Klotz, 'Iohann Winckelmanns, Praesidentens der Alterthümer zu Rom und Scrittore der vaticanischen Bibliothek &c, Geschichte der Kunst des Alterthums', *Acta Litteraria* 1, no. 3 (1764): 336–53, and 'Dresden', *Göttingsche Anzeigen von Gelehrten Sachen* 33/34 (1765): 265–79.

6 Klotz, 'Dresden', 266.

7 Christian Adolph Klotz, *Mores eruditorum* (n.p., 1760) and *Genius seculi* (Altenburg, n. d.). On Mencke and the tradition of satirical writings, see Leonard Forster, '"Charlataneria eruditorum" zwischen Barock und Aufklärung in Deutschland', in *Res Publica Literaria: Die Institution der Gelehrsamkeit in der frühen Neuzeit*, ed. Sebastian Neumeister and Conrad Wiedemann, vol. 1 (Wiesbaden: Harrassowitz, 1987), 203–20.

8 Christian Adolph Klotz, *Ueber das Studium des Alterthums* (Halle, 1766), 42.

9 Ibid., 10–11.

10 Christian Adolph Klotz, *Ueber den Nutzen und Gebrauch der alten geschnittenen Steine und ihre Abdrücke* (Altenburg, 1768), 14–5.

11 Ibid., 9.

12 Ibid., 15. Also, Friederich Just Riedel, *Sämmtliche Schriften*, vol. 4: *Verschiedene Briefe* (Vienna, 1787), 311–2.

13 On Lippert, Christina Kerschner, 'Philipp Daniel Lippert (1702–1785) und seine Daktyliothek zum "Nutzen der Schönen Künste und Künstler"', in *Daktyliotheken: Götter und Caesaren aus der Schublade: antike Gemmen in Abdrucksammlungen des 18. und 19. Jahrhunderts*, Daktyliotheken, ed. Valentin Kockel, Daniel Graepler and Gergana Angelova (Munich: Biering und Brinkmann, 2006), 60–8, and Justi, *Winckelmann und seine Zeitgenossen*, vol. 1, 417–31.

14 Philipp Daniel Lippert, *Dactyliothec: Das ist Sammlung geschnittener Steine der Alten aus denen vornehmsten Museis in Europa zum Nutzen der schönen Künste und Künstler*, vol. 1 (Leipzig, 1767), iv.

15 Klotz, *Ueber den Nutzen*, 61.

16 Ibid., 63.

17 Ibid., 63–5, 131, 13 and 73. Also, Ulf R. Hansson, 'Die Quelle des guten Geschmacks ist nun geöffnet: Philipp Daniel Lipperts Dactyliotheca Universalis', in *Tankemönster. En festskrift till Eva Rystedt*, ed. Fanni Faegersten, Jenny Wallensten and Ida Östenberg (Lund: Faegersten, 2010), 92–101.

18 Lippert, *Dactyliothec*, vol. 1, 280.

19 Klotz, *Ueber den Nutzen*, 241.
20 On Socrates in the German Enlightenment, Benno Böhm, *Sokrates im 18. Jahrhundert* (Neumünster: Wachholtz, 1966) and Daniel Orrells, *Classical Culture and Modern Masculinity* (Oxford: Oxford University Press, 2011), 62–76. Also, for the French discussion, Russell Goulbourne, 'Voltaire's Socrates', in *Socrates from Antiquity to the Enlightenment*, ed. Michael Trapp (London: Ashgate, 2007), 229–47.
21 Christoph August Heumann, 'Ehren-Rettung der Xanthippe', *Acta philosophorum, das ist: Gründl. Nachrichten aus der Historia Philosophica, nebst beygefügten Urtheilen von denen dahin gehörigen alten und neuen Büchern* 1, no. 1 (1715): 103–25.
22 Klotz, *Ueber den Nutzen*, 199.
23 Riedel, *Sämmtliche*, 121.
24 Klotz, *Ueber den Nutzen*, 84.
25 Ibid., 89 and 236.
26 Christian Adolph Klotz, *Beytrag zur Geschichte des Geschmacks und der Kunst aus Münzen* (Altenburg, 1767), 3.
27 Winckelmann, *Geschichte*, vol. 2, 407.
28 Klotz, *Beytrag zur Geschichte*, 28 and 159–60.
29 Ibid., 63, 65, 17, 15 and 64.
30 Mager, 'Die Theologische'. Also, on the German radical underground, Martin Mulsow, *Moderne aus dem Untergrund: Radikale Frühaufklärung in Deutschland 1680–1720* (Hamburg: Meiner, 2002).
31 Johann Fisch, 'Zivilisation, Kultur', in *Geschichtliche Grundbegriffe*, ed. Otto Brunner, Werner Conze and Reinhart Koselleck, vol. 7 (Stuttgart: Klett-Cotta, 1992), 679–774, and Joseph Niedermann, *Kultur, Werden und Wandlungen des Begriffs und seiner Ersatzbegriffe von Cicero bis Herder* (Firenze: Bibliopolis, 1941).
32 Hochstrasser, *Natural Law Theories*, 95–8, and Michael C. Carhart, *The Science of Culture in Enlightenment Germany* (Cambridge: Harvard University Press, 2007).
33 Johann Gottfried Herder, *Ueber die neuere Deutsche Litteratur: Fragmente*, vol. 2 (Riga, 1767), 262.
34 Anonymous, 'Ueber die neue deutsche Litteratur, erste und zwote Sammlung von Fragmenten', *Deutsche Bibliothek der schönen Wissenschaften* 1, no. 1 (1767): 161–80, on 164.
35 Johann Gottfried Herder. *Briefe: Gesamtausgabe, 1763–1803*, ed. Wilhelm Dobbek and Günter Arnold, vol. 1: *Briefe. April 1763–April 1771* (Weimar: Hermann Böhlaus Nachfolger, 1977), 86, 110, 113 and 130.
36 Herder, *Kritische Wälder*, vol. 2, 10–1, 13–4 and 21.
37 Ibid., vol. 3, 96.

38 Carl Renatus Hausen, *Pragmatische Geschichte der Protestanten in Deutschland* (Halle, 1767), 121.
39 Herder, *Kritische Wälder*, vol. 3, 169 and 171.
40 VR, 'Kritische Wälder, Oder Betrachtungen über die Wissenschaft und Kunst der Schönen. Erstes und zweytes Wäldchen', *Deutsche Bibliothek der schönen Wissenschaften* 3, no. 10 (1769): 334–62, on 337.
41 Herder, *Briefe: Gesamtausgabe,* vol. 1, 161 and 172.
42 Meinecke, *Die Entstehung*, vol. 2, 387–416,
43 John H. Zammito, *Kant, Herder, and the Birth of Anthropology* (Chicago: Chicago University Press, 2002), 160. For another recent example, see Damien Valdez, *German Philhellenism: The Pathos of the Historical Imagination from Winckelmann to Goethe* (Basingstoke: Palgrave Macmillan, 2014). Valdez dedicates two chapters to a discussion of 'Winckelmann and the Young Herder', but only mentions Klotz in passing as an opponent to Lessing.
44 For example, J. Gurlitt, *Ueber die Gemmenkunde: Zur Ankündigung einer Schulfeierlichkeit im Kloster Bergen* (Magdeburg, 1798), and Johann Ferdinand Roth, *Mythologische Daktyliothek: Nebst vorausgeschichter Abhandlung geschnittenen Steinen* (Nürnberg, 1805), 69–77.
45 Christian Gottlob Heyne, ed., 'Vorrede', in Johann Gottfried von Herder, *Sämmtliche Werke zur schönen Literatur und Kunst*, vol. 1 (Stuttgart, 1827), 24–30, on 29–30.
46 For example, MS Ruppert 2056, Herzogin Anna Amalia Bibliothek, Weimar, 16–17. Also, for a programmatic description, Christian Gottlob Heyne, *Einleitung in das Studium der Antike, oder Grundriß einer Anführung zur Kenntniß der alten Kunstwerke* (Göttingen, 1772).
47 MS Ruppert 2056, 21.
48 MS Frederik Stoud, Vorlesungen des Hofraths Heine über die Archæologie, 1789 und 1792, Ny Kongelig Samling, Det Kongelige Bibliotek, Copenhagen, unpag, section 1.
49 The most dramatic examples may be the nineteenth-century divisions of history into 'history' and 'prehistory' and of the world population into 'historical people' and 'ahistorical people'. On these divisions, see also Kasper Risbjerg Eskildsen, 'The Language of Objects: Christian Jürgensen Thomsen's Science of the Past', *Isis* 103, no. 1 (2012): 24–53.

Chapter 5

1 Quoted in Johann Christoph Gatterer, *Praktische Diplomatik* (Göttingen, 1799), 142–3.

2   Ibid., 145–6, on 146.
3   Ibid., 132–52.
4   Martin Gierl, *Geschichte als präzisierte Wissenschaft: Johann Christoph Gatterer und die Historiographie des 18. Jahrhunderts im ganzen Umfang* (Stuttgart: Fromman-Holzboog, 2012).
5   Johann Christoph Gatterer, 'Abhandlung vom Standort und Gesichtspunct des Geschichtschreibers oder der teutsche Livius', *Allgemeine historische Bibliothek* 5 (1768): 3–29, on 11 and 13.
6   Ibid., 14–5.
7   Gatterer, *Praktische Diplomatik*, 133.
8   For example, Johann Christoph Gatterer, 'Vorrede von der Evidenz in der Geschichtskunde', in *Die Allgemeine Welthistorie die in England durch eine Gesellschaft von Gelehrten ausgefertiget worden: In einem vollständigen und pragmatischen Auszuge*, ed. F. E. Boysen, vol. 1 (Halle, 1767), 1–38, on 24.
9   On Gatterer and *Diplomatik*, Gierl, *Geschichte*, 128–61. Gierl quotes Gatterer's condition for membership on 139.
10 Gatterer, *Elementa*, 81–6. Also, Gierl, *Geschichte*, 187–217, and Martin Gierl, 'Das Alphabet der Natur und das Alphabet der Kultur im 18. Jahrhundert: Botanik, Diplomatik, Linguistik und Etnographie nach Carl von Linné, Johann Christop Gatterer und Christian Wilhelm Büttner', *NMT Zeitschrift für Geschichte der Wissenschaften, Technik und Medizin* 18 (2010): 1–27.
11 Johann Christoph Gatterer, 'Nähere Nachricht von der neuen Ausgabe der gleichzeitigen Schriftsteller über die Teutsche Geschichte', *Allgemeine Historische Bibliothek* 8 (1768): 3–22, on 10.
12 Gatterer, *Praktische Diplomatik*, 133–4.
13 Gatterer, 'Vorrede von der Evidenz', 27.
14 Ibid., 27–8. Also, Gatterer, *Handbuch der Universalhistorie*, 74–7.
15 Gatterer, *Praktische Diplomatik*, 142.
16 Gotthold Ephraim Lessing, *Laokoon: oder über die Grenzen der Mahlerey und Poesie* (Berlin, 1766), preface, unpag.
17 Johan Hinric Lidén, *Dagböcker*, vol. 2, MS X 397, Uppsala Universitetsbibliotek, 187, 197 and 245. Also, for other similar descriptions, Gierl, *Geschichte*, 152–3.
18 Carl Boell, *Sendschreiben über die Anfrage in was für einem Zustand sich die Rechtsgelehrsamkeit auf der blühenden Georg Augusta befinde* (Colmar, 1775), 27.
19 Johann Stephan Pütter, *Versuch einer academischen Gelehrten-Geschichte von der Georg-August-Universität zu Göttingen*, vol. 1 (Göttingen, 1765), 273.
20 Gatterer, *Praktische Diplomatik*, 140.

21 Still in 1876 Hermann Wesendonck could declare Gatterer, together with his Göttingen colleague Schlözer, one of the founders of German historiography in *Die Begründung der neueren deutschen Geschichtsschreibung durich Gatterer und Schlözer* (Leipzig, 1876). In a footnote to *Die Entstehung des Historismus*, Meinecke briefly dismissed Wesendonck's work, vol. 2, 308. Gatterer was not even mentioned in Eduard Fueter's otherwise comprehensive *Geschichte der neueren Historiographie* (Munich: Oldenbourg, 1936).

22 Reill, *The German Enlightenment*. Also, 'History and Hermeneutics in the Aufklärung: The Thought of Johann Christoph Gatterer', *Journal of Modern History* 45, no. 1 (1973): 24–51, and 'Johann Christoph Gatterer', in *Deutsche Historiker*, ed. Hans Ulrich Wehler, vol. 6 (Göttingen: Vandenhoeck und Ruprecht, 1980), 7–22.

23 Martin Gierl, 'Change of Paradigm as a Squabble Between Institutions: The Institute of Historical Sciences, the Society of Sciences, and the Separation of Cultural and Natural Sciences in Göttingen in the Second Half of the Eighteenth Century', in *Scholars in Action: The Practice of Knowledge and the Figure of the Savant in the Eighteenth Century*, ed. André Holenstein, Hubert Steinke and Martin Stuber, vol. 2 (Leiden: Brill, 2013), 267–87.

24 Johann Christoph Gatterer, 'Zufällige Gedanken über die teutsche Geschichte', *Allgemeine historische Bibliothek* 2 (1767): 23–34, on 29.

25 Gatterer, 'Vorrede von der Evidenz', 5, 4 and 11.

26 Gatterer, 'Zufällige Gedanken', 34.

27 Johann Christoph Gatterer, 'Vorrede', *Historisches Journal* 1 (1772): unpag.

Chapter 6

1 Paul W. Schroeder, *The Transformation of European Politics 1763–1848* (Oxford: Oxford University Press, 1994), 666–711.

2 Leopold von Ranke, *Das Briefwerk*, ed. Walther Peter Fuchs (Hamburg: Hoffmann und Campe, 1949), 222–4 and 231–2.

3 Friedrich von Gentz, *Briefe von und an Friedrich von Gentz*, ed. Friedrich Carl Wittichen, vol. 1 (Munich: Oldenbourg, 1909), 345.

4 Leopold Ranke, *Ueber die Verschwörung gegen Venedig, im Jahre 1618: Mit Urkunden aus dem Venezianischen Archive* (Berlin, 1831).

5 Also, on Ranke's early years, Theodore H. von Laue, *Leopold Ranke: The Formative Years* (Princeton: Princeton University Press, 1950) and Siegfried Baur, *Versuch über die Historik des jungen Ranke* (Berlin: Duncker und Humblot, 1998).

6 Also, Michael Harbsmeier, 'World Histories Before Domestication: The Writing of Universal Histories, Histories of Mankind and World Histories in Late Eighteenth-Century Germany', *Culture and History* 5 (1989): 93–131, and Andreas Urs Sommer, 'Historischer Pyrrhonismus und die Entstehung der spekulativ-universalistischen Geschichtsphilosophie', in *Unsicheres Wissen: Skeptizismus und Wahrscheinlichkeit 1550–1850*, ed. Carlos Spoerhase, Dirk Werle and Markus Wild (Berlin: Walter de Gruyter, 2009), 201–14.
7 Barthold Georg Niebuhr, 'Einleitung zu den Vorlesungen über Römische Alterthümer 1811', in idem, *Kleine historische und philologische Schriften*, vol. 2 (Bonn, 1843), 1–19, on 5 and 9.
8 Leopold von Ranke, 'Idee der Universalhistorie', in idem, *Aus Werk und Nachlass*, ed. Walther Peter Fuchs and Theodor Schieder, vol. 4: *Vorlesungseinleitungen*, ed. Volker Dotterweich and Walther Peter Fuchs (Munich: Oldenbourg, 1975), 72–89.
9 Also Baur, *Versuch über die Historik*, 112–23.
10 Karl August Varnhagen von Ense, *Werke*, ed., Konrad Feilchenfeldt, vol. 5 (Frankfurt am Main: Deutscher Klassiker Verlag, 1994), 420.
11 Anonymous, 'Die Berliner Historiker', *Hallische Jahrbücher für deutsche Wissenschaft und Kunst* 4 (1841): 421–2, 425–7 and 429–39, on 430. Günter Berg considered Karl Friedrich Köppen, a friend of Engels and Marx, the author of this article. Siegfried Baur has proposed Arnold Ruge as another possibility. Günter Berg, *Leopold Ranke als akademischer Lehrer: Studien zu seinen Vorlesungen und seinem Geschichtsdenken* (Göttingen: Vandenhoeck und Ruprecht, 1968), 57 and Baur, *Versuch über die Historik*, 31, note 48.
12 Leopold Ranke, *Zur Kritik neuerer Geschichtschreiber* (Leipzig, 1824), 181.
13 Also, Kasper Risbjerg Eskildsen, 'Inventing the Archive: Testimony and Virtue in Modern Historiography', *History of the Human Sciences* 26, no. 3 (2013): 8–26.
14 Kasper Risbjerg Eskildsen, 'Leopold von Ranke (1795–1886): Criticizing an Early Modern Historian', *History of Humanities* 4, no. 2 (2019): 257–62.
15 Ranke, *Zur Kritik*, 173 and 72–4.
16 Also, Gino Benzoni, 'Ranke's Favorite Source: The Venetian Relazioni. Impressions with Allusions to Later Historiography', in *Leopold von Ranke and the Shaping of the Historical Discipline*, ed. Georg G. Iggers and James M. Powell (Syracuse: Syracuse University Press, 1990), 45–57.
17 Leopold Ranke, *Fürsten und Völker von Süd-Europa im sechzehnten und siebzehnten Jahrhundert. Vornehmlich aus ungedruckten Gesandtschafts-Berichten* (Hamburg, 1827), ix.
18 Ranke, *Briefwerk*, 84–5.

19 Ibid., 156–63.
20 Ranke, *Fürsten und Völker*, viii.
21 For a historiographical overview, see Richard Mackenney, '"A Plot Discover'd." Myth, Legend, and the "Spanish" Conspiracy against Venice in 1618', in *Venice Reconsidered: The History and Civilization of an Italian City-State 1297–1797*, ed. John Jeffries Martin and Dennis Romano (Baltimore: Johns Hopkins University Press, 2000), 185–216.
22 Ranke, *Ueber die Verschwörung*, 1.
23 Also Claudio Povolo, 'The Creation of Venetian Historiography', in *Venice Reconsidered: The History and Civilization of an Italian City-State 1297–1797*, ed. John Jeffries Martin and Dennis Romano (Baltimore: Johns Hopkins University Press, 2000), 491–519.
24 Ranke, *Ueber die Verschwörung*, 12.
25 Ibid., 17.
26 Ibid., 52.
27 Ranke, 'Idee der Universalhistorie', 84.
28 Ranke, *Ueber die Verschwörung*, 53–62, Also S. Rossi Minutelli, 'Archivi e biblioteche', in *Storia di Venezia*, vol. 2: *L'Ottocento e il Novecento*, ed. Mario Isnenghi and Stuart Woolf (Rome: Istituto della Enciclopedia italiana, 2002), 1081–122, esp. 1084–92, and Claudio Povolo, *Il romanziere e l'archivista. De un processo veneziano del '600 all' anonimo manoscritto dei Promessi sposi* (Venice: Istituto Veneto di Scienze Lettere ed Arti, 1993), esp. 71–95.
29 Shapin and Schaffer, *Leviathan and the Air-Pump*, 60–5.
30 Ranke, *Ueber die Verschwörung*, 54.
31 Ibid., 54–5 and 44.
32 Ranke, *Briefwerk*, 121–2, 131–2, 172, and 194.
33 Also, on Ranke's letters, Ulrich Muhlack, 'Leopold Ranke, seine Geschichtsschreibung und seine Briefe', in Leopold von Ranke, *Briefwechsel: Historisch-kritische Ausgabe*, ed. Ulrich Muhlack and Oliver Ramonat, vol. 1 (Munich: Oldenbourg, 2007), 3–49.
34 Nicholas Jardine, 'Naturphilosophie and the Kingdoms of Nature', in *Cultures of Natural History*, ed. Nicholas Jardine, James A. Secord and E. C. Spary (Cambridge: Cambridge University Press, 1996), 230–45, on 231.
35 Ranke, *Briefwerk*, 128, 130, 154–5, 186–7 and 208.
36 Ibid., 115, 121–2, 123 and 126.
37 Leopold von Ranke, *Neue Briefe*, ed. Bernard Hoeft (Hamburg: Hoffmann und Campe, 1949), 108, n 2.
38 Ranke, *Briefwerk*, 164, 195, 214, 203 and 206.

39 Leopold Kammerhofer, 'Die Gründung des Haus-, Hof- und Staatsarchivs 1749', in *Speicher des Gedächtnisses: Bibliotheken, Museen, Archive*, vol 2: *Die Erfindung des Ursprungs, die Systematisierung der Zeit*, ed. Moritz Csáky (Vienna: Passagen Verlag, 2001), 81–99, and Wolfgang Ernst, *Im Namen der Geschichte*: *Sammeln – Speichern- Er/Zählen. Infrastrukturelle Konfigurationen des deutschen Gedächtnisses* (Munich: Wilhelm Fink Verlag, 2003), 586–613.

40 Jennifer S. Milligan, "What is an Archive?' in the History of Modern France', in *Archive Stories: Facts, Fictions, and the Writing of History*, ed. Antoinette M. Burton (Durham: Duke University Press, 2005), 159–83, on 161.

41 Reinhold Koser, ed., *Die Neuordnung des Preussischen Archivwesens durch den Staatskanzler Fürsten von Hardenberg* (Leipzig: Hirzel, 1904), 6 and 21.

42 Ludwig Bittner, ed., *Gesamtinventar des Wiener Haus-, Hof- und Staatsarchivs*, vol. 1 (Vienna: Holzhausen, 1936), 163–9, on 167.

43 Ibid., 175–80.

44 Ranke, *Briefwerk*, 171.

45 Ibid., 119, 111, 191 and 171. Also, on involvement of diplomats, Bittner, *Gesamtinventar*, vol. 1, 182.

46 Barbara Dorn, *Friedrich von Gentz und Europa: Studien zu Stabilität und Revolution 1802-1822* (PhD diss., University of Bonn, 1993) and Günther Kronenbitter, *Wort und Macht: Friedrich Gentz als politischer Schriftsteller* (Berlin: Duncker und Humblot, 1994).

47 Bittner, *Gesamtinventar*, vol. 1, 182–3.

48 Ranke, *Briefwerk*, 126–7.

49 Leopold von Ranke, 'Ausgewählte Briefe', in idem, *Sämmtliche Werke*, vol. 53/54: *Zur eigenen Lebensgeschichte*, ed. by Alfred Dove (Leipzig, 1890), 77–565, on 181.

50 Bittner, *Gesamtinventar*, vol. 1, 182–3.

51 Ranke, *Neue Briefe*, 109 and 110.

52 Ranke, *Briefwerk*, 169–70. Also, Ugo Tucci, 'Ranke Storico di Venezia', in *Venezia nel Cinquecento*, ed. Leopold von Ranke, trans. Ingeborg Zapperi Walter (Rome: Istituto della Enciclopedia italiana, 1974), 1–69, esp. 3–18, and 'Ranke and the Venetian Document Market', in *Leopold von Ranke and the Shaping of the Historical Discipline*, ed. Georg G. Iggers and James M. Powell (Syracuse: Syracuse University Press, 1990), 99–107, esp. 100.

53 Ranke, *Briefwerk*, 126–7.

54 Ranke, *Neue Briefe*, 113 and 137–8.

55 Ranke, *Briefwerk*, 220–1.

56 Ranke, *Ueber die Verschwörung*, 57.

57 Ranke, *Briefwerk*, 221.

58 Heinrich Heine, 'Französische Zustände', in idem, *Historisch-kritische Gesamtausgabe der Werke*, ed. Manfred Windfuhr, vol. 12:1, ed. Jean-René Derré and Christiane Giesen (Hamburg: Hoffmann und Campe, 1980), 63–226, on 70.
59 Anonymous, 'Die Berliner', 431.
60 Ludewig, *Rechtliche Erleuterung*, xciii–xciv.
61 Robert von Mohl, *Die Geschichte und Literatur der Staatswissenschaften*, vol. 2 (Erlangen, 1856), 238–9.
62 On Ranke and historical continuity, also Rudolf Vierhaus, 'Die Idee der Kontinuität im historiographischen Werk Leopold von Rankes', in *Leopold von Ranke und die moderne Geschichtswissenschaft*, ed. Wolfgang J. Mommsen (Stuttgart: Klett-Cotta, 1988), 166–75.
63 John E. Toews, *Becoming Historical: Cultural Reformation and Public Memory in Early Nineteenth-Century Berlin* (Cambridge: Cambridge University Press, 2004), esp. 372–418.
64 Ranke, *Briefwerk*, 231–2.
65 Leopold Ranke, 'Einleitung', *Historisch-politische Zeitschrift* 1 (1832): 1–8, on 2, 1 and 3.
66 Leopold von Ranke, 'Am neunzigsten Geburtstag 21. December 1885', in idem, *Sämmtliche Werke*, vol. 51/52: *Abhandlungen und Versuche*, ed. Alfred Dove and Theodor Wiedemann (Leipzig, 1888), 592–8, on 597.
67 For a discussion, see Gabriele Lingelbach, *Klio macht Karriere: Die Institutionalisierung der Geschichtswissenschaft in Frankreich und den USA in der zweiten Hälfte des 19. Jahrhunderts* (Göttingen: Vandenhoeck und Ruprecht, 2003) and Herman Paul, 'German Thoroughness in Baltimore: Epistemic Virtues and National Stereotypes', *History of Humanities* 3, no. 2 (2018): 327–50.
68 Georg G. Iggers, 'The Image of Ranke in American and German Historical Thought', *History and Theory* 2, no. 1 (1962): 17–40, on 18.
69 Iggers, *The German Conception*, 4.
70 Toews, *Becoming Historical*, 373.
71 For the sciences, see David Cahan, ed., *From Natural Philosophy to the Sciences: Writing the History of Nineteenth Century Science* (Chicago: Chicago University Press, 2003).

Chapter 7

1 Bärbel Schwager, *Das Göttinger Auditoriengebäude von 1862/65: Ein Beitrag zur Universitätarchitektur im 19. Jahrhundert und zur Hannoverschen Variante des Rundbogenstils* (Göttingen: Peter Lang, 1995), 310–1.

2 For contemporary views on Waitz's 'scholarly persona' also Herman Paul, 'The Virtues of a Good Historian in Early Imperial Germany: Georg Waitz's Contested Example', *Modern Intellectual History* 15, no. 3 (2018): 681–709.

3 Hartmut Boockmann, 'Geschichtsunterricht und Geschichtsstudium in Göttingen', in *Geschichtswissenschaft in Göttingen: Eine Vorlesungsreihe*, ed. Hartmut Boockmann and Hermann Wellenreuter (Göttingen: Wandenhoeck und Ruprecht, 1987), 161–85, esp. 175–8. For descriptions of Waitz and his teaching style by his former students, see Ferdinand Frensdorff, 'Georg Waitz', in *Allgemeine Deutsche Biographie*, vol. 40 (Leipzig, 1886), 602–29, Gabriel Monod, 'Georges Waitz', *Revue historique* 11, no. 31 (1886): 383–90, Hermann Grauert, 'Georg Waitz', in *Historisches Jahrbuch. Im Auftrage der Görres-Gesellschaft*, vol. 8 (Munich, 1887), 48–100, Ludwig Wieland, 'Georg Waitz', *Abhandlungen der Königlichen Gesellschaft der Wissenschaften zu Göttingen* 33 (1886): 1–15, and Dietrich Schäfer, *Mein Leben* (Berlin: Köhler, 1926), 75–7. For his own description of his teaching practices, Georg Waitz, *Die historischen Übungen zu Göttingen: Glückwunschschreiben an Leopold von Ranke zum Tage der Feier seines funfzigjährigen Doctorjubiläums. 20. Februar 1867* (Göttingen, 1867).

4 Weiland, 'Georg Waitz', 12–3.

5 Monod, 'Georges Waitz', 383–4.

6 For a discussion of the moral significance of epistemic virtues for Monod and Waitz, see also Paul, 'The Virtues of a Good Historian' and Camille Creyghton, Pieter Huistra, Sarah Keymeulen and Herman Paul, 'Virtue Language in Historical Scholarship: The Cases of Georg Waitz, Gabriel Monod, and Henri Pirenne', *History of European Ideas* 42, no. 7 (2016): 924–36. Also, on the significance of moral and epistemic virtues in late-nineteenth-century humanistic scholarship, Kasper Risbjerg Eskildsen, 'Scholarship as a Way of Life: Character and Virtue in the Age of Big Humanities', *History of the Humanities* 1, no. 2 (2016): 387–97.

7 Konrad H. Jarausch, *Deutsche Studenten, 1800–1970* (Frankfurt am Main: Suhrkamp, 1984), 129.

8 On the natural sciences, David Kaiser, ed., *Pedagogy and the Practice of Science. Historical and Contemporary Perspectices* (Cambridge: MIT Press, 2005).

9 William Clark, 'On the Dialectical Origins of the Research Seminar', *History of Science* 27, no. 2 (1989): 111–54, and Carlos Spoerhase and Mark-Georg Dehrmann, 'Die Idee der Universität: Friedrich August Wolf und die Praxis des Seminars', *Zeitschrift für Ideengeschichte* 5, no. 1 (2011): 105–17.

10 For an overview, Konrad H. Jarausch, 'Universität und Hochschule', in *Handbuch der deutschen Bildungsgeschichte*, vol. 4: *1870–1918. Von*

Reichsgründung bis zum Ende des Ersten Weltkriegs, ed. Christa Berg (Munich: C.H. Beck, 1991), 313–45, Bernhard vom Brocke, 'Wege aus der Krise: Universitätsseminar, Akademiekommission oder Forschungsinstitut. Formen der Institutionalisierung in den Geistes- und Naturwissenschaften 1810-1900-1995', in *Konkurrenten in der Fakultät. Kultur, Wissen und Universität um 1900*, ed. Christoph König and Eberhard Lämmert (Frankfurt am Main: Fischer, 1999), 191–218, and 'Die Entstehung der deutschen Forschungsuniversität ihre Blüte und Krise um 1900', in *Humboldt International: Der Export des deutschen Universitätsmodells*, ed. Rainer Christoph Schwinges (Basel: Schwabe, 2001), 367–401. Also, Gert Schubring, 'Kabinett – Seminar – Institut: Raum und Rahmen des forschenden Lernens', *Berichte zur Wissenschaftsgeschichte* 23, no. 3 (2000): 269–85.

11 Also, Kathryn M. Olesko, 'Commentary: On Institutes, Investigations, and Scientific Training', in *The Investigative Enterprise: Experimental Physiology in Nineteenth-Century Medicine*, ed. William Coleman and Frederic L. Holmes (Berkeley: University of California Press, 1988), 295–332.

12 Paul Fredericq, *L'Enseignement supérieur de l'histoire: Notes et impressions de voyage* (Gent, 1899). On Fredericq and his notebooks, also Jo Tollebeek, 'A Stormy Family. Paul Fredericq and the Formation of an Academic Historical Community in the Nineteenth Century', *Storia della Storiografia* 53 (2008): 59–73, and *Fredericq en Zonen: Een antropologie van de moderne geschiedwetenschap* (Amsterdam: Bert Bakker, 2008).

13 MS Kristian Erslev, Tyske Universitetsstudier, Breve, 19, Diverse, Ny Kongelige Samling, 4604, 4, Det Kongelige Bibliotek, Copenhagen.

14 G. Stanley Hall, *Methods of Teaching History* (Boston, 1883). Also, for an international overview, Frank Hadler, Gabriele Lingelbach and Matthias Middell, ed. *Historische Institute im internationalen Vergleich* (Leipzig: AVA, 2001) and, on the introduction of historical seminars in the United States, Gabriele Lingelbach, *Klio macht Karriere*, Bonnie G. Smith, 'Gender and the Practices of Scientific History: The Seminar and Archival Research in the Nineteenth Century', *The American Historical Review* 100, no. 4 (1995): 1150–76, and Anthony Grafton, 'In Clio's American Atelier', in *Social Knowledge in the Making*, ed. Charles Camic, Neil Gross, und Michèle Lamont (Chicago: University of Chicago Press, 2011), 89–117.

15 Georg Waitz, *Friedrich Christoph Dahlmann: Gedächtnisrede gehalten in der Aula der Universität Kiel am 13. Mai 1885* (Kiel, 1885), 5.

16 Georg von Below and K. Vogel, 'Briefe von K. W. Nitzsch an W. Schrader (1868–80)', *Archiv für Kulturgeschichte* 10 (1912): 49–110, on 59.

17 Waitz, *Die historischen Übungen*, 7. See also Waitz, *Friedrich Christoph Dahlmann*, 5, and Fredericq, *L'Enseignement supérieur*, 46.
18 Julius von Pflugk-Harrtung, 'Heinrich von Sybel', *Westermanns illustrierte deutsche Monatshefte* 64 (1888): 331–46, on 341.
19 Leopold Ranke, 'Vorrede', in *Jahrbücher des Deutschen Reichs unter dem Sächsischen Hause*, ed. idem, 1, no. 1 (Berlin, 1837): v–xii, on vii and ix.
20 Waitz, *Die historischen Übungen*, 8.
21 Anthony Grafton, *The Footnote: A Curious History* (Cambridge: Harvard University Press, 1999), 64–8.
22 Wilhelm Junghans, *Die Geschichte der fränkischen Könige Childerich und Chlodevech, kritisch untersucht* (Göttingen, 1857) and Rudolf Usinger, *Die dänischen Annalen und Chroniken des Mittelalters, kritisch untersucht* (Hannover, 1861).
23 Siegfried Hirsch and Georg Waitz, 'Kritische Prüfung der Echtheit und des historischen Wertes des Chronicon Corbejense', in *Jahrbücher des Deutschen Reichs unter dem Sächsischen Hause*, ed. Leopold Ranke, vol. 3, no. 1 (Berlin, 1839), v–viii and 1–139, on v–vi.
24 Ibid., on 42–4.
25 For the history of the chronicle, and different theories about the falsification, see also Kasper Risbjerg Eskildsen, 'Fälschung', in *Enzyklopädie der Genauigkeit*, ed. Markus Krajewski, Antonia von Schöning and Mario Wimmer (Konstanz: Konstanz University Press, 2021), 130–9.
26 Hirsch and Waitz, 'Kritische Prüfung', 86–100, quotes on 98 and 91.
27 Herman Hildebrand, *Die Chronik Heinrichs von Lettland. Ein Beitrag zu Livlands Historiographie und Geschichte* (Berlin, 1865), 46–7. The dissertation was defended in Dorpat, but had first been presented in Waitz's exercises in Göttingen, and Waitz considered it as a product of his school.
28 Karl Wittich, 'Richer über die Herzoge Giselbert von Lothringen und Heinrich von Sachsen', *Forschungen zur deutschen Geschichte* 3 (1863): 105–41, on 108.
29 For example, Junghans, *Die Geschichte der fränkischen Könige*, Carl Simonis, *Versuch einer Geschichte des Alarichs Königs der Westgothen* (Göttingen, 1858), Eduard Winkelmann, *Geschichte Kaiser Friedrichs des Zweiten und seiner Reiche, 1212-1235* (Berlin, 1863).
30 For example, August Kluckhohn, *Geschichte des Gottesfriedens* (Leipzig, 1857), iv, Usinger, *Die dänischen Annalen*, 6, August von Druffel, *Kaiser Heinrich IV. und seine Söhne* (Regensburg, 1862), unpag., Theodor Knochenhauer, *Geschichte Thüringens in der karolingischen und sächsischen Zeit* (Gotha, 1863), ix–x., Hildebrand, *Die Chronik Heinrichs*, unpag, and Arnold Busson, *Die Doppelwahl*

des Jahres 1257 und das römische Königthum Alfons X. von Castilien (Münster, 1866), vi.
31 Monod, 'Georges Waitz', 383.
32 Weiland, 'Georg Waitz', 12–3.
33 Hans-Jürgen Pandel, 'Von der Teegesellschaft zum Forschungsinstitut. Die historischen Seminare vom Beginn des 19. Jahrhunderts bis zum Ende des Kaiserreichs', in *Transformationen des Historismus. Wissenschaftsorganisation und Bildungspolitik vor dem Ersten Weltkrieg*, ed. Horst Walter Blanke (Waltrop: Wilhelm Fink, 1994), 1–31, and 'Die Entwicklung der historischen Seminare in Deutschland', in *Halle und die deutsche Geschichtswissenschaft um 1900*, ed. Werner Freitag (Halle: Mitteldeutscher Verlag, 2002), 25–36. Also, Hermann Heimpel, 'Über Organisationsformen historischer Forschung in Deutschland', *Historische Zeitschrift* 189 (1959): 139–222, esp. 140–50, Paul Egon Hübinger, *Das historische Seminar der rheinischen Friedrich-Wilhelms-Universität zu Bonn* (Bonn: Röhrscheid, 1963), and Markus Huttner, 'Historische Gesellschaften und die Entstehung historischer Seminare: Zu den Anfängen institutionalisierter Geschichtsstudien an den deutschen Universitäten des 19. Jahrhunderts', in *Historische Institute im internationalen Vergleich*, ed. Frank Hadler, Gabriele Lingelbach and Matthias Middell (Leipzig: AVA, 2001), 39–83.
34 Ibid., esp. 39–43.
35 Max Lenz, *Geschichte der Königlichen Friedrich-Wilhelms-Universität zu Berlin*, vol. 3: *Wissenschaftlichen Anstalten* (Halle: Buchhandlung des Waisenhauses, 1910), 255.
36 Ibid., 255–7.
37 *Historisches Seminar an der Universität Leipzig. Ratschläge für das Studium der mittleren und neueren Geschichte*. Copy in Kristian Erslev, Breve, 19, Tryksager, Ny kgl. Samling, 4604, 4, Det Kongelige Bibliotek, Copenhagen.
38 Ibid.
39 Wilhelm Arndt, ed., *Kleine Denkmäler aus der Merovingerzeit* (Hannover, 1874), v.
40 [George Burton Adams], 'Historical Seminar Methods at Leipzig', *The Nation*, 1265 (26 September 1889): 252 and Fredericq, *L'Enseignement*, 28.
41 Wilhelm Maurenbrecher, 'Lebensbild C. v. Noordens', in Carl von Noorden, *Historische Vorträge*, ed. Wilhelm Maurenbrecher (Leipzig, 1884), 1–52, about the exercises, 38–40.
42 MS. Kristian Erslev, Tyske Universitetsstudier, Breve, 19, Diverse, Ny Kongelig Samling, 4604, 4, Det Kongelige Bibliotek, Copenhagen. Erslev's travel journal

includes two hectograph copies from Weitzsäcker's exercises on 24 June and 1 July 1885.

43 Georg Waitz, 'Falsche Richtungen: Schreiben an den Herausgeber', *Historische Zeitschrift* 1, no 1. (1859): 17–28, on 24.

44 On Waitz's political viewpoints and the connection to his historical works, see Robert L. Benson and Loren J. Weber, 'Georg Waitz', in *Medieval Scholarship: Biographical Studies on the Formation of a Discipline*, ed. Helen Damico and Joseph B. Zavadil, vol. 1 (New York: Routledge, 1995), 63–75, and Niklas Lenhard-Schramm, *Konstrukteure der Nation: Geschichtsprofessoren als politische Akteure in Vormärz und Revolution 1848/49* (Münster: Waxmann, 2014), especially 50–4 and 94–103.

45 Georg Waitz, *Ueber die Gründung des deutschen Reichs durch den Vertrag zu Verdun* (Kiel, 1843), 24–5.

46 Peter Novick, *That Noble Dream: The 'Objectivity Question' and the American Historical Profession* (Cambridge: Cambridge University Press, 1988), 4.

Epilogue

1 Herbert Butterfield, *The Whig Interpretation of History* (New York: Norton, 1965), 16.

2 Karl Heussi, *Die Krisis des Historismus* (Tübingen: J. C. B Mohr, 1932), 6.

3 Steven Shapin, *The Scientific Life: A Moral History of a Late Modern Vocation* (Chicago: University of Chicago Press, 2008), esp. 21–91.

4 Max Weber, 'Science as a Vocation', in *From Max Weber: Essays in Sociology*, trans. H. H. Gerth and C. Wright Mills (London: Routledge, 2009), 129–56, on 152.

5 Julie E. Reuben, *The Making of the Modern University: Intellectual Transformation and the Marginalization of Morality* (Chicago: University of Chicago Press, 1996).

6 Butterfield, *The Whig Interpretation of History*, 67. Also, 126–7.

7 Dipesh Chakrabarty, *Provincializing Europe: Postcolonial Thought and Historical Difference* (Princeton: Princeton University Press, 2000).

8 For recent discussions, Daniel Woolf, *A Concise History of History: Global Historiography from Antiquity to the Present* (Cambridge: Cambridge University Press, 2019), esp. 196–212, and Stefan Tanaka, *History without Chronology* (Amherst: Lever Press, 2019).

References

Printed sources

Adams, George Burton. 'Historical Seminar Methods at Leipzig'. *The Nation* 1265 (26 September 1889): 252.
Adelung, Johann Christoph. 'Die Urkunde'. In *Grammatisch-kritisches Wörterbuch der Hochdeutschen Mundart*, vol. 4, 963–4. Leipzig, 1801.
Ahnert, Thomas. *Religion and the Origins of the German Enlightenment: Faith and the Reform of Learning in the Thought of Christian Thomasius*. Rochester: University of Rochester Press, 2006.
Albrect, Michael. 'Thomasius – kein Eklektiker?' In *Christian Thomasius 1655–1728: Interpretation zu Werk und Wirkung*, edited by Werner Schneiders, 73–94. Hamburg: Meiner, 1989.
Albrect, Michael. *Eklektik: Eine Begriffsgeschichte mit Hinweisen auf die Philosophie- und Wissenschaftsgeschichte*. Stuttgart: Frommann-Holzboog, 1994.
Algazi, Gadi. 'Scholars in Households: Refiguring the Learned Habitus, 1480–1550'. *Science in Context* 16, no. 1/2 (2003): 9–42.
Anonymous. 'Philosophe'. In *Le Dictionnaire de l'Académie françoise, dédié au Roy*, vol. 2, 229. Paris, 1694.
Anonymous. 'Wohlmeinendes Gutachten über Herrn Thomas bißherige Art zu schreiben'. In Christian Thomasius, *Allerhand bißher publicirte kleine teutsche Schrifften mit Fleiß colligiret und zusammen getragen: Nebst etlichen Beylagen und einer Vorrede*, 271–340. Halle, 1701.
Anonymous. 'Ueber die neue deutsche Litteratur, erste und zwote Sammlung von Fragmenten'. *Deutsche Bibliothek der schönen Wissenschaften* 1, no. 1 (1767): 161–80.
Anonymous. 'Die Berliner Historiker'. *Hallische Jahrbücher für deutsche Wissenschaft und Kunst* 4 (1841): 421–2, 425–7, 429–39.
Anonymous. *Historisches Seminar an der Universität Leipzig. Ratschläge für das Studium der mittleren und neueren Geschichte*. N. p., n. d.
Arndt, Wilhelm, ed. *Kleine Denkmäler aus der Merovingerzeit*. Hannover, 1874.
Arnold, Gottfried. *Unpartheyischen Kirchen- und Ketzer-Historie*, 2 vols. 1688–1700. 2nd edn. Frankfurt am Main, 1729.

Bachmann, Georg August. *Ueber Archive deren Natur und Eigenschaften: Einrichtung und Benutzung*. Amberg, 1801.

Baur, Siegfried. *Versuch über die Historik des jungen Ranke*. Berlin: Duncker und Humblot, 1998.

Beiser, Frederick C. *The German Historicist Tradition*. Oxford: Oxford University Press, 2011.

von Below, Georg and K. Vogel. 'Briefe von K. W. Nitzsch an W. Schrader (1868–80)'. *Archiv für Kulturgeschichte* 10 (1912): 49–110.

Benson, Robert L. and Loren J. Weber. 'Georg Waitz'. In *Medieval Scholarship: Biographical Studies on the Formation of a Discipline*, edited by Helen Damico and Joseph B. Zavadil, vol. 1, 63–75. New York: Routledge, 1995.

Benthem, Henrich Ludolff. *Engeländischer Kirch- und Schulen-Staat*. Lüneburg, 1694.

Benthem, Henrich Ludolff. *Holländischer Kirch- und Schulen-Staat*. 2 Vols. Merseburg, 1698.

Benthem, Henrich Ludolph. *Pacifici Verini ohnmaßgebliches Bedencken, ob und wie die heutiges Tages gesuchte Vereinigung derer, welche die ohnveränderte Augspurgische Confession angenommen, mit den übrigen diene zum Wohlstande der Kirche Christi*. 1700.

Bentzen, Siegfried. *Christianus minime christianus, oder das Eben-Bild Christian Thomasii*. Ratzeburg, 1692.

Benzoni, Gino. 'Ranke's Favorite Source: The Venetian Relazioni. Impressions with Allusions to Later Historiography'. In *Leopold von Ranke and the Shaping of the Historical Discipline*, edited by Georg G. Iggers and James M. Powell, 45–57. Syracuse: Syracuse University Press, 1990.

Berg, Günter. *Leopold Ranke als akademischer Lehrer: Studien zu seinen Vorlesungen und seinem Geschichtsdenken*. Göttingen: Vandenhoeck und Ruprecht, 1968.

Berkvens-Stevelinck, Christinane, Jonathan Israel and G.H.M. Posthumus Meyjes, eds. *The Emergence of Tolerance in the Dutch Republic*. Brill: Leiden, 1997.

Bientjes, Julia. *Holland und der Holländer im Urteil deutscher Reisender 1400–1800*. Gronningen: J. B. Wolters, 1967.

Bierling, Friedrick Wilhelm. *Commentatio de pyrrhonismo historico*. Leipzig, 1724.

Bittner, Ludwig, ed. *Gesamtinventar des Wiener Haus-, Hof- und Staatsarchivs*, vol. 1. Vienna: Holzhausen, 1936.

Blanke, Horst Walter and Dirk Fleischer, eds. *Theoretiker der deutschen Aufklärungshistorie*. 2 Vols. Stuttgart: Frommann-Holzboog, 1990.

Boell, Carl. *Sendschreiben über die Anfrage in was für einem Zustand sich die Rechtsgelehrsamkeit auf der blühenden Georg Augusta befinde*. Colmar, 1775.

Böhm, Benno. *Sokrates im 18. Jahrhundert*. Neumünster: Wachholtz, 1966.

Boockmann, Hartmut. 'Geschichtsunterricht und Geschichtsstudium in Göttigen'. In *Geschichtswissenschaft in Göttingen: Eine Vorlesungsreihe*, edited by Hartmut Boockmann and Hermann Wellenreuter, 161–85. Göttingen: Wandenhoeck und Ruprecht, 1987.

Brewer, John and Silvia Sebastiani, eds. 'Closeness and Distance in the Age of Enlightenment'. Forum section in *Modern Intellectual History* 11, no. 3 (2014).

vom Brocke, Bernhard. 'Wege aus der Krise: Universitätsseminar, Akademiekommission oder Forschungsinstitut. Formen der Institutionalisierung in den Geistes- und Naturwissenschaften 1810–1900–1995'. In *Konkurrenten in der Fakultät. Kultur, Wissen und Universität um 1900*, edited by Christoph König and Eberhard Lämmert, 191–218. Frankfurt am Main: Fischer, 1999.

vom Brocke, Bernhard. 'Die Entstehung der deutschen Forschungsuniversität ihre Blüte und Krise um 1900'. In *Humboldt International: Der Export des deutschen Universitätsmodells*, edited by Rainer Christoph Schwinges, 367–401. Basel: Schwabe, 2001.

Brühl, Carlrichard. 'Die Entwicklung der diplomatischen Methode im Zusammenhang mit dem Erkennen von Fälschungen'. In *Fälschungen im Mittelalter. Internationale Kongreß der Monumenta Germaniae Historica*, edited by Detlev Jasper, vol. 3, 11–27. Hannover: Hahnsche Buchhandlung, 1988.

vom Bruch, Rüdiger. 'Mommsen und Harnack: Die Geburt von Big Science aus den Geisteswissenschaften'. In *Theodor Mommsen. Wissenschaft und Politik im 19. Jahrhundert*, edited by Alexander Demandt, Andreas Goltz and Heinrich Schlange-Schöningen, 121–41. Berlin: De Gruyter, 2005.

Bunge, Wien van. *The Early Enlightenment in the Dutch Republic, 1650–1750*. Leiden: Brill, 2003.

Bursian, Conrad. 'Klotz, Christian Adolph'. In *Allgemeine Deutsche Biographie*, vol. 16, 228–31. Leipzig, 1882.

Busson, Arnold. *Die Doppelwahl des Jahres 1257 und das römische Königthum Alfons X. von Castilien*. Münster, 1866.

Butterfield, Herbert. *The Whig Interpretation of History*. New York: Norton, 1965.

Cahan, David, ed. *From Natural Philosophy to the Sciences: Writing the History of Nineteenth Century Science*. Chicago: Chicago University Press, 2003.

Carhart, Michael C. *The Science of Culture in Enlightenment Germany*. Cambridge: Harvard University Press, 2007.

Cassius, Georg Andreas. *Ausführliche Lebensbeschreibung des um die gelehrte Welt Hochverdienten D. Christoph August Heumanns*. Kassel, 1768.

de Certeau, Michel. *The Writing of History*, translated by Tom Conly. New York: Columbia University Press, 1992.

Chakrabarty, Dipesh. *Provincializing Europe: Postcolonial Thought and Historical Difference*. Princeton: Princeton University Press, 2000.

Clark, William. 'On the Dialectical Origins of the Research Seminar'. *History of Science* 27, no. 2 (1989): 111–54.

Clark, William. *Academic Charisma and the Origins of the Research University*. Chicago: University of Chicago Press, 2006.

Condren, Conal, Stephen Gaukroger and Ian Hunter, eds. *The Philosopher in Early Modern Europe: The Nature of a Contested Identity*. Cambridge: Cambridge University Press, 2006.

Creyghton, Camille, Pieter Huistra, Sarah Keymeulen and Herman Paul. 'Virtue language in historical scholarship: the cases of Georg Waitz, Gabriel Monod, and Henri Pirenne'. *History of European Ideas* 42, no. 7 (2016): 924–36.

Daston, Lorraine. *Classical Probability in the Enlightenment*. Princeton: Princeton University Press, 1988.

Deichsel, Johann Gottlieb. 'Reise durch Deutschland nach Holland und England in den Jahren 1717–1719'. *Johann Bernoulli's Archiv zur neuern Geschichte, Geographie, Natur- und Menschenkenntniß* 3 (1786): 137–88 and 7 (1787): 151–212.

Descartes, René. 'Discourse on the Method of Rightly Conducting One's Reason and Seeking Truth in the Sciences'. In idem, *The Philosophical Writings*, edited and translated by John Cottingham, Robert Stoothoff and Dugald Murdoch, vol. 1, 111–51. Cambridge: Cambridge University Press, 1985.

Dilthey, Wilhelm. *Einleitung in die Geisteswissenschaften: Versuch einer Grundlegung für das Studium der Gesellschaft und der Geschichte*. Leipzig, 1883.

Dilthey, Wilhelm. *Aufbau der geschichtlichen Welt in den Geisteswissenschaften*. Berlin: Königliche Akademie der Wissenschaften, 1910.

von Döllinger, Ignaz. *Die Universitäten sonst und jetzt*. Munich, 1867.

Dorn, Barbara. *Friedrich von Gentz und Europa: Studien zu Stabilität und Revolution 1802-1822*. PhD diss., University of Bonn, 1993.

Dotterweich, Volker. *Heinrich von Sybel. Geschichtswissenschaft in politischer Absicht (1817–1861)*. Göttingen: Vandenhoeck und Ruprecht, 1978.

Dreitzel, Horst. 'Zur Entwicklung und Eigenart der "eklektischen Philosophie"'. *Zeitschrift für historische Forschung* 18 (1991): 281–343.

von Dreyhaupt, Johann Christoph. *Pagus neletici et nudzici, oder ausführliche diplomatisch-historische Beschreibung des zum ehemaligen Primat und Ertz-Stifft, nunmehr aber durch den westphälischen Friedens-Schluss secularisirten Hertzogthum Magdeburg gehörigen Saal-Creÿses, und aller darinnen befindlichen Städte, Schlösser, Aemter*. 2 Vols. Halle, 1755.

Droysen, Johann Gustav. *Grundriss der Historik*. Leipzig, 1868.

von Druffel, August. *Kaiser Heinrich IV. und seine Söhne*. Regensburg, 1862.
Durchhardt, Heinz, Matthias Schnettger and Martin Vogt, eds. *Der Friede von Rijswijk 1697*. Mainz: Philipp von Zabern, 1998.
Elias, Norbert. *Die höfische Gesellschaft. Untersuchungen zur Soziologie des Königtums und der höfischen Aristokratie*. 1969. Reprinted. Frankfurt am Main: Suhrkamp, 1997.
Engel, Johann. 'Die deutschen Universitäten und die Geschichtswissenschaft'. *Historische Zeitschrift* 189, no. 1 (1959): 223–378.
Engfer, Hans-Jürgen. 'Christian Thomasius: Erste Proklamation und erste Krise der Aufklärung in Deutschland'. In *Christian Thomasius 1655–1728: Interpretation zu Werk und Wirkung*, edited by Werner Schneiders, 21–36. Hamburg: Meiner, 1989.
Ernst, Wolfgang. *Im Namen der Geschichte: Sammeln – Speichern- Er/Zählen. Infrastrukturelle Konfigurationen des deutschen Gedächtnisses*. Munich: Wilhelm Fink Verlag, 2003.
Eskildsen, Kasper Risbjerg. 'The Language of Objects: Christian Jürgensen Thomsen's Science of the Past'. *Isis* 103, no. 1 (2012): 24–53.
Eskildsen, Kasper Risbjerg. 'Inventing the Archive: Testimony and Virtue in Modern Historiography'. *History of the Human Sciences* 26, no. 3 (2013): 8–26.
Eskildsen, Kasper Risbjerg. 'Scholarship as a Way of Life: Character and Virtue in the Age of Big Humanities'. *History of the Humanities* 1, no. 2 (2016): 387–97.
Eskildsen, Kasper Risbjerg. 'Leopold von Ranke (1795–1886): Criticizing an Early Modern Historian'. *History of Humanities* 4, no. 2 (2019): 257–62.
Eskildsen, Kasper Risbjerg. 'Fälschung'. In *Enzyklopädie der Genauigkeit*, edited by Markus Krajewski, Antonia von Schöning and Mario Wimmer, 130–9. Konstanz: Konstanz University Press, 2021.
Fasolt, Constantin. *The Limits of History*. Chicago: University of Chicago Press, 2004.
Fisch, Johann. 'Zivilisation, Kultur'. In *Geschichtliche Grundbegriffe*, edited by Otto Brunner, Werner Conze and Reinhart Koselleck, vol. 7, 679–774. Stuttgart: Klett-Cotta, 1992.
Fisch, Stefan. 'Auf dem Weg zur Aufklärungshistorie: Prozesse des Wandels in der protestantischen Historiographie'. *Geschichte und Gesellschaft* 23, no. 1 (1997): 115–33.
Forster, Leonard. "Charlataneria eruditorum' zwischen Barock und Aufklärung in Deutschland'. In *Res Publica Literaria: Die Institution der Gelehrsamkeit in der frühen Neuzeit*, edited by Sebastian Neumeister and Conrad Wiedemann, vol. 1, 203–20. Wiesbaden: Harrassowitz, 1987.
Franke, Konrad. 'Zacharias Conrad von Uffenbach als Handschriftensammler: Ein Beitrag zur Kulturgeschichte des 18. Jahrhunderts'. *Börsenblatt für den Deutschen Buchhandel – Franfurter Ausgabe* 51 (July 29, 1965): 1235–338.

Fredericq, Paul. *L'Enseignement supérieur de l'histoire: Notes et impressions de voyage.* Gent, 1899.

Frensdorff, Ferdinand. 'Georg Waitz'. In *Allgemeine Deutsche Biographie*, vol. 40, 602–29. Leipzig, 1886.

Fueter, Eduard. *Geschichte der neueren Historiographie.* Munich: Oldenbourg, 1936.

Fulda, Daniel. *Wissenschaft aus Kunst: Die Entstehung der modernen deutschen Geschichtsschreibung, 1760–1860.* Berlin: De Gruyter, 1996.

Fulda, Daniel. 'Sattelzeit. Karriere und Problematik eines kulturwissenschaftlichen Zentralbegriffs'. In *Sattelzeit: Historiographiegeschichtliche Revisionen*, edited by Elisabeth Décultot and Daniel Fulda, 1–16. Berlin: De Gruyter, 2016.

Fustel de Coulanges, Numa Denis. 'Da la manière d'écrire l'historie en France et en Allemagne depuis cinquante ans'. *Revue des Deux Mondes* 101 (September 1, 1872): 241–51.

Garber, Daniel. 'Philosophia, Historia, Mathematica: Shifting Sands in the Disciplinary Geography of the Seventeenth Century'. In *Scientia in Early Modern Philosophy: Seventeenth-Century Thinkers on Demonstrative Knowledge from First Principles*, edited by Tom Sorell, G.A.J Rogers and jill Kraye, 1–17. Dordrecht: Springer, 2010.

Gatterer, Johann Christoph. *Elementa artis diplomaticae universalis.* Göttingen, 1765a.

Gatterer, Johann Christoph. *Handbuch der Universalhistorie nach ihrem gesamten Umfange*, vol. 1. Göttingen, 1765b.

Gatterer, Johann Christoph. 'Zufällige Gedanken über die teutsche Geschichte'. *Allgemeine historische Bibliothek* 2 (1767a): 23–34.

Gatterer, Johann Christoph. 'Vorrede von der Evidenz in der Geschichtskunde'. In *Die Allgemeine Welthistorie die in England durch eine Gesellschaft von Gelehrten ausgefertiget worden: In einem vollständigen und pragmatischen Auszuge*, edited by F. E. Boysen, vol. 1, 1–38. Halle, 1767b.

Gatterer, Johann Christoph. 'Abhandlung vom Standort und Gesichtspunct des Geschichtschreibers oder der teutsche Livius'. *Allgemeine historische Bibliothek* 5 (1768a): 3–29.

Gatterer, Johann Christoph. 'Nähere Nachricht von der neuen Ausgabe der gleichzeitigen Schriftsteller über die Teutsche Geschichte'. *Allgemeine Historische Bibliothek* 8 (1768b): 3–22.

Gatterer, Johann Christoph. 'Vorrede'. *Historisches Journal* 1 (1772): unpag.

Gatterer, Johann Christoph. *Abriss der Diplomatik.* Göttingen, 1798.

Gatterer, Johann Christoph. *Praktische Diplomatik.* Göttingen, 1799.

von Gentz, Friedrich. *Briefe von und an Friedrich von Gentz*, edited by Friedrich Carl Wittichen, vol. 1. Munich: Oldenbourg, 1909.

Gerlach, Hans-Martin, ed. *Christian Wolff: Seine Schule und seine Gegner*. Hamburg: Meiner, 2001.

Gierl, Martin. 'Das Alphabet der Natur und das Alphabet der Kultur im 18. Jahrhundert: Botanik, Diplomatik, Linguistik und Etnographie nach Carl von Linné, Johann Christop Gatterer und Christian Wilhelm Büttner'. *NMT Zeitschrift für Geschichte der Wissenschaften, Technik und Medizin* 18 (2010): 1–27.

Gierl, Martin. *Geschichte als präzisierte Wissenschaft: Johann Christoph Gatterer und die Historiographie des 18. Jahrhunderts im ganzen Umfang*. Stuttgart: Fromman-Holzboog, 2012.

Gierl, Martin. 'Change of Paradigm as a Squabble Between Institutions: The Institute of Historical Sciences, the Society of Sciences, and the Separation of Cultural and Natural Sciences in Göttingen in the Second Half of the Eighteenth Century'. In *Scholars in Action: The Practice of Knowledge and the Figure of the Savant in the Eighteenth Century*, edited by André Holenstein, Hubert Steinke and Martin Stuber, vol. 2, 267–87. Leiden: Brill, 2013.

von Giesebrecht, Wilhelm. *Gedächtnissrede auf Leopold von Ranke*. Munich, 1887.

Goulbourne, Russell. 'Voltaire's Socrates'. In *Socrates from Antiquity to the Enlightenment*, edited by Michael Trapp, 229–47. London: Ashgate, 2007.

Grafton, Anthony. *The Footnote: A Curious History*. Cambridge: Harvard University Press, 1999.

Grafton, Anthony. *What was History? The Art of History in Early Modern Europe*. Cambridge: Cambridge University Press, 2007.

Grafton, Anthony. 'In Clio's American Atelier'. In *Social Knowledge in the Making*, edited by Charles Camic, Neil Gross und Michèle Lamont, 89–117. Chicago: University of Chicago Press, 2011.

Grauert, Hermann. 'Georg Waitz'. In idem, *Historisches Jahrbuch: Im Auftrage der Görres-Gesellschaft*, vol. 8, 48–100. Munich, 1887.

Gruber, Johann Daniel. 'Hofrath J. D. Gruber an Gerl. Adolf von Münchhausen über den Zustand und die Blüthe der deutschen Universitäten'. In *Die Gründung der Universität Göttingen: Entwürfe, Berichte und Briefe der Zeitgenossen*, edited by E. F. Rössler, 458–67. Göttingen, 1855.

Grunert, Frank. 'Zur Aufgeklärten Kritik am theokratischen Absolutismus. Der Streit zwischen Hector Gottfried Masius und Christian Thomasius über Ursprung und Begründung der summa potestas'. In *Christian Thomasius (1655–1728): Neue Forschungen im Kontext der Frühaufklärung*, edited by Friedrich Vollhardt, 51–78. Tübingen: Niemeyer, 1997.

Gundling, Nikolaus Hieronymus. *Ausfürlicher und vollständiger Discours über dessen Abriß einer Rechten Reichs-Historie*. Frankfurt am Main, 1732.

Gundling, Nikolaus Hieronymus. 'Vorbericht zu denen Winter-lectionen'. In idem, *Sammlung kleiner teutscher Schriften*, vol. 1, 94–142. Halle, 1737.

Günter, H. 'Das historische Seminar'. In *Die wissenschaftlichen Anstalten der Ludwig-Maximilians-Universität zu München*, edited by Karl Alexander von Müller, 193–9. Munich: De Gruyter, 1926.

Gurlitt, J. *Ueber die Gemmenkunde: Zur Ankündigung einer Schulfeierlichkeit im Kloster Bergen*. Magdeburg: Kloster Bergen, 1798.

Hadler, Frank, Gabriele Lingelbach and Matthias Middell, eds. *Historische Institute im internationalen Vergleich*. Leipzig: AVA, 2001.

Hadot, Pierre. *Qu'est-ce que la philosophie antique?* Paris: Gallimard, 1995.

Hamann, Julian. 'Boundary Work Between Two Cultures: Demarcating the Modern Geisteswissenschaften'. *History of Humanities* 3, no. 1 (2018): 27–38.

Hammerstein, Notker. *Jus und Historie: Ein Beitrag zur Geschichte des historischen Denkens an deutschen Universitäten im späten 17. und 18. Jahrhundert*. Göttingen: Vandenhoeck und Ruprecht, 1972.

Hammerstein, Notker. 'Reichs-Historie'. In *Aufklärung und Geschichte: Studien zur deutschen Geschichtswissenschaft im 18. Jahrhundert*, edited by Hans Erich Bödeker, Georg G. Iggers, Jonathan B. Knudsen and Peter Hanns Reill, 82–104. Göttingen: Vandenhoeck und Ruprecht, 1986.

Hansson, Ulf R. 'Die Quelle des guten Geschmacks ist nun geöffnet: Philipp Daniel Lipperts Dactyliotheca Universalis'. In *Tankemönster. En festskrift till Eva Rystedt*, edited by Fanni Faegersten, Jenny Wallensten and Ida Östenberg, 92–101. Lund: Faegersten, 2010.

Harbsmeier, Michael. 'World histories before domestication: The writing of universal histories, histories of mankind and world histories in late eighteenth-century Germany'. *Culture and History* 5 (1989): 93–131.

Harloe, Katherine. *Winckelmann and the Invention of Antiquity: History and Aesthetics in the Age of Altertumswissenschaft*. Oxford: Oxford University Press, 2013.

Hartmann, Andreas. 'Reisen und Aufschreiben'. In *Reisekultur: Von Pilgerfahrt zum modernen Tourismus*, edited by Hermann Bausinger, Klaus Beyrer and Gottfried Korff, 152–9. Munich: C. H. Beck, 1991.

Hartog, François. *Regimes of Historicity: Presentism and Experiences of Time*, translated by Saskia Brown. New York: Columbia University Press, 2015.

Hausen, Carl Renatus. *Pragmatische Geschichte der Protestanten in Deutschland*. Halle, 1767.

Heimpel, Hermann. 'Über Organisationsformen historischer Forschung in Deutschland'. *Historische Zeitschrift* 189 (1959): 139–222.

Heine, Heinrich. 'Französische Zustände'. In idem, *Historisch-kritische Gesamtausgabe der Werke*, edited by Manfred Windfuhr, vol. 12:1, edited by Jean-René Derré and Christiane Giesen, 63–226. Hamburg: Hoffmann und Campe, 1980.

Herder, Johann Gottfried. *Ueber die neuere Deutsche Litteratur: Fragmente*. 2 Vols. Riga, 1767.

Herder, Johann Gottfried. *Kritische Wälder: oder einige Betrachtungen über die Wissenschaft und Kunst der Schönen*. 3 Vols. Riga, 1769.

Herder, Johann Gottfried. *Briefe: Gesamtausgabe 1763–1803*, edited by Wilhelm Dobbek and Günter Arnold, vol. 1: *Briefe. April 1763–April 1771*, Weimar: Hermann Böhlaus Nachfolger, 1977.

Heumann, Christoph August. 'Der Einleitung zur Historia Philosophica. Das 1. Capitel/ von deren Nutzbarkeit'. *Acta philosophorum, das ist: Gründl. Nachrichten aus der historia philosophica, nebst beygefügten Urtheilen von denen dahin gehörigen alten und neuen Büchern* 1, no. 1 (1715a): 1–63.

Heumann, Christoph August. 'Ehren-Rettung der Xanthippe'. *Acta philosophorum, das ist: Gründl. Nachrichten aus der historia philosophica, nebst beygefügten Urtheilen von denen dahin gehörigen alten und neuen Büchern* 1, no. 1 (1715b): 103–25.

Heumann, Christoph August. 'Der Einleitung zur Historia Philosophica. Sechstes Capitel von dem Ingenio Philosophico'. *Acta philosophorum, das ist: Gründl. Nachrichten aus der historia philosophica, nebst beygefügten Urtheilen von denen dahin gehörigen alten und neuen Büchern* 1, no. 4 (1716): 567–670.

Heumann, Christoph August. *Conspectus reipublicae literariae sive via ad historiam literariam iuventuti studiosae aperta*. Hanover, 1718.

Heumann, Christoph August. *Erweiß daß die Lehre der Reformirten Kirche von dem Heil. Abendmahle die rechte und wahre sey*. Eisleben, 1764.

Heussi, Karl. *Die Krisis des Historismus*. Tübingen: J. C. B Mohr, 1932.

Heyne, Christian Gottlob. *Einleitung in das Studium der Antike, oder Grundriß einer Anführung zur Kenntniß der alten Kunstwerke*. Göttingen, 1772.

Heyne, Christian Gottlob. 'Vorrede'. In Johann Gottfried von Herder, *Sämmtliche Werke zur schönen Literatur und Kunst*, vol. 1, 24–30. Stuttgart, 1827.

Hildebrand, Herman. *Die Chronik Heinrichs von Lettland. Ein Beitrag zu Livlands Historiographie und Geschichte*. Berlin, 1865.

Hirsch, Siegfried and Georg Waitz. 'Kritische Prüfung der Echtheit und des historischen Wertes des Chronicon Corbejense'. In *Jahrbücher des Deutschen Reichs unter dem Sächsischen Hause*, edited by Leopold Ranke, vol. 3, no. 1, v–viii and 1–139. Berlin, 1839.

Hochstrasser, T. J. *Natural Law Theories in the Early Enlightenment*. Cambridge: Cambridge University Press, 2000.

Hoffbauer, Johann Christoph. *Geschichte der Universität zu Halle bis zum Jahre 1805*. Halle, 1805.

Holzhey, Helmut. 'Initiert Thomasius einen neuen Philosophentypus?' In *Christian Thomasius 1655–1728: Interpretation zu Werk und Wirkung*, edited by Werner Schneiders, 37–51. Hamburg: Meiner, 1989.

Hübinger, Paul Egon. *Das historische Seminar der rheinischen Friedrich-Wilhelms-Universität zu Bonn*. Bonn: Röhrscheid, 1963.

Hull, William I. *William Sewel of Amsterdam 1654–1720: The first Quaker historian of Quakerism*. Philadelphia: Paterson and White Company, 1933.

Hunter, Ian. *Rival Enlightenments: Civil and Metaphysical Philosophy in Early Modern Germany*. Cambridge: Cambridge University Press, 2001.

Hunter, Ian. 'The University Philosopher in Early Modern Germany'. In *The Philosopher in Early Modern Europe: The Nature of a Contested Identity*, edited by Conal Condren, Stephen Gaukroger and Ian Hunter, 35–65. Cambridge: Cambridge University Press, 2006.

Hunter, Ian. *The Secularisation of the Confessional State: The Political Thought of Christian Thomasius*. Cambridge: Cambridge University Press, 2007.

Huttner, Markus. 'Historische Gesellschaften und die Entstehung historischer Seminare: Zu den Anfängen institutionalisierter Geschichtsstudien an den deutschen Universitäten des 19. Jahrhunderts'. In *Historische Institute im internationalen Vergleich*, edited by Frank Hadler, Gabriele Lingelbach and Matthias Middell, 39–83. Leipzig: AVA, 2001.

Iggers, Georg G. 'The Image of Ranke in American and German Historical Thought'. *History and Theory* 2, no. 1 (1962): 17–40.

Iggers, Georg G. *The German Conception of History: The National Tradition of Historical Thought from Herder to the Present*. Middletown, CT: Wesleyan University Press, 1968.

Israel, Jonathan. *The Dutch Republic: Its Rise, Greatness, and Fall, 1477–1806*. Oxford: Clarendon Press, 1995.

Israel, Jonathan. *Radical Enlightenment: Philosophy and the Making of Modernity 1650–1750*. Oxford: Oxford University Press, 2001.

Israel, Jonathan. *Enlightenment Contested: Philosophy, Modernity, and the Emancipation of Man 1670–1752*. Oxford: Oxford University Press, 2006.

Jaeger, Friedrich and Jörn Rüsen. *Geschichte des Historismus: Eine Einführung*. Munich: C. H. Beck, 1992.

Jarausch, Konrad H. *Deutsche Studenten, 1800–1970*. Frankfurt am Main: Suhrkamp, 1984.

Jarausch, Konrad H. 'The Institutionalization of History in 18th-Century Germany'. In *Aufklärung und Geschichte: Studien zur deutschen Geschichtswissenschaft im 18. Jahrhundert*, edited by Hans Erich Bödeker, Georg G. Iggers, Jonathan B. Knudsen and Peter H. Reill, 26–48. Göttingen: Vandenhock und Ruprecht, 1986.

Jarausch, Konrad H. 'Universität und Hochschule'. In *Handbuch der deutschen Bildungsgeschichte, vol. 4: 1870–1918. Von Reichsgründung bis zum Ende des Ersten Weltkriegs*, edited by Christa Berg, 313–45. Munich: C.H. Beck, 1991.

Jardine, Nicholas. 'Naturphilosophie and the Kingdoms of Nature'. In *Cultures of Natural History*, edited by Nicholas Jardine, James A. Secord and E. C. Spary, 230–45. Cambridge: Cambridge University Press, 1996.

Jardine, Nicholas. *The Scenes of Inquiry: On the Reality of Questions in the Sciences*. Oxford: Oxford University Press, 2000.

Jones, Matthew L. *The Good Life in the Scientific Revolution: Descartes, Pascal, Leibniz, and the Cultivation of Virtue*. Chicago: University of Chicago Press, 2006.

Junghans, Wilhelm. *Die Geschichte der fränkischen Könige Childerich und Chlodevech, kritisch untersucht*. Göttingen, 1857.

Justi, Carl. *Winckelmann und seine Zeitgenossen*. 3 Vols. Cologne: Phaidon, 1956.

Kahlert, Torsten. '"Große Projekte": Mommsens Traum und der Diskurs um Big Science und Großforschung'. In *Wissenskulturen: Bedingungen wissenschaftlicher Innovation*, edited by Harald Müller and Florian Eßer, 67–86. Kassel: Kassel University Press, 2012.

Kaiser, David, ed. *Pedagogy and the Practice of Science. Historical and Contemporary Perspectices*. Cambridge: MIT Press, 2005.

Kammerhofer, Leopold. 'Die Gründung des Haus-, Hof- und Staatsarchivs 1749'. In *Speicher des Gedächtnisses: Bibliotheken, Museen, Archive, vol. 2: Die Erfindung des Ursprungs, die Systematisierung der Zeit*, edited by Moritz Csáky, 81–99. Vienna: Passagen Verlag, 2001.

Kannegieter, J. Z. *Geschiedenis van de vroegere quakergemeenschap te Amsterdam 1656 tot begin negentiende eeuw*. Amsterdam: Scheltema en Holkema, 1971.

Kerschner, Christina. 'Philipp Daniel Lippert (1702–1785) und seine Daktyliothek zum "Nutzen der Schönen Künste und Künstler"'. In *Daktyliotheken: Götter und Caesaren aus der Schublade: antike Gemmen in Abdrucksammlungen des 18. und 19. Jahrhunderts, Daktyliotheken*, edited by Valentin Kockel, Daniel Graepler and Gergana Angelova, 60–8. Munich: Biering und Brinkmann, 2006a.

Kerschner, Christina and Valentin Kockel. 'Die Editionsgeschichte der Lippertschen Daktyliotheken'. In *Daktyliotheken: Götter und Caesaren aus der Schublade: antike Gemmen in Abdrucksammlungen des 18. und 19. Jahrhunderts, Daktyliotheken*, edited by Valentin Kockel, Daniel Graepler and Gergana Angelova, 69–75. Munich: Biering und Brinkmann, 2006b.

Kertscher, Hans-Joachim. '"Klotz und die Klotzianer" als Autoren des halleschen Gebauer-Verlags'. In idem, *Literatur und Kultur in Zeitalter der Aufklärung: Aufsätze zum geselligen Leben in einer deutschen Universitätsstadt*, 381–96. Hamburg: Kovac, 2007.

Klotz, Christian Adolph. *Mores eruditorum*. N. p., 1760.

Klotz, Christian Adolph. *Genius seculi*. Altenburg, n. d.

Klotz, Christian Adolph. 'Iohann Winckelmanns, Praesidentens der Alterthümer zu Rom, und Scrittore der vaticanischen Bibliothek &c, Geschichte der Kunst des Alterthums'. *Acta Litteraria* 1, no. 3 (1764): 336–53.

Klotz, Christian Adolph. 'Dresden'. *Göttingsche Anzeigen von Gelehrten Sachen* 33/34 (1765): 265–79.

Klotz, Christian Adolph. *Ueber das Studium des Alterthums*. Halle, 1766.

Klotz, Christian Adolph. *Beytrag zur Geschichte des Geschmacks und der Kunst aus Münzen*. Altenburg, 1767.

Klotz, Christian Adolph. *Ueber den Nutzen und Gebrauch der alten geschnittenen Steine und ihre Abdrücke*. Altenburg, 1768.

Kluckhohn, August. *Geschichte des Gottesfriedens*. Leipzig, 1857.

Kniggen, Hermann. 'Lebens-Lauf des Wohlseeligen Herrn General-Superintendenten'. In Henrich Ludolph Benthem, *Vorstellung und Betrachtung der Schrifften der alten Kirchen-Lehrer von der Wahrheit und Göttlichkeit Christlicher Religion*, unpag. Hamburg, 1727.

Knochenhauer, Theodor. *Geschichte Thüringens in der karolingischen und sächsischen Zeit*. Gotha, 1863.

Kohler, Robert E. 'Place and Practice in Field Biology'. *History of Science* 40, no. 2 (2002a): 189–210.

Kohler, Robert E. *Landscapes and Labscapes: Exploring the Field-Lab Boundary*. Chicago: University of Chicago Press, 2002b.

Kohler, Robert E. and Henrika Kuklick. 'Introduction'. *Osiris* 11 (1996): 1–14.

Koselleck, Reinhart. 'Einleitung'. In *Geschichtliche Grundbegriffe*, edited by Otto Brunner, Werner Conze and Reinhart Koselleck, vol. 1, xiii–xxvii. Stuttgart: Ernst Klett Verlag, 1972.

Koselleck, Reinhart. *Vergangener Zukunft: Zur Semantik geschichtlicher Zeiten*. Frankfurt am Main: Suhrkamp, 1979.

Koser, Reinhold, ed. *Die Neuordnung des Preussischen Archivwesens durch den Staatskanzler Fürsten von Hardenberg*. Leipzig: Hirzel, 1904.

Kronenbitter, Günther. *Wort und Macht: Friedrich Gentz als politischer Schriftsteller*. Berlin: Duncker und Humblot, 1994.

Lämmermann, Christoph August. 'Litterarische Anekdoten, die Elzevirische Buchdruckerey in Leiden, und die beiden dasigen Gelehrten, Herm. Boerhave und Thom. Crenius'. *Historisch-litterarisch-bibliographisches Magazin* 3, no. 6 (1792): 99–109.

Landfester, Rüdiger. *Historia magistra vitæ: Untersuchungen zur humanistischen Geschichtstheorie des 14. bis 16. Jahrhunderts*. Geneva: Droz, 1972.

Landgren, Per. *Det aristoteliska historiebegreppet: Historieteori i renässansens Europa och Sverige*. Gothenburg: Acta Universitatis Gothoburgensis, 2008.

Latour, Bruno. *Science in Action: How to Follow Scientists and Engineers Through Society*. Cambridge: Harvard University Press, 1987.

von Laue, Theodore H. *Leopold Ranke: The Formative Years*. Princeton: Princeton University Press, 1950.

Lehmann-Brauns, Sicco. *Weisheit der Weltgeschichte: Philosophiegeschichte zwischen Barock und Aufklärung*. Tübingen: Max Niemeyer Verlag, 2004.

Lenhard-Schramm, Niklas. *Konstrukteure der Nation: Geschichtsprofessoren als politische Akteure in Vormärz und Revolution 1848/9*. Münster: Waxmann, 2014.

Lenz, Max. *Geschichte der Königlichen Friedrich-Wilhelms-Universität zu Berlin, vol. 3: Wissenschaftlichen Anstalten*. Halle: Buchhandlung des Waisenhauses, 1910.

Leporin, Christian Polycarp. *Germania literata vivens, oder das jetzt lebende Gelehrte Deutschland*. Quedlinburg, 1724.

Lessing, Gotthold Ephraim. *Laokoon: oder über die Grenzen der Mahlerey und Poesie*. Berlin, 1766.

Lessing, Gotthold Ephraim. *Briefe, antiquarischen Inhalts*. 2 Vols. Berlin, 1768–1769.

Lifschitz, Avi. *Language and Enlightenment: The Berlin Debates of the Eighteenth Century* Oxford: Oxford University Press, 2012.

Lippert, Philipp Daniel. *Dactyliothecae universalis signorum*. 3 Vols. Leipzig, 1755–62.

Lippert, Philipp Daniel. *Dactyliothec: Das ist Sammlung geschnittener Steine der Alten aus denen vornehmsten Museis in Europa zum Nutzen der schönen Künste und Künstler*. 2 Vols. Leipzig, 1767.

Lingelbach, Gabriele. *Klio macht Karriere: Die Institutionalisierung der Geschichtswissenschaft in Frankreich und den USA in der zweiten Hälfte des 19. Jahrhunderts*. Göttingen: Vandenhoeck und Ruprecht, 2003.

Livingstone, David. *Putting Science in Its Place: Geographies of Scientific Knowledge*. Chicago: University of Chicago Press, 2003.

Lorenz, Chris and Berber Bevernage, eds. *Breaking up Time: Negotiating the Borders between Present, Past and Future*. Göttingen: Vandenhoeck und Ruprecht, 2013.

Lotz-Heumann, Ute and Matthias Pohlig. 'Confessionalization and Literature in the Empire, 1555–1700'. *Central European History* 40, no. 1 (2007): 35–61.

von Ludewig, Johann Peter. 'Gebrauch und Mißbrauch der Zeitungen/ bey Eröffnung eines collegii geführt. Anno 1700'. In idem, *Gesamte kleine teutsche Schriften*, 80–111. Halle, 1705a.

von Ludewig, Johann Peter. 'Über die Riswikische Friedens-Handlung und dessen Instrumentum wird der Studirenden Jugend ein collegium eröffnet. Anno 1698'. In idem, *Gesamte kleine teutsche Schriften*, 321–35. Halle, 1705b.

von Ludewig, Johann Peter. 'Zulängliche Antwort auf die liederlige Zunöthigung Herrn Tobias Pfanners'. In idem, *Gesamte kleine teutsche Schriften*, 358–409. Halle, 1705c.

von Ludewig, Johann Peter. *Vollständige Erläuterung der Güldenen Bulle*. 2 Vols. Frankfurt am Mail, 1716–9.

von Ludewig, Johann Peter. 'Praefatio'. In idem, *Opuscula miscella*, 13–36. Halle, 1720.

von Ludewig, Johann Peter. *Reliquiae manuscriptorum omnis aevi*. 12 Vols. Frankfurt am Main, 1720–41.

von Ludewig, Johann Peter. *Rechtliche Erleuterung der Reichs-Historie von erstem Ursprung biß 1734*. Halle, 1735.

von Ludewig, Johann Peter. 'Auswertiger Todes-Fall des Heßischen Cantzlers, Wilhelm Ludewigs von Maskowsky'. In idem, *Gelehrte Anzeigen, in alle Wissenschaften, so wol geistlicher als weltlicher, alter und neuer Sachen*, vol. 1, 337–9. Halle, 1743.

von Ludewig, Johann Peter. *Erläuterte Germania Princeps, das ist: Historisch-Politisch- und Rechtliche Anmerckungen über desselben Teutsche Fürsten-Staaten*, edited by H. von Finsterwald. Frankfurt am Main, 1744.

Mackenney, Richard. "A Plot Discover'd.' Myth, Legend, and the 'Spanish' Conspiracy against Venice in 1618'. In *Venice Reconsidered: The History and Civilization of an Italian City-State 1297–1797*, edited by John Jeffries Martin and Dennis Romano, 185–216. Baltimore: Johns Hopkins University Press, 2000.

Mager, Inger. 'Die theologische Lehrfreiheit in Göttingen und ihre Grenzen: Der Abendmahlskonflikt um Christian August Heumann'. In *Theologie in Göttingen: Eine Vorlesungsreihe*, edited by B. Moeller, 41–57. Göttingen: Vandenhoeck und Ruprecht, 1987.

Mannheim, Karl. 'Historismus'. In idem, *Wissenssoziologie: Auswahl aus dem Werk*, edited by Kurt H. Wolff, 246–307. 1964. Reprinted. Neuwied am Rhein: Luchterhand, 1970.

Marshall, John. *John Locke, Toleration and Early Enlightenment Culture: Religious Intolerance and Arguments for Religious Toleration in Early Modern and 'Early Enlightenment' Europe*. Cambridge: Cambridge University Press, 2006.

Matytsin, Anton M. *The Spectre of Skepticism in the Age of Enlightenment*. Baltimore: Johns Hopkins University Press, 2016.

Maurenbrecher, Wilhelm. 'Lebensbild C. v. Noordens'. In Wilhelm Maurenbrecher and Carl von Noorden, *Historische Vorträge*, 1–52. Leipzig, 1884.

Mazón, Patricia M. *Gender and the Modern Research University: The Admission of Women to German Higher Education, 1865–1914*. Stanford: Stanford University Press, 2003.

McKeon, Michael. *The Secret History of Domesticity: Public, Private, and the Division of Knowledge*. Baltimore: Johns Hopkins University Press, 2005.

Meier, Christian, Odilo Engels, Günter Horst and Reinhart Koselleck. 'Geschichte, Historie'. In *Geschichtliche Grundbegriffe*, edited by Otto Brunner, Werner Conze and Reinhart Koselleck, vol. 2, 593–718. Stuttgart: Ernst Klett Verlag, 1975.

Meinecke, Friedrich. *Die Entstehung des Historismus*. 2 Vols. Munich: Oldenbourg, 1936.

Mencke, Johann Burkhard. *Das Holländische Journal 1698–1699: (Ms. Germ. oct. 82 der Staatsbibliothek Berlin)*, edited by Hubert Laeven. Hildesheim: Olms, 2005.

Miller, Peter N., ed. *Momigliano and Antiquarianism: Foundations of the Modern Cultural Sciences*. Toronto: University of Toronto Press, 2007.

Milligan, Jennifer S. "What is an Archive?' in the History of Modern France'. In *Archive Stories: Facts, Fictions, and the Writing of History*, edited by Antoinette M. Burton, 159–83. Durham: Duke University Press, 2005.

Minutelli, S. Rossi. 'Archivi e biblioteche'. In *Storia di Venezia, vol. 2: L'Ottocento e il Novecento*, edited by Mario Isnenghi and Stuart Woolf, 1081–122. Rome: Istituto della Enciclopedia italiana, 2002.

von Mohl, Robert. *Die Geschichte und Literatur der Staatswissenschaften*. 3 Vols. Erlangen, 1856–8.

Momigliano, Arnaldo. 'Ancient History and the Antiquarian'. *Journal of the Warburg and Courtauld Institutes* 13, no. 3/4 (1950): 285–315.

Monod, Gabriel. 'Georges Waitz'. *Revue historique* 11, no. 31 (1886): 383–90.

Muhlack, Ulrich. *Geschichtswissenschaft im Humanismus und in der Aufklärung: Die Vorgeschichte des Historismus*. Munich: Beck, 1991.

Muhlack, Ulrich. 'Leopold Ranke, seine Geschichtsschreibung und seine Briefe'. In Leopold von Ranke, *Briefwechsel: Historisch-kritische Ausgabe*, edited by Ulrich Muhlack and Oliver Ramonat, vol. 1, 3–49. Munich: Oldenbourg, 2007.

Mulsow, Martin. 'Gundling versus Buddeus: Competing Models of the History of Philosophy'. In *History and the Disciplines. The Reclassification of Knowledge in Early Modern Europe*, edited by Donald R. Kelley, 103–26. Rochester: University of Rochester Press, 1997.

Mulsow, Martin. *Moderne aus dem Untergrund: Radikale Frühaufklärung in Deutschland 1680–1720*. Hamburg: Meiner, 2002.

Mulsow, Martin. *Die unanständige Gelehrtenrepublik: Wissen, Libertinage und Kommunikation in der Frühen Neuzeit*. Stuttgart: J. B. Metzler, 2007.

Mulsow, Martin. *Prekäres Wissen: Eine andere Ideengeschichte der Frühen Neuzeit*. Franfurt am Main: Suhrkamp, 2012.

Mulsow, Martin, Kasper Risbjerg Eskildsen and Helmut Zedelmaier, eds *Christoph August Heumann (1681-1764): Gelehrte Praxis zwischen christlichem Humanismus und Aufklärung*. Stuttgart: Franz Steiner Verlag, 2017.

Nadel, Georg H. 'Philosophy of History before Historicism'. *History and Theory* 3, no. 3 (1964): 291-315.

Niebuhr, Barthold Georg. 'Einleitung zu den Vorlesungen über Römische Alterthümer 1811'. In idem, *Kleine historische und philologische Schriften*, vol. 2, 1-19. Bonn, 1843.

Niedermann, Joseph. *Kultur, Werden und Wandlungen des Begriffs und seiner Ersatzbegriffe von Cicero bis Herder*. Firenze: Bibliopolis, 1941.

Novick, Peter. *That Noble Dream: The "Objectivity Question" and the American Historical Profession*. Cambridge: Cambridge University Press, 1988.

Oexle, Otto Gerhard. *Geschichtswissenschaft im Zeichen des Historismus: Studien zu Problemgeschichten der Moderne*. Göttingen: Vandenhoeck und Ruprecht, 1996.

Ophir, Adi and Steven Shapin. 'The Place of Knowledge: A Methodological Survey'. *Science in Context* 4, no. 1 (1991): 3-21.

Olesko, Kathryn M. 'Commentary: On Institutes, Investigations, and Scientific Training'. In *The Investigative Enterprise. Experimental Physiology in Nineteenth-Century Medicine*, edited by William Coleman and Frederic L. Holmes, 295-332. Berkeley: University of California Press, 1988.

Orrells, Daniel. *Classical Culture and Modern Masculinity*. Oxford: Oxford University Press, 2011.

Pandel, Hans-Jürgen. 'Von der Teegesellschaft zum Forschungsinstitut. Die historischen Seminare vom Beginn des 19. Jahrhunderts bis zum Ende des Kaiserreichs'. In *Transformationen des Historismus. Wissenschaftsorganisation und Bildungspolitik vor dem Ersten Weltkrieg*, edited by Horst Walter Blanke, 1-31. Waltrop: Wilhelm Fink, 1994.

Pandel, Hans-Jürgen. 'Die Entwicklung der historischen Seminare in Deutschland'. In *Halle und die deutsche Geschichtswissenschaft um 1900*, edited by Werner Freitag, 25-36. Halle: Mitteldeutscher Verlag, 2002.

Paul, Herman. 'The Virtues of a Good Historian in Early Imperial Germany: Georg Waitz's Contested Example'. *Modern Intellectual History* 15, no. 3 (2018a): 681-709.

Paul, Herman. 'German Thoroughness in Baltimore: Epistemic Virtues and National Stereotypes'. *History of Humanities* 3, no. 2 (2018b): 327-50.

Paul, Herman and Adriaan van Veldhuizen, eds. *Historicism: A Travelling Concept*. London: Bloomsbury, 2020.

Pfanner, Tobias. 'Bedencken von dem principio fidei historicae zumahlen wie selbiges auf denen Gesandtschaffts- und andern Acten geründet'. In Johann Peter von Ludewig, *Gesamte kleine teutsche Schriften*, 336-57. Halle, 1705.

von Pflugk-Harrtung, Julius. 'Heinrich von Sybel'. *Westermanns illustrierte deutsche Monatshefte* 64 (1888): 331–46.

Phillips, Mark Salber. *On Historical Distance*. New Haven: Yale University Press, 2013.

Pomata, Gianna and Nancy Siraisi, eds. *Historia: Empiricism and Erudition in Early Modern Europe*. Cambridge: MIT Press, 2005.

Poovey, Mary. *A History of the Modern Facts: Problems of Knowledge in the Sciences of Wealth and Society*. Chicago: Chicago University Press, 1998.

Popper, Karl. *The Poverty of Historicism*. London: Routledge, 1957.

Povolo, Claudio. *Il romanziere e l'archivista: De un processo veneziano del '600 all' anonimo manoscritto dei Promessi sposi*. Venice: Istituto Veneto di Scienze Lettere ed Arti, 1993.

Povolo, Claudio. 'The Creation of Venetian Historiography'. In *Venice Reconsidered: The History and Civilization of an Italian City-State 1297–1797*, edited by John Jeffries Martin and Dennis Romano, 491–519. Baltimore: Johns Hopkins University Press, 2000.

Proesler, Hans. *Das Problem einer Entwicklungsgeschichte des historischen Sinnes*. Berlin: Ebering, 1920.

Pütter, Johann Stephan. *Versuch einer academischen Gelehrten-Geschichte von der Georg-August-Universität zu Göttingen*. 2 Vols. Göttingen, 1765–88.

Ranke, Leopold. *Zur Kritik neuerer Geschichtschreiber*. Leipzig, 1824.

Ranke, Leopold. *Fürsten und Völker von Süd-Europa im sechzehnten und siebzehnten Jahrhundert. Vornehmlich aus ungedruckten Gesandtschafts-Berichten*. Hamburg, 1827.

Ranke, Leopold. *Ueber die Verschwörung gegen Venedig, im Jahre 1618: Mit Urkunden aus dem Venezianischen Archive*. Berlin, 1831.

Ranke, Leopold. 'Einleitung'. *Historisch-politische Zeitschrift* 1 (1832): 1–8.

Ranke, Leopold. 'Vorrede'. In *Jahrbücher des Deutschen Reichs unter dem Sächsischen Hause*, edited by idem, vol. 1, no. 1, v–xii. Berlin, 1837.

von Ranke, Leopold. 'Am neunzigsten Geburtstag 21. December 1885'. In idem, *Sämmtliche Werke, 51/52: Abhandlungen und Versuche*, edited by Alfred Dove and Theodor Wiedemann, 592–8. Leipzig, 1888.

von Ranke, Leopold. 'Ausgewählte Briefe'. In idem, *Sämmtliche Werke, 53/54: Zur eigenen Lebensgeschichte*, edited by Alfred Dove, 77–565. Leipzig, 1890.

von Ranke, Leopold. *Das Briefwerk*, edited by Walther Peter Fuchs. Hamburg: Hoffmann und Campe, 1949a.

von Ranke, Leopold. *Neue Briefe*, edited by Bernard Hoeft. Hamburg: Hoffmann und Campe, 1949b.

von Ranke, Leopold. 'Idee der Universalhistorie'. In idem, *Aus Werk und Nachlass*, edited by Walther Peter Fuchs and Theodor Schieder, vol. 4:

Vorlesungseinleitungen, edited by Volker Dotterweich and Walther Peter Fuchs, 72–89. Munich: Oldenbourg, 1975.

Raspe, Rudolf Erich. *Anmerkungen über die neueste Schrift des Hernn Geheimden Rath Klotz in Halle vom Nutzen und Gebrauch der geschnittenen Steine und ihrer Abdrücke*. Cassel, 1768.

von Raumer, Georg Wilhelm. 'Christian Thomasius und die Entstehung der Universität Halle'. In *Neues Allgemeines Archiv für Geschichtskunde des Preußichen Staates*, edited by Leopold von Ledebur, vol. 1, 185–95. Berlin, 1836.

Reill, Peter Hanns. 'History and Hermeneutics in the Aufklärung: The Thought of Johann Christoph Gatterer'. *Journal of Modern History* 45, no. 1 (1973): 24–51.

Reill, Peter Hanns. *The German Enlightenment and the Rise of Historicism*. Berkeley: University of California Press, 1975.

Reill, Peter Hanns. 'Johann Christoph Gatterer'. In *Deutsche Historiker*, edited by Hans Ulrich Wehler, vol. 6, 7–22. Göttingen: Vandenhoeck und Ruprecht, 1980.

Reuben, Julie E. *The Making of the Modern University: Intellectual Transformation and the Marginalization of Morality*. Chicago: University of Chicago Press, 1996.

Riedel, Friederich Just. *Sämmtliche Schriften*, vol. 4: *Verschiedene Briefe*. Vienna, 1787.

Roth, Johann Ferdinand. *Mythologische Daktyliothek: Nebst vorausgeschichter Abhandlung geschnittenen Steinen*. Nürnberg, 1805.

Rowold, Katharina. *The Educated Woman: Minds, Bodies, and Women's Higher Education in Britain, Germany, and Spain, 186–1914*. London: Routledge, 2010.

Rüsen, Jörn. *Konfigurationen des Historismus: Studien zur deutschen Wissenschaftskultur*. Frankfurt am Main: Suhrkamp, 1993.

Sawilla, Jan Marco. "'Geschichte': En Produkt der deutschen Aufklärung? Eine Kritik an Reinhart Kosellecks Begriff des 'Kollektivsingulars Geschichte'". *Zeitschrift für Historische Forschung* 31, no. 3 (2004), 381–428.

Sawilla, Jan Marco. 'Das Zeugnis des Historiographen. Anwesenheit und gestufte Plausibilität in der Geschichtsschreibung der Frühen Neuzeit'. In *Zeugnis und Zeugenschaft: Perspektiven aus der Vormoderne*, edited by Wolfram Drews and Heike Schlie, 311–35. Munich: Wilhelm Fink, 2011.

Scattola, Merio. "'Historia literaria' als 'Historia pragmatica': Die pragmatische Bedeutung der Geschichtsschreibung im intellektuellen Unternehmen der Gelehrtengeschichte'. In *Historia literaria: Neuordnung des Wissens im 17. und 18. Jahrhundert*, edited by Frank Grunert und Friedrich Vollhardt, 37–63. Berlin: Akademie Verlag, 2007.

Schäfer, Dietrich. *Mein Leben*. Berlin: Köhler, 1926.

Scheele, Meta. *Wissen und Glaube in der Geschichtswissenschaft: Studien zum historischen Pyrrhonismus in Frankreich und Deutschland*. Heidelberg: Carl Winters Universitätsbuchhandlung, 1930.

Scherer, Emil Clemens. *Geschichte und Kirchengeschichte an den deutschen Universitäten: Ihre Anfänge im Zeitalter des Historismus und ihre Ausbildung zu selbständigen Disziplinen*. Freiburg im Breisgau: Herder, 1927.

Schilling, Heinz. 'Die Konfessionalisierung im Reich: Religiöser und gesellschaftlicher Wandel in Deutschland zwischen 1555 und 1620'. *Historische Zeitschrift* 246, no. 1 (1988): 1–45.

Schlüter, Gisela, ed. '*Historischer Pyrrhonismus*'. Special issue of *Das Achtzehnte Jahrhundert* 31, no. 2 (2007).

Schmauß, Johann Jacob. *Kurzer Begriff der Reichs-Historie*. Leipzig, 1729.

Schneider, Ulrich Johannes. 'Eclecticism and the History of Philosophy'. In *History and the Disciplines. The Reclassification of Knowledge in Early Modern Europe*, edited by Donald R. Kelley, 83–101. Rochester: University of Rochester Press, 1997.

Schneiders, Werner. 'Nicht "plump", nicht "säuisch", nicht "sauertöpfisch": Zu Thomasius' Idee einer Philosophie für alle'. In *Die Philosophie und die Belles-Lettres*, edited by Martin Fontius and Werner Schneiders, 11–20. Berlin: Akademie Verlag, 1997.

Schneppen, Heinz. *Niederländische Universitäten und deutsches Geistesleben: Von der Gründung der Universität Leiden bis ins späte 18. Jahrhundert*. Münster: Aschendorffsche Verlagsbuchhandlung, 1960.

Schroeder, Paul W. *The Transformation of European Politics 1763–1848*. Oxford: Oxford University Press, 1994.

Schubring, Gert. 'Kabinett – Seminar – Institut: Raum und Rahmen des forschenden Lernens'. *Berichte zur Wissenschaftsgeschichte* 23, no. 3 (2000): 269–85.

Schwager, Bärbel. *Das Göttinger Auditoriengebäude von 1862/5: Ein Beitrag zur Universitätarchitektur im 19. Jahrhundert und zur Hannoverschen Variante des Rundbogenstils*. Göttingen: Peter Lang, 1995.

Seifert, Arno. *Cognitio historica: Die Geschichte als Namengeberin der frühneuzeitlichen Emperie*. Berlin: Duncker und Humblot, 1976.

Shapin, Steven. 'The House of Experiment in Seventeenth-Century England'. *Isis* 79, no. 3 (1988): 373–404.

Shapin, Steven. "The Mind is Its Own Place': Science and Solitude in Seventeenth-Century England'. *Science in Context* 4, no. 1 (1990): 191–218.

Shapin, Steven. 'Why the Public Ought to Understand Science-in-the-Making'. *Public Understanding of Science* 1, no. 1 (1992): 27–30.

Shapin, Steven. 'Placing the View from Nowhere: Historical and Sociological Problems in the Location of Science'. *Transactions of the Institute of British Geographers* 23, no. 1 (1998): 5–12.

Shapin, Steven. *The Scientific Life: A Moral History of a Late Modern Vocation*. Chicago: University of Chicago Press, 2008.

Shapin, Steven and Simon Schaffer. *Leviathan and the Air-Pump: Hobbes, Boyle, and the Experimental Life*. 1985. Reprinted. Princeton: Princeton University Press, 1989.

Shapiro, Barbara J. *A Culture of Fact: England 1550–1720*. Ithaca: Cornell University Press, 2000.

Simonis, Carl. *Versuch einer Geschichte des Alarichs Königs der Westgothen*. Göttingen, 1858.

Smith, Bonnie G. 'Gender and the Practices of Scientific History: The Seminar and Archival Research in the Nineteenth Century'. *The American Historical Review* 100 (1995): 1150–76.

Sommer, Andreas Urs. 'Historischer Pyrrhonismus und die Entstehung der spekulativ-universalistischen Geschichtsphilosophie'. In *Unsicheres Wissen: Skeptizismus und Wahrscheinlichkeit 1550–1850*, edited by Carlos Spoerhase, Dirk Werle and Markus Wild, 201–14. Berlin: De Gruyter, 2009.

Sparn, Walter. 'Philosophische Historie und dogmatische Heterodoxie: Der Fall des Exegeten Christoph August Heumann'. In *Historische Kritik und biblischer Kanon in der deutschen Aufklärung*, edited by Henning Graf Reventlow, Walter Sparn and John Woodbridge, 171–92. Wiesbaden: Harrassowitz, 1988.

Spener, Philipp Jakob. *Pia desideria: Oder herzliches Verlangen nach Gottgefälliger Besserung der wahren Evangelischen Kirchen*. 1675. Reprinted. Frankfurt am Main, 1680.

Spieß, Philipp Ernst. *Von Archiven*. Halle, 1777.

Spoerhase, Carlos. 'Big humanities: "Größe" und "Großforschung" als Kategorien geisteswissenschaftlicher Selbstbeobachtung'. *Geschichte der Germanistik* 37/38 (2010): 9–27.

Spoerhase, Carlos and Mark-Georg Dehrmann. 'Die Idee der Universität: Friedrich August Wolf und die Praxis des Seminars'. *Zeitschrift für Ideengeschichte* 5, no. 1 (2011): 105–17.

Sprat, Thomas. *The History of the Royal-Society of London for the Improving of Natural Knowledge*. London, 1667.

Stanley Hall, G. *Methods of Teaching History*. Boston, 1883.

Stolle, Gottlieb. *Eine Reise durch die Gelehrtenrepublik: Reisejournal 1703/1704*, edited by Martin Mulsow. Stuttgart: Franz Steiner Verlag, forthcoming.

Stolleis, Michael. *Geschichte des öffentlichen Rechts in Deutschland*. 4 Vols. Munich: C. H. Beck, 1988–92.

von Sybel, Heinrich. 'Ueber den Stand der neueren deutschen Geschichtschreibung'. In idem, *Kleine historische Schriften*, 343–59. Munich, 1863.

Tanaka, Stefan. *History without Chronology*. Amherst: Lever Press, 2019.

Thomasius, Christian. *Discours welcher Gestalt man denen Frantzosen in gemeinen Leben und Wandel nachahmen solle?* N. p, n. d.

Thomasius, Christian. *Introductio ad philosophiam aulicam*. Leipzig, 1688.

Thomasius, Christian. *Einleitung zu der Vernunfft-Lehre, worinnen durch eine leichte/ und allen vernünfftigen Menschen/ waserley Standes oder Geschlechts sie seyn/ verständliche Manier der Weg gezeiget wird/ ohne die Syllogisticâ das wahre/ wahrscheinliche und falsche von einander zu entscheiden/ und neue Warheiten zu erfinden*. Halle, 1691.

Thomasius, Christian. *Von der Arzeney wieder die unvernünfftige Liebe, und der zuvor nöthigen Erkäntnß sein Selbst. Oder: Ausübung der Sitten Lehre*. Halle, 1696.

Thomasius, Christian. *Summarischer Entwurf der Grundlehren, die einem Studio Juris zu wissen/ und auff Universitäten zu lernen nöthig sind*. Halle, 1699.

Thomasius, Christian. 'Kurtzer Entwurff/ was auff der Chur-Brandenburgischen Friedrichs Universität zu Halle Christian Thomas/ JCtus und P.P. voriges Jahr gelesen/ und küfftig für Lectiones und Collegia zu halten besonnen sey. Publicirt 1694. am Sonntag Cantate'. In idem, *Allerhand bißher publicirte kleine teutsche Schrifften mit Fleiß colligiret und zusammen getragen; Nebst etlichen Beylagen und einer Vorrede*, 631–54. Halle, 1701a.

Thomasius, Christian. *Dreyfache Rettung des Rechts Evangelischer Fürsten in Kirchen-Sachen*, edited by Johann Gottfried Zeidlern. Frankfurt am Main, 1701b.

Thomasius, Christian. *Höchstnötige Cautelen welche ein Studiosus Juris, der sich zu Erlernung der Rechts-Gelahrheit auff eine kluge und geschickte Weise vorbereiten will/ zu beobachten hat*. Halle, 1713.

Thomasius, Christian. 'Erinnerung wegen derer über den dritten Theil seiner Grund-Lehren/ bißher gehaltenen Lectionum privatissimarum und deren Verwandelung in Lectiones privatas'. In idem, *Außerlesene und in deutsch noch nie gedruckte Schrifften*, vol. 2, 193–220. Halle, 1714a.

Thomasius, Christian. 'Erinnerung wegen zweyer Collegiorum über den vierdten Theil seiner Grund-Lehren'. In idem, *Außerlesene und in deutsch noch nie gedruckte Schrifften*, vol. 2, 221–52. Halle, 1714b.

Thomasius, Christian. 'Erinnerung wegen zweyer Collegiorum über den ersten Theil seiner Grund-Lehren'. In idem, *Außerlesene und in deutsch noch nie gedruckte Schrifften*, vol. 2, 253–84. Halle, 1714c.

Thomasius, Christian. 'Summarische Erzehlung von der Verjagung des Autoris aus seinem Vaterlande'. In idem, *Vernünfftige und Christliche aber nicht Scheinheilige Thomasischen Gedancken und Erinnerungen uber allerhand Gemischte Philosophische und Juristische Händel*, vol. 2, 44–201. Halle, 1724a.

Thomasius, Christian. 'Mein Anno 1689. Herrn M. August Herman Francken ertheiltes Responsum Juris'. In idem, *Vernünfftige und Christliche aber nicht Scheinheilige Thomasischen Gedancken und Erinnerungen uber allerhand Gemischte Philosophische und Juristische Händel*, vol. 2, 352–492. Halle, 1724b.

Thomasius, Christian. *Kurtzer Entwurff der politischen Klugheit*. Frankfurt am Main, 1728.

Thomasius, Christian. *Briefwechsel: Historisch-kritische Edition*, edited by Frank Grunert, Matthias Hambrock and Martin Kühnel, vol. 1. Berlin: De Gruyter, 2017.

Thompson, Martyn P. 'The History of Fundamental Law in Political Thought from the French Wars of Religion to the American Revolution'. *The American Historical Review* 91, no. 5 (1986): 1103–28.

Toews, John E. *Becoming Historical: Cultural Reformation and Public Memory in Early Nineteenth-Century Berlin*. Cambridge: Cambridge University Press, 2004.

Tollebeek, Jo. 'A Stormy Family. Paul Fredericq and the Formation of an Academic Historical Community in the Nineteenth Century'. *Storia della Storiografia* 53 (2008a): 59–73.

Tollebeek, Jo. *Fredericq en Zonen: Een antropologie van de moderne geschiedwetenschap*. Amsterdam: Bert Bakker, 2008b.

Toulmin, Steven. *Cosmopolis: The Hidden Agenda of Modernity*. Chicago: University of Chicago Press, 1990.

Trevor-Roper, Hugh. *History and the Enlightenment*. New Haven, CT: Yale University Press, 2010.

Troeltsch, Ernst. *Der Historismus und seine Probleme*. Tübingen: J. C. B. Mohr, 1922.

Troeltsch, Ernst. 'Die Krisis des Historismus'. In idem., *Kritische Gesamtausgabe*, vol. 15: *Schriften zur Politik und Kulturphilosophie (1918–1923)*, Berlin: Walter de Gruyter, 2002, 437–55.

von Uffenbach, Zacharias Conrad. *Merkwürdige Reisen durch Niedersachsen Holland und Engelland*, 3 vols. Frankfurt am Main, 1753–4.

von Tschirnhauß auf Hackenau, Wolff Bernhard. *Getreuer Hofmeister auf Academien und Reisen*. Hanover, 1727.

Tucci, Ugo. 'Ranke Storico di Venezia'. In Leopold von Ranke, *Venezia nel Cinquecento*, translated by Ingeborg Zapperi Walter, 1–69. Rome: Istituto della Enciclopedia italiana, 1974.

Tucci, Ugo. 'Ranke and the Venetian Document Market'. In *Leopold von Ranke and the Shaping of the Historical Discipline*, edited by Georg G. Iggers and James M. Powell, 99–107. Syracuse: Syracuse University Press, 1990.

Usinger, Rudolf. *Die dänischen Annalen und Chroniken des Mittelalters, kritisch untersucht*. Hannover, 1861.

Valdez, Damien. *German Philhellenism: The Pathos of the Historical Imagination from Winckelmann to Goethe*. Basingstoke: Palgrave Macmillan, 2014.

Varnhagen von Ense, Karl August. *Werke in fünf bänden*, edited by Konrad Feilchenfeldt. 5 Vols. Frankfurt am Main: Deutscher Klassiker Verlag, 1987–1994.

Vierhaus, Rudolf. 'Die Idee der Kontinuität im historiographischen Werk Leopold von Rankes'. In *Leopold von Ranke und die moderne Geschichtswissenschaft*, edited by Wolfgang J. Mommsen, 166-75. Stuttgart: Klett-Cotta, 1988.

Völkel, Markus. *'"Pyrrhonismus historicus" und "fides historica": Die Entwicklung der deutschen historischen Methodologie under dem Geschichtspunkt der historischen Skepsis'*. Frankfurt am Main: Peter Lang, 1987.

Völkel, Markus. 'Historischer Pyrrhonismus und Antiquarismus-Konzeption bei Arnaldo Momigliano'. *Das Achtzehnte Jahrhundert* 31, no. 2 (2007): 179-90.

Völkel, Markus. 'The "Historical Consciousness" of the Holy Roman Empire of the German Nation (Sixteenth to Eighteenth Century)'. In *The Holy Roman Empire 1495-1806*, edited by R. J. W. Evans, Michael Schnaich and Peter H. Wilson, 323-45. Oxford: Oxford University Press, 2011.

Völkel, Markus. 'German Historical Writing from the Reformation to the Enlightenment'. In *The Oxford History of Historical Writing*, edited by Daniel Wolf, vol. 3, 324-46. Oxford: Oxford University Press, 2012.

VR. 'Kritische Wälder, Oder Betrachtungen über die Wissenschaft und Kunst der Schönen. Erstes und zweytes Wäldchen'. *Deutsche Bibliothek der schönen Wissenschaften* 3, no. 10 (1769): 334-362.

Waitz, Georg. *Ueber die Gründung des deutschen Reichs durch den Vertrag zu Verdun*. Kiel, 1843.

Waitz, Georg. 'Falsche Richtungen: Schreiben an den Herausgeber'. *Historische Zeitschrift* 1, no 1. (1859): 17-28.

Waitz, Georg. *Die historischen Übungen zu Göttingen: Glückwunschschreiben an Leopold von Ranke zum Tage der Feier seines funfzigjährigen Doctorjubiläums. 20. Februar 1867*. Göttingen, 1867.

Waitz, Georg. *Friedrich Christoph Dahlmann: Gedächtnisrede gehalten in der Aula der Universität Kiel am 13. Mai 1885*. Kiel, 1885.

Weber, Max. 'Science as a Vocation'. In *From Max Weber: Essays in Sociology*, translated by H. H. Gerth and C. Wright Mills, 129-56. London: Routledge, 2009.

Wesendonck, Hermann. *Die Begründung der neueren deutschen Geschichtsschreibung durch Gatterer und Schlözer*. Leipzig, 1876.

White, Hayden. *Metahistory: The Historical Imagination in Nineteenth Century Europe*. Baltimore: Johns Hopkins University Press, 1972.

Wieland, Ludwig. 'Georg Waitz'. *Abhandlungen der Königlichen Gesellschaft der Wissenschaften zu Göttingen* 33 (1886): 1-15.

Wielema, Michiel. *The March of the Libertines: Spinozists and the Dutch Reformed Church (1660-1750)*. Hilversum: Uitgeverij Verloren, 2004.

Winkelmann, Eduard. *Geschichte Kaiser Friedrichs des Zweiten und seiner Reiche, 1212-1235*. Berlin, 1863.

Winkelmann, Johann Joachim. *Geschichte der Kunst des Alterthums*. 2 Vols. Dresden, 1764.

Wittich, Karl. 'Richer über die Herzoge Giselbert von Lothringen und Heinrich von Sachsen'. *Forschungen zur deutschen Geschichte* 3 (1863): 105–41.

Wittkau, Annette. *Historismus: Zur Geschichte des Begriffs und des Problems*. Göttingen: Vandenhoeck und Ruprecht, 1992.

Wolff, Christian. *Preliminary Discourse on Philosophy in General*, translated by Richard J. Blackwell. Indianapolis: Bobbs-Merrill, 1963.

Woolf, Daniel. *A Concise History of History: Global Historiography from Antiquity to the Present*. Cambridge: Cambridge University Press, 2019.

Wotschke, Theodor. 'Eine Kollektenreise von Leipzig nach Wolfenbüttel im Jahre 1721'. *Thüringisch-Sächsische Zeitschrift für Geschichte und Kunst* 16, no. 1 (1927): 79–94.

Wundt, Max. *Die deutsche Schulphilosophie im Zeitalter der Aufklärung*. Tübingen: Mohr, 1945.

Wustmann, Gustav. 'Verbotene Bücher'. In idem, *Aus Leipzigs Vergangenheit: Gesammelte Aufsätze*, vol. 1, 194–235. Leipzig, 1885.

Zammito, John H. *Kant, Herder, and the Birth of Anthropology*. Chicago: Chicago University Press, 2002.

Zedelmaier, Helmut. *Der Anfang der Geschichte: Studien zur Urspungsdebatte im 18. Jahrhundert*. Hamburg: Meiner, 2003.

Zelle, Carsten, ed. *"Vernünftige Ärtze": Hallesche Psychomediziner und die Anfänge der Anthropologie der deutschsprachigen Frühaufklärung*. Tübingen: Max Niemeyer Verlag, 2001.

Manuscript sources

Erslev, Kristian. *Breve*, Ny Kongelige Samling, 4604, 4. Copenhagen: Det Kongelige Bibliotek.

Lidén, Johan Hinric. *Dagböcker*, MS X 397, Uppsala: Uppsala Universitetsbibliotek.

Ruppert 2056. *Herzogin Anna Amalia Bibliothek*. Weimar. From www.heyne-digital.de.

Stoud, Frederik. *Vorlesungen des Hofraths Heine über die Archæologie, 1789 und 1792*. Copenhagen: Ny Kongelig Samling, Det Kongelige Bibliotek.

Index

Abby of Corvey 112
Acta eruditorum (Acts of the Learned) (journal) 37
Acta philosophorum (Acts of the Philosophers) (journal) 36, 64
Adams, Herbert Baxter 109
Addison, Joseph 70
Adelung, Johann Christoph 139 n.17
Ahnert, Thomas 130 n.9
Alberti, Valentin 19
Algazi, Gadi 31
Allgemeine historische Bibliothek (General Historical Library) (journal) 77
Altenstein, Karl vom Stein zum 98
antiquarianism 81
　archaeology and 73–4
　battle over 57–8, 72, 73, 75
　enlightened 58–60
　revived 70–1
archive. *See also* princely archive; state archive
　centralization of 97–8, 102
Archives Nationales 97
Arndt, Wilhelm 115–16
Arnim, Bettina von 98
Arnold, Gottfried 39–41
Ars formularia (art of formulas) 79, 80
art cabinet 11–12, 14, 73–5
　and antiquarianism
　　battle over 57–8
　　enlightened 58–60
　　imprints 60–3
　kultur and Klotz and 68–73
　libertine glyptography and 64–6
　radical numismatics and 66–8
Auch eine Philosophie der Geschichte zur Bildung der Menschheit (This Too a Philosophy of History for the Formation of Humanity) (Herder) 72

Austria 14, 87, 88, 91, 92, 94, 97, 98, 100–2, 105
auxiliary sciences 77, 83, 86, 115

Bacchus 65
Bachmann, Georg August 50
Baron Munchausen (Raspe) 58
Baur, Siegfried 146 n.11
Bayle, Pierre 26, 40
belief in archives (*fides archivorum*) 50–3
bella diplomatica (document wars) 51
Benson, Robert L. 154 n.44
Benthem, Henrich Ludolff 37–9, 41, 42, 135 n.13, 136 n.15
Bentinck, Hans Willem 47
Berg, Günter 146 n.11
Beytrag zur Geschichte des Geschmacks und der Kunst aus Münzen (Contribution to the History of Taste and Art from Coins) (Klotz) 67
Bibliothek der elenden Scribenten (Library of Miserable Writers) (journal) 58
Bientjes, Julia 134 n.2
Bittner, Ludwig 148 n.45
Bodin, Jean 21
Böhm, Benno 142 n.20
Böhme, Jacob 42, 43
Bonde, Carl 47
Boockmann, Hartmut 150 n.3
Boufflers, Marshal Louis-François 47
Breckling, Friedrich 40, 41
Briefe, antiquarischen Inhalts (Letters of Antiquarian Content) (Lessing) 58
Bunge, Wien van 134 n.4
Bursian, Conrad 140 n.1
Butterfield, Herbert 119–21

Cahan, David 149 n.71
Carlsbad Decrees (1819) 99
Casaubon, Isaac 21
Cassius, Georg Andreas 36
Chakrabarty, Dipesh 122
Chambrier, Jean Pierre de 93
character 27, 71, 113
   assessment 91, 97
   exercise of 107–8
   German 54, 117
   moral 49, 58, 91, 108, 111, 112
   scholarly 20, 82, 83
Charlemagne 4, 40, 54
Christianity 14, 57, 60, 67, 68, 71, 73
   institutionalized 40
Chronicon Corbejense (Corvey Chronicle) 111
Claus, Jacob 39, 41
Codex diplomaticus Quedlinburgensis (Diplomatic Codex of Quedlinburg) (Erath) 81
collegium privatissimum (most private class) 23–5, 29, 32
Condren, Conal 131 n.13
confessions/confessional 3, 4, 13, 14, 18–19, 33, 96, 117, 130 n.9
   art cabinet and 57, 68
   fieldwork and 35, 39, 44
   princely archive and 47, 51
Congress of Vienna 87, 99, 103
conjectural history 5
Conring, Hermann 55
Conspectus reipublicae literariae (Overview of the Republic of Letters) (Heumann) 36, 45–6
credibility 49, 52, 95, 111, 113. *See also* trust
   of historian 82–4
Crenius, Thomas. *See* Crusius, Thomas Theodor
Creyghton, Camille 150 n.6
Croese, Gerard 41
Crusius, Thomas Theodor 40

Dactyliothec (Lippert) 62, 65
Daru, Pierre 93
Daston, Lorraine 51
De charlataneria eruditorum (On the Charlatanry of the Learned) (Mencke) 59

Deichsel, Johann Gottlieb 37, 43
De jure naturae et gentium (The Law of Nature and Nations) (Pufendorf) 69
De re diplomatica (On Diplomatics) (Mabillon) 51
Der junge Gelehrte (The Young Scholar) (Lessing) 59
Descartes, René 44, 45
Deutsche Bibliothek der schönen Wissenschaften (German Library of the Literary and Fine Arts) (Klotz) 69
Deutsche Verfassungsgeschichte (German Constitutional History) (Waitz) 117
Dialogues upon the Usefulness of Ancient Medals (Addison) 70
Dilthey, Wilhelm 5
diplomata. *See* official documents
Diplomatik (diplomatics) 77, 79–84, 86
diplomatisches Gutachten (diplomatic expert opinion) 80
diplomatisches Responsum (diplomatic response) 80
Discours de la méthode (Discourse on Method) (Descartes) 44
Döllinger, Ignaz von 5
doubt, avoiding 52–3
Dresden Academy of Art 61
Droysen, Johann Gustav 11, 114

eclecticism 4, 21, 28, 36, 43, 45
Ehrenberg, Bonifacius Heinrich 36, 38
Einleitung zur Vernunfft-Lehre (Introduction to the Art of Reasoning) (Thomasius) 20, 28
Engels, Odilo 128 n.31
epistemic virtues 43, 112, 116, 150 n.6
epistemology 48, 51, 84–6, 89
   purpose of 116
equality
   exercise of 27–30
   place of 30–3
Erath, Anton Ulrich von 81
Erslev, Kristian 109, 116, 153–4 n.42
exercises. *See Übungen* (exercises)

Falcke, Johann Friedrich 112
Fasolt, Constantin 4

Fench fashions, in German
        everyday life   18
fieldwork
    academic journey as   35–7
    history as   41–3
    as moral education   43–5
    philosophy and history
        compared and   45–6
    travel guides and   37–40
Forschungen zur deutschen Geschichte
        (Research on German
        History)   111
Forster, Leonard   141 n.7
Fox, George   39
Francke, August Hermann   23, 24, 27
Frankfurt National Assembly   117
Frari archive   97, 100
Frederick the Great   45, 57, 59
Fredericq, Paul   109, 151 n.12
French ideals   18
Frensdorff, Ferdinand   150 n.3
Friedrich III   38
Friedrich Wilhelm IV   103, 105
Fritzsche, Peter   8
Fueter, Eduard   145 n.21
Fulda, Daniel   128 n.30
Fürsten und Völker von Süd-Europa (The
        Princes and People of Southern
        Europe) (Ranke)   91

Gatterer, Johann Christoph   14, 76–84,
        139 n.17, 145 n.21
    credibility of   82–4
    disciplinarity between
        jurisprudence and
        philosophy and   84–6
    Klotz and   81–2
    Lidén and   83
    Livy and   77–8
    as statesman and historian   77–8
Gaukroger, Stephen   131 n.13
Genius seculi (Spirit of the Age)
        (Klotz)   59, 70
Gentz, Friedrich von   88, 99–101
Gerlach, Hans-Martin   137 n.38
German Conception of History, The
        (Iggers)   7, 104
*German Enlightenment and the
        Rise of Historicism, The*
        (Reill)   84

German universities, significance of   12
Geschichte der Kunst des Alterthums
        (History of the Art of Antiquity)
        (Winckelmann)   58–9, 67
*Geschichten der romanischen und
        germanischen Völker* (Histories of
        the Roman and Germanic
        People) (Ranke)   90
Gesichtspunct (viewpoint)   77, 78
Gierl, Martin   77, 84
Giovio, Paolo   91
glyptography   61, 73
    libertine   64–6
Goethe, Johann Wolfgang von   7, 13
Goulbourne, Russell   142 n.20
Gracián, Baltasar   17
Grafton, Anthony   111, 151 n.14
Graphik/Graphica (graphics)   79–81, *80*
Grauert, Hermann   150 n.3
gravestone   75–7. *See also* Gatterer,
        Johann Christoph
    Linnean graphics and   79–81
    reproduction problem and   81–2
Gundling, Nikolaus Hieronymus   49–50,
        55, 85, 138 n.12
Günter, Martin   29

Hackenau, Wolff   135 n.13
Hadler, Frank   151 n.14
Hadot, Pierre   20, 131 n.14
Hall, G. Stanley   109, 151 n.14
Hallensleben, Georg
        Christoph   75, 78, 81–3
Hallische Jahrbücher (Halle
        Yearbooks)   89, 102
Hammerstein, Notker   32–3, 55
Hardenberg, Karl August von   98
Harloe, Katherine   141 n.4
Hartmann, Andreas   135 n.13
Hartog, François   8
Haus-, Hof- und Staatsarchivs   97
Hausen, Carl Renatus   71
Heine, Heinrich   101
Henrici   38
Henry of Livonia   112–13
Henry the Fowler   4, 54, 75, 76, 78, 80,
        81, 110–12
Herder, Johann Gottfried   2, 7–8, 14, 57,
        58, 68–71, 78, 84, 104
    on Klotz   69–73

Index

Heumann, Christoph August 13, 36–43, 45–6, 64, 68, 135 n.5
Heussi, Karl 120, 121
Heyne, Christian Gottlob 73
Hildebrand, Hermann 112–13, 152 n.27
Hirsch, Siegfried 111, 112
historia (historical knowledge). *See* historical knowledge
historia magistra vitae, tradition of 3, 21
   rejection of 13, 25, 54, 57
   revival of 85
Historia Quakeriana (Quaker History) (Croese) 41
historical belief 26, 48, 50–2, 81, 91
historical discipline 14, 73–4, 88–9, 103, 110
   modern 10, 88
   morals and politics of 116–18, 121
   politics of 104–5
historical knowledge 2–3, 6, 9, 12, 33, 45, 85, 86, 115, 125–6 n.5
   historical Pyrrhonism and 26
   importance of 22
   princely archive and 51, 53
   production of 13, 88, 94, 102, 103
historical Pyrrhonism 26, 52, 90, 132 n.34
historical revolt 4
historical scholarship 1–15, 33, 46, 84–6, 117
   art cabinet and 58, 73–4
   crisis of historicism and 6–7
   differences and 2
   historiography purpose and 119–23
   institutionalization of 45, 77
   new paradigm and 1–2
   princely archive and 54–6
   state archive and 89, 102, 105
   Waitz on 116
historiography 7, 9, 57, 107, 126 n.5, 147 n.21. *See also individual entries*
   European 4
   German 84, 85, 104, 145 n.21
   in making 10–11
   politics of 119–20
   purpose of history of 121–3
   state archive and 89, 92, 93–4, 101
   without politics 120–1
Historische Journal (Historical Journal) 77, 86
Historisch-politische Zeitschrift (Historical-Political Journal) 88, 103
history. *See also individual entries*
   age of 1–2, 6, 119
   and historicism compared 6–9
   morals of 9
   and theory compared 2–6
History of the Royal Society (Sprat) 32
Holland. *See* fieldwork
Holländischer Kirch- und Schulen-Staat (Dutch Church and School State) (Benthem) 37–8
Holy Roman Empire 4, 40, 47, 51, 54–6, 71, 77, 80, 81, 87, 102, 105, 117, 122
'How One Should Imitate the French in Everyday Life' (Thomasius) 27
Hoym, Friedrich von 81
Huistra, Pieter 150 n.6
Humboldt, Alexander von 99
Humboldt, Wilhelm von 104
Hunter, Ian 33, 130 nn.8–9, 131 n.13, 137 n.40

Iggers, Georg G. 7, 104
imperial history. *See Reichshistorie* (imperial history)
institutionalization 7
   of Christianity 40
   of discipline 108–10
   of exercises 114–16
   of historical scholarship 45, 77
   modern 14–15
   of seminars 33, 109–10, 114, 115
   Waitz on 15
Introductio ad philosophiam aulicam (Introduction to Court Philosophy) (Thomasius) 21
Israel, Jonathan 134 n.4, 136 n.23
Italy 14, 45, 61, 62, 68, 87, 88, 91–3, 95–100

Jahrbücher des Deutschen Reichs unter dem Sächsischen Hause (Yearbooks of the German Empire under the Saxon House) 110
Jansen, Albert 42
Jardine, Nicholas 96, 129 n.37
Johns Hopkins University Studies in Historical and Political Science (Adams) 109
Jones, Matthew 21

Index

July Revolution 87, 103
juridical approach 85
Jurieu, Pierre 40
Justi, Carl 141 n.4

Kaiser, David 150 n.8
Karl, Adam Franz 47
Kertscher, Hans-Joachim 140 n.1
Keymeulen, Sarah 150 n.6
Klotz, Christian Adolph 14, 57–61,
    140 n.1, 141 n.7, 143 n.43
  Gatterer and 81–2
  glyptography and 61, 64–6
  kultur and 68–73
  Lippert and 61–3, 65
  numismatics and 67
  on Socrates 64
Klotzianer 58, 64, 69, 71–2
Knechtl, Josef 99–100
knowledge, definition of 2–3, 5–6, 20,
    33, 45, 53, 85, 89
Kohler, Robert 11
Kohlhans, Casper 41
Königliche Institut der historischen
    Wissenschaften zu
    Göttingen 14, 77, 79, 83, 84
Königliche Sozietät der
    Wissenschaften 85, 86
Königsberg 114
Köppen, Karl Friedrich 146 n.11
Koselleck, Reinhart 2, 8, 121,
    128 nn.30–1
Kritische Wälder (Critical Forests)
    (Herder) 58, 70–3
Kultur (culture) 14, 57, 58
  Klotz and 68–73
Kunstrichter (art critic) 82
Kurtzer Entwurf der politischen Klugheit
    (Short Sketch of Political
    Prudence) (Thomasius) 25

Lämmermann, Christoph August 37
Landgren, Per 126 n.5
L'Antiquité expliquée et représentée en
    figures (Antiquity Explained
    and Represented in Figures)
    (Montfaucon) 63
lecture hall
  and equality
    exercise of 27–30
    place of 30–3

    self in 22–7
Leda, swan, and Amor 65
Leibniz, Gottfried Wilhelm 45
Lenhard-Schramm, Niklas 154 n.44
Lessing, Gotthold Ephraim 7, 58, 59, 68,
    70, 82, 143 n.43
Lidén, Johan Hinric 83
Liebhaber (connoisseur) 82–3
Lillieroot, Nils 47
Lingelbach, Gabriele 151 n.14
Linnean graphics 79–81, *80*
Lippert, Philipp Daniel 61–4, 73
Livingstone, David 129 n.37
Livy 77–8, 84
Louis XIV 35, 48
Ludewig, Johann Peter von 10, 13, 47–8,
    56–7, 85, 102, 140 n.28
  distrust in archives for 48–50
  history and law and 53–5
  on trust in documents 52–3

Mabillon, Jean 51
Mackenney, Richard 147 n.21
Mannheim, Karl 6
Marshall, John 136 n.23
Maskowsky, Wilhelm Ludwig von 148
Matytsin, Anton M. 132 n.34
mediation, places of 11–12
Meier, Christian 128 n.31
Meinecke, Friedrich 7, 72, 145 n.21
Mencke, Johann Burkhard 37,
    59, 141 n.7
Metahistory (White) 8
Metternich, Klemens von 87,
    98–101, 103–5
Middell, Matthias 151 n.14
Miller, Peter N. 139 n.16
Mohl, Robert von 102
Momigliano, Arnaldo 50, 139 n.16
Monatsgespräche (Monthly Conversations)
    (journal) 19
Monod, Gabriel 108, 113, 150 nn.3, 6
Montaigne, Michel de 26
Montfaucon, Bernard de 63
Monumenta Germaniae Historica
    (Historical Monuments of
    Germany) 115
moral character 49, 58, 91, 108, 111, 112
moral education 13, 21, 25, 121
  fieldwork as 43–5
moral philosophy 23, 25, 55

moral purpose   6, 116, 117, 121
morals of history   9–10
moral virtues   43, 112, 116, 150 n.6
Mores eruditorum (Manners of the Learned) (Klotz)   59
Möser, Justus   7
Mulsow, Martin   134 n.1, 135 n.5, 142 n.30
Münzenberg gravestone   75–8, 81, 82, 84. *See also* gravestone

Nani, Battista   93
new paradigm, of historical comprehension   1–2
Nicolai, Friedrich   70, 72
Niebuhr, Barthold Georg   89
Noorden, Carl von   114–16
Novick, Peter   117
numismatics   66–8, 73

official documents   51, 79, 80, 83, 90
Ophir, Adi   129 n.37
organized religion   71
Orrells, Daniel   142 n.20
Ottonian dynasty/Saxon kings and emperors   4, 19, 40, 54, 59, 75, 108, 110
Otto the Great   4

past, as not the present   20–2
Paul, Herman   150 nn.2, 6
Penn, William   39
Perthes, Friedrich   88
Pfanner, Tobias   51
Phaedrus (Plato)   64
philosopher, meaning and significance of   20
Pia desidera (Pious Desires) (Spener)   24
Picart, Bernard   63
Pierre, Jacques   92
politics of history   116–20
Pomata, Gianna   126 n.5
Poovey, Mary   126 n.9
Popper, Karl   8
pragmatic history   84, 85
present, as not the past   17–19
princely archive   11, 12, 13
  distrust in   48–50
  history and law and   53–5
  history between theology and jurisprudence and   55–6

Rijswijk and   47–8
trust in documents and   50–3
private classes/teaching   12, 15, 33. *See also Übungen* (exercises)
  significance of   31–2
  of Thomasius   23–5, 29, 32
Prösler, Hans   1
public and private classes   23
public lectures   23, 30, 32
Pufendorf, Samuel   5, 68–9
purpose   11, 14–15, 50, 89, 100
  art cabinet and   59, 65, 70
  epistemological   116
  fieldwork and   43, 44
  of historiography   119–23
  of history of historiography   121–3
  moral   6, 116, 117, 121
  official   66
  pedagogical   26
  political   13, 105, 117, 121
Pyrrhonism   26, 52, 63, 90, 132 n.34

Ranke, Heinrich   96
Ranke, Leopold von   7, 10, 14, 15, 87–9, 117, 149 n.62
  action and reaction in archive for   101–4
  archival and universal history and   89–90
  archival self and   96–7
  archive access for   97–101
  archive discovery and   90–2
  document history and   92–4
  entering the archive for   94–5
  historical discipline politics and   104–5
  on true politics   103
  on yearbooks and exercises   110–11
Raspe, Rudolf Erich   58
Raumer, Johann George von   24–5, 27, 28
Reichs-Grund-Gesetze (imperial fundamental laws)   54–5
Reichshistorie (imperial history)   13, 47, 55–6, 79, 85, 102, 140 n.28
Reichshofrat (Vienna)   51
Reichskammergericht (Wetzlar)   51
Reill, Peter Hanns   5, 84, 86
relativism   9, 13, 118, 121
  modern   7, 8, 13
religious intolerance, antidote to   44–5

Reuben, Julie E.   121
Richer of Reims   113
Riedel, Friedrich Just   64
Riga   57, 58, 72
Ritter, Heinrich   96, 97, 99
Rousseau, Jean Jacques   7, 72
Ruge, Arnold   146 n.11

St. Real, Abbé de   93
Santa Maria Gloriosa dei Frari
    convent   94, 95
Sattelzeit (threshold period)   8
Sawilla, Jan Marco   128 n.31
scepticism   26, 48, 50, 52, 63, 122
Schäfer, Dietrich   150 n.3
Schaffer, Simon   94, 126 n.9
Scheele, Meta   132 n.34
Scheffner, Johann Georg   69
Schlözer, August Ludwig von   145 n.21
Schlüter, Gisela   132 n.34
Schmauß, Johann Jakob   55
Schneppen, Heinz   134 n.2
Seifert, Arno   126 n.5
Seilern, Johann Friedrich von   47
self, exercise of   22–7
self-reflection   20, 25
seminar
    institutionalized   109–10, 114–15
    institutionalized exercises
        and   114–16
Semiotik/Semiotica (semiotics)   79, 80
Sextus Empiricus   26
Shapin, Steven   10, 94, 126 n.9, 129 n.37
Shapiro, Barbara J.   126 n.9
Siraisi, Nancy   126 n.5
Smith, Bonnie G.   151 n.14
Socrates   64, 142 n.20
*Sommario della congiura contra la citta
    di Venetia* (Summary of the
    Conspiracy Against the City of
    Venice) (anonymous)   93
Spener, Philipp Jakob   24, 28, 41
Spieß, Philipp Ernst   50
Spinoza, Baruch   36, 42
Sprat, Thomas   32
Staatsarchiv   97
Standort (place)   77, 78
state archive   14
    access of   97–101
    action and reaction in   101–4
    archival self and   96–7

    discovery of   90–2
    entering of   94–5
    historical discipline
        politics and   104–5
    history of documents and   92–4
    revolution and   87–9
    universal history and   89–90
    statesman and historian   77–9
Stegern, Adrian   20
Stolle, Gottlieb   36–7, 40, 42
Sybel, Heinrich von   5
Symposium (Plato)   64

Tanaka, Stefan   154 n.8
Téllez-Girón, Pedro   92
testimonies   48–52, 63, 78, 81, 90–2
Thomasius, Christian   4, 13, 17–19, 116,
    130 n.9, 132 n.30, 137 n.40
    age of history and   32–3
    and equality
        exercise of   27–30
        place of   30–2
    in exile   19
    on historical examples   25–7
    on historical knowledge   53
    on historical studies   21–2
    private classes and   23–4, 29, 32
    Raumer and   24–5, 27, 28
    on self   22–7
    on Stegern   20
    on universities   19
Thompson, Martyn P.   140 n.28
Toews, John   102–3, 105
Tollebeek, Jo   151 n.12
Troeltsch, Ernst   6, 7
trust   12, 26–7, 42, 47, 49, 78, 81, 112–13
    in documents   50–3

Übungen (exercises)   107
    of equality   27–30
    exercising character and   107–8
    historians of past and present
        and   111–14
    institutionalized   114–16
    of Ranke   110–11
    of Waitz   107–8, 111
Ueber das Studium des Alterthums (On the
    Study of Antiquity) (Klotz)   60
*Ueber den Nutzen und Gebrauch der alten
    geschnittenen Steine und ihre
    Abdrücke* (On the Benefits

and Use of Ancient Engraved Stones and their Imprints) (Klotz) 64
Ueber die neuere Deutsche Litteratur (On Recent German Literature) (Herder) 69
Ueber die Verschwörung gegen Venedig im Jahre 1618 (On the Conspiracy Against Venice in the Year of 1618) (Ranke) 88, 92
Uffenbach, Zacharias Conrad von 28–9, 37, 40, 43, 135 n.10
undocumented history 94
universal history 4, 5, 55–6, 86, 89–90, 94
University of Berlin 88, 89, 109, 114
University of Göttingen 3, 36, 53, 76, 77, 84
University of Halle 3, 19, 23, 27, 30, 45, 47–50, 55, 61
University of Jena 36
University of Leipzig 17, 23, 24, 27, 114, 115
Unpartheyische Kirchen- und Ketzerhistorie (Impartial History of the Church and Heretics) (Arnold) 39–40
Urkunden. *See* official documents
Urkundenschrift-Gebiet/regnum diplomaticum (official document realm). *See* official documents

Valdez, Damien 143 n.43
Varmod, Thomas 41
Varnhagen von Ense, Karl August 89, 99
vice and virtues 25, 54, 112, 113
Vienna 96–8
Vierhaus, Rudolph 149 n.62
virtual witnessing 94–5
virtues 60, 64, 68
  epistemic 43, 112, 116, 150 n.6
  modern 9
  moral 43, 112, 116, 150 n.6
  vices and 25, 54, 112, 113

Völkel, Markus 4, 132 n.34, 139 n.16
Vossius, Gerardus Johannes 21

Waitz, Georg 15, 107–8, 111–12, 116, 150 nn.2–3, 6, 152 n.27, 154 n.44
  exercises of 107–8, 111
  historical discipline and 116–17
  importance of 111–14
  on institutionalized seminars 109–10
  Monod on 113–14
  morals and politics of historical discipline and 116–18
  moral significance of 108
Weber, Loren J. 154 n.44
Weber, Max 121
Weigh House 30, *31*, 32
Weizsäcker, Julius 114–16
Wesendonck, Hermann 145 n.21
Whig Interpretation of History, The (Butterfield) 119
White, Hayden 1, 2, 8, 119
Wieland, Ludwig 150 n.3
Wielema, Michiel 134 n.4
William of Orange 47
William the Silent 35
Winckelmann, Johann Joachim 7, 58, 61, 67, 141 n.4
Winckler, Johann 41
wissenschaftliche Evidenz (scholarly evidence) 85
Wittich, Karl 113
Wolff, Christian 45, 53, 85, 137 nn.38, 40
Woolf, Daniel 154 n.8
world monarchies 4, 13, 40, 51, 54, 55, 122, 123
Wundt, Max 137 n.40

Zammito, John H. 72, 143 n.43
Zedelmaier, Helmut 135 n.5
Zeidlern, Johann Gottfried 29, 30
Zeitgeist (spirit of time) 14, 57, 58, 68, 70–3
Zelle, Carsten 132 n.30

www.ingramcontent.com/pod-product-compliance
Lightning Source LLC
Chambersburg PA
CBHW061834300426
44115CB00013B/2373